D0387268

Eddy Arnold
I'll Hold You
in My Heart

Eddy Arnold
I'll Hold You in My Heart

Don Cusic

RUTLEDGE HILL PRESS
Nashville, Tennessee

Published in Nashville, Tennessee, by Rutledge Hill Press, Inc., 211 Seventh Avenue North, Nashville, Tennessee 37219. Distributed in Canada by H. B. Fenn & Company, Ltd., 34 Nixon Road, Bolton, Ontario L7E 1W2. Distributed in Australia by Millennium Books, 33 Maddox Street, Alexandria, NSW 2015. Distributed in New Zealand by Tandem Press, 2 Rugby Road, Birkenhead, Aukland 10. Distributed in the United Kingdom by Verulam Publishing, Ltd., 152a Park Street Lane, Park Street, St. Albans, Hertfordshire AL2 2AU.

All photographs courtesy of Eddy Arnold

Cover and book design by Harriette Bateman
Typography by E.T. Lowe, Nashville, Tennessee

Library of Congress Cataloging-in-Publication Data
Cusic, Don.
    Eddy Arnold : I'll hold you in my heart / Don Cusic.
      p. cm.
    ISBN 1-55853-492-X
    1. Arnold, Eddy. 2. Country musicians—United States—Biography.
I. Title.
ML420.A77C87   1997
782.421642'092—dc21
[B]   97-7218
                                                  CIP
                                                  MN

Printed in the United States of America

1 2 3 4 5 6 7 8 9   01 00 99 98 97

This book is dedicated to
the man it is written
about—Eddy Arnold

Contents

Preface

During the period of researching and writing this book, I spent many hours with Eddy Arnold. Some of that time was spent doing interviews where I asked him a set of questions, but a lot of time was spent just listening to him reminisce—in his office, on the road during personal appearances, and at lunch. A number of the quotes in this book came from Mr. Arnold during these conversations. In addition, Mr. Arnold had saved a large number of articles written about him throughout his career. His wife, Sally, clipped, collected, and saved articles about him. In the 1960s he had a clipping agency that saved these articles. These articles are in Eddy Arnold's office, and I used them extensively. Sometimes the date and name of the newspaper were not on them, or the page numbers were missing. However, whenever possible, I have documented them as accurately as possible.

The Country Music Foundation is invaluable for people who do research into country music, and I owe staff members there a great debt of gratitude, especially Ronnie Pugh, Bob Pinson, and John Rumble. Their files on people such as Steve Sholes, Paul Cohen, and others involved in the early country music industry were especially helpful.

Although no parts of this book have been published, I have presented papers on Eddy Arnold at academic conferences of the Popular Culture Association, the Tennessee Folklore Society, and the International Association for the Study of Popular Music, and at the International Country Music Conference held in Meridian, Mississippi, in conjunction with Jimmie Rodgers Days.

In addition to Mr. Arnold, I owe a great debt of gratitude to his manager, Jerry Purcell, who was always available to answer any questions and who helped immeasurably with the book. I also owe a great debt of gratitude to those who shared their time and thoughts: Mr. and Mrs. Robert Jones (who live on the farm where Eddy Arnold grew up), Owen Bradley, Bill Denny, Brad McCuen, Chet Atkins, Ronnie Pugh, Floyd Cramer, Frances Preston, Joe Talbot, Joe Galante, Charles Brown, Roy Wiggins, Charles Wolfe, Otto Kittsinger, Keith Bilbrey, Kyle Cantrell, LeAnn Rimes, Bobby Campbell, Robert Edging, Joe Allison, Vallo Nickalau, and Sally Arnold.

I would also like to thank my family—my wife, Jackie, and children Delaney, Jesse, Eli, and Alex—for allowing me to spend days and nights away from home while working on this project.

Finally, readers may know that Eddy Arnold has been portrayed as frugal and even a tightwad by many individuals. However, although it is true that he does not like to waste money, I have come to know another side of him throughout this project. The Eddy Arnold I have come to know is a warm and generous man. There are numerous examples of his helping people in a variety of ways, but he doesn't want them publicized, so they are not in this book. But I know he has helped other performers—often without their knowledge. He has helped former business associates get started in business and helped others who have fallen on hard times. And he has bought me more lunches than I can count.

1

Growing Up

It's not a long way from Chester County to Nashville if you measure only the miles. But if you look at a poor sharecropper farm boy and then at a world-famous entertainer whose voice has reached millions, the distance seems immeasurable. Eddy Arnold was that penniless farm boy who made the journey to country music superstardom. But his story is not his alone. It is also the story of country music's journey from the rural South to fame and fortune in the big cities of this nation. In many ways the stories of Eddy Arnold and country music run parallel, both starting out poor and a bit backward but, in the end, reaching from Tennessee to the ends of the earth.

Tennessee is a long, narrow state, about five hundred miles from the northeast city of Bristol to Memphis in the southwest corner. As you travel west from the Smoky Mountains on the eastern border, Tennessee first becomes hilly through the Cumberland Plateau and then gets flatter as the traveler gets closer to Memphis and the Mississippi River, which serves as the western border. Nashville is located near the middle of the state; Memphis sits about two hundred miles west of Nashville. Jackson is about halfway between Nashville and Memphis or about a hundred miles away from Nashville. By this time the land has gotten pretty flat with some rolling hills while the dirt has grown dark and rich.

South of Jackson about twenty miles is the small town of Pinson; turning east near the Pinson Mounds, you enter into Chester County, whose county seat, Henderson, is about fifteen miles farther south. In 1918, the roads were not paved and there was no electricity; it was mostly small farms while the towns of Pinson and

Henderson consisted of a handful of stores and a school, although Henderson also had a courthouse sitting up on a hill.

In May 1918, American soldiers were in Europe fighting World War I. Under General John J. Pershing, most American forces were in France on the western front, digging trenches and trying to break the back of the German army. President Woodrow Wilson had abandoned his promise to "keep America out of the European War" and joined the Allies, Great Britain and France, to defeat Germany. It was the first war in the air, and Eddie Rickenbacker downed twenty-six enemy planes over France. A backwoods farm boy from the mountains of Jamestown, Tennessee, named Alvin York would become a hero for capturing 132 Germans single-handedly. Later that year, in the November elections, the Republicans took control of both houses of Congress.

At the beginning of 1918, President Wilson proposed a fourteen-point peace plan. Daylight savings time was put in motion on March 31 to help the war effort by cutting electricity needs in the nation. Throughout the summer about a million American troops were fighting in the Great War. On November 11, the Armistice was signed, ending the war, and on December 4, President Wilson sailed to the Versailles peace conference, where he would present his idea for the League of Nations to the Europeans.

Out on a 240-acre Tennessee farm about halfway between Pinson and Henderson in Chester County, Richard Edward Arnold was born on May 15, 1918. Both parents had been married before and widowed. Will C. Arnold's first wife, Mary Etta, had died on April 7, 1905; they had nine children. On September 4, 1906, Will Arnold married Georgia Wright, who had two surviving children from her first marriage to J. D. Ingle. Will and Georgia had five children of their own: a daughter, Patty; then two sons, W. D. and John; a daughter who died at eighteen months; then the son they named Richard Edward Arnold. Edd, as he was called, was born when his dad was fifty-eight and his mother was forty-four. "I must've been quite a surprise for them," the grown Eddy Arnold observes. In the combined two families, Edd Arnold was the youngest of fourteen children born to Will Arnold and the youngest of sixteen when the families of both parents were combined.

Edd's dad, Will, was a farmer and entrepreneur. The farm was located beside a dirt road and had a creek running through it. The adjoining farm belonged to the Lathams, and Edd and the Latham boys spent endless hours playing in the fields and branch between the two houses. Edd had also shown an interest in music; around 1928, young Edd had received a harmonica, which gave him his first taste of playing music, and he obtained a guitar when he was ten. He had music in him, "in his bones," as country folks would say, because his daddy could play the fiddle and his mother could sing. His mother, who played the guitar and sang around the house, taught Edd his first chords. His Grandfather Wright could not see, but he encouraged the boy with his music, although Edd was often told to "keep quiet" in the house because his father was sick and couldn't stand the noise from a young boy trying to learn the guitar. But learning the guitar was a labor of love, and young Edd kept clanging away.

> ➤ *He had music in him, "in his bones," as country folks would say, because his daddy could play the fiddle and his mother could sing.*

In addition to his farm, where he grew cotton, peas, corn, hay, and potatoes, and raised some livestock, Will C. Arnold had a gristmill and sawmill. He was a successful, respected man in the community, and people often came by to talk and get advice. But Will had high blood pressure, and as Edd was growing up, his dad grew sick. On Edd's eleventh birthday, May 15, 1929, as he was playing at a nearby farm in a field with the Latham boys across the branch from his house, he heard the dinner bell ringing out in the late afternoon. As soon as heard it, young Edd Arnold knew his father had died.

The boyhood days of fun and frolic were forever changed. The next day, May 16, was Edd's brother W. D.'s birthday, and the day after that, their father was buried on a little knoll in a graveyard beside the white clapboard Friendship Baptist Church. As friends and family gathered for the funeral, young Edd thought his heart would break, and he couldn't imagine how times could be tougher or something could hurt deeper.

Problems arose immediately. On April 24, 1924, Will C. Arnold had borrowed $1,980 from D. S. Parker and given a deed of trust for the loan. The loan had been partially repaid, but when Will Arnold died, Parker came to collect his money. A series of documents were filed in court to sell the 167-acre farm where the family lived as well as two other 35-acre tracts that Will owned. After some delays, the farm was auctioned at the Henderson Court House on October 25,

Eddy Arnold at about the age of six with his parents, wearing a suit his mother made for him.

1930, to Parker, who bought the three tracts for a total of $1,745. Then in December, the Arnolds' neighbors, the Lathams, purchased the land from Parker for $2,344; a week and a half later the Lathams sold the land to A. A. Arnold, son of Will C. and Mary Etta and Edd's half brother. A. A. Arnold let Georgia and the three boys still home—W. D., John, and Edd—live on the farm as sharecroppers.

Out in the country, there is a big gap between being a landowner and being a sharecropper. A landowner has social status, respect, and prestige. Owning land means owning something, having some control of your destiny, having a connection to the earth and a stake in the community. But being a sharecropper means having no status or prestige—you're just a short step away from being hired help. Being a sharecropper puts you on the bottom rung of the economic ladder, subject not only to the usual pitfalls of farming—too much or too little rain and crops that sometimes fail—but also to the whims of the landowner. It helped a little that the landowner was Edd's half brother, but it was still a big comedown for the Arnold family to go from being a family headed by a respected landowner to a family of sharecroppers. The loss of self-respect that comes from not owning your own land was even bigger than the loss of the farm implements and animals the Arnolds had to see auctioned off.

There was a lot of turmoil during the years 1929 and 1930 for the Arnold family; papers were filed and family members had to appear in court. For young Edd it turned his world topsy-turvy; he experienced a boiling cauldron of emotions because he didn't know if the family would remain on the farm or not. And an eleven-year-old boy is left out of the loop when family decisions are made; the eight older half brothers and half sister (one half brother had died in 1927) were heirs to the property in addition to the four Arnold children.

In the sale in October 1930, much of the personal property was also sold to clear the debt; Arnold remembers they were allowed to keep a couple of cows, some pigs, two mules, and some farm equipment—but he had to watch as the rest of the property was sold to others. He felt a deep sense of loss as well as a personal emptiness; he did not know what was going to happen to him or his family. Sixty-five years later he could still close his eyes and recall those feelings that day.

The year 1929 was a particularly formative one for young Edd. First, his father died, and he had to face growing up without a dad. He felt a deep gap in his heart and soul his entire life because he didn't have a dad. As a young boy he had been learning to play the guitar during the year his father died, and he was often told to "keep quiet" because his father was ill and the playing bothered him. After his father's death Edd would feel a great deal of guilt that he had not realized just how sick his father was, or that somehow his boyish noisiness had been partly responsible for his father's death.

> *Edd's family bought a phonograph, and he ordered some records from the Sears catalog; his favorite artist became Gene Autry.*

In December of that year, Grandfather Wright, who regaled the family with stories from the Civil War (he had been a soldier in that conflict) and who had encouraged young Edd in the boy's efforts to learn to play the guitar, also died. Finally, Edd watched the family's farm and the family's possessions sold off, and that left him with a deep, abiding fear that one day all he owned might also be lost. Never a wealthy family, the Arnolds plunged into poverty in 1929. It would cause him to scrimp and save his whole life, be careful with his money and, even when he was making more money than he could spend, always carry in the back of his mind that it could all be gone tomorrow.

The one bright spot of 1929 was a phonograph that Edd's sister Patty brought home with her from St. Louis at Christmas. It was the first time Edd had seen a phonograph, and he sat enthralled as he listened to the records. As he got older, Edd's family bought a phonograph, and he ordered some records from the Sears catalog; his favorite artist became Gene Autry, and the first Autry song he fell in love with was "When Jimmie Rodgers Said Good-Bye."

When you grow up poor on a farm out in the country, you spend a lot of time alone with your dreams. While some farm boys immerse themselves in the day-to-day activities of farming, planting crops, worrying about the weather, and feeding the livestock, others let their minds wander to wonder what life would be like without the chores of farming.

Farming is a hard way to make a living. First, enormous risks are involved; there are no guarantees that once you plant a crop, the rains will come at the right times or that, when a crop is ready for harvest, a storm won't come along and wipe out a whole year's work. Next, the farmer is at the mercy of the buyer for the price he gets; he must take what he can when he delivers it because there is no way to drive a bargain when your whole crop will rot if it isn't sold soon.

Most boys who grow up on the farm want to get away from farming. Farming might sound glamorous and appealing to city folks—breathing fresh air, getting in touch with the land and all that—but the truth of the matter is that it is never-ending hard work. Some boys move off the farm and go into town to take a job in a store or with some factory or manufacturing company. Edd's brother W. D. went to barber school, then set up a barbershop in Jackson.

Making a living is only part of life. To some, it is the major part and so they try to get a job as soon as possible, get married, have a family, and try to pay the bills. But some boys have dreams that are bigger—they want to matter, want to go beyond just making a living to making a mark in this world. Edd Arnold was such a boy.

What could a farm boy do in the 1930s? Jobs were scarce—it was, after all, the Great Depression—so most people stayed put if they had a job of any kind. With farming, at least you could grow some of your own food. Most boys never finished high school because they couldn't afford to stay in school. Besides, you were more likely to get hired by somebody for being a hard worker than for having an education. People needed hard workers, not scholars.

A boy could stay on the farm or go into town and look for a job in a store or office. But if he could sing, the whole wide world was open to him. Here was a chance for a farm boy to make some money having fun—it was like being paid to do nothing or being paid to do what he would be doing anyhow—and he could get recognition and attention in the community. People would know who he was—he wouldn't be just another struggling nobody; if he could sing on the radio, he could be *somebody*. Edd Arnold wanted to be somebody.

2

Earliest Performances

Eddy Arnold remembers hearing early Jimmie Rodgers's records and reading about Rodgers's death in 1933 in the newspaper (Edd had just turned fifteen when Rodgers died). The following year, 1934, Edd had four music "lessons" when a traveling musician drew some chord diagrams on the schoolhouse blackboard and demonstrated the fingering to Arnold; the four lessons cost 75 cents each.

When Edd was sixteen, he went with his school to visit the radio station in Jackson, and he knew when he walked in the door that it was the life for him, singing out over the airwaves. Things were starting to click in his mind; singing was a way to get off the farm and out into the world at large, and he could sing pretty good. Arnold remembers the impact the radio station had on him at the time: "I want to do that!" The radio station "looked so big to me, to see an engineer in there turning the knobs. I didn't know what he was doing, but I knew it was something important." The wheels were turning: "I'm saying all the time in my mind, this is what I want to do—sing on the radio!"

In 1934, Edd Arnold was picked by his school to sing a song at the Madison County Fair; he sang "If You'll Let Me Be Your Little Sweetheart." Later, he played at house parties for $1 a night. The school choir, with Edd as a member, sang at a county fair, and the radio station came down and broadcast it. It might not have been the big break of Edd's career, but it was one more step in seeing his dream of being a singer on the radio come true. A salesman helped him with another step.

"One day I was down on the farm," remembers Arnold. "You work in the morning and come in at twelve and have dinner and I'd clang on my guitar. Eat and strum the guitar. Sometimes I'd sit out on the front porch. One day a man came selling subscriptions to *The Jackson Sun* in Jackson, Tennessee, and they owned radio station WTJS. He was trying to sell us a subscription and I was sitting there with the guitar and he said, 'Why don't you come down and I'll get you an audition?' So I did."

> ➤ *The wheels were turning: "I'm saying all the time in my mind, this is what I want to do—sing on the radio!"*

Arnold quit school when he was sixteen, after he had finished the ninth grade. At that time, it was rare to find someone who *did* finish high school, especially in the rural South. If somebody had a strong back and was willing to work hard, he could make a way in this life, support a family, and even climb the ladder of success. Hard work and experience were what counted, and the sooner he got some experience, the better off he was.

Another turning point occurred for Arnold when he was sixteen. After his father died, W. D., the eldest brother, took young Edd under his wing, was good and kind to him, and became a father figure. But John, Edd's other brother who was seven years older than Edd, was a different story. The two fought constantly, or more accurately, John beat up the younger, smaller Edd constantly. They just couldn't get along, possibly because John was a bit jealous of the attention Edd got from W. D., possibly because that's what older brothers do, or maybe because that was the way he was.

But when Edd was sixteen, strong as a horse with lots of stamina, the tables turned. John had been plowing with some mules and Edd went out to help. The mules were tired and sweaty, and Edd thought they should be given a rest. John was adamantly against that and told Edd to keep on plowing. Then John reached down, picked up the singletree from the plow (a piece of wood about a foot and a half long that connects the mules to the plow), and hit Edd over the head with it, drawing blood. Edd lit into him with his fists, leaving bruises and a black eye. Their mother was upset, especially after seeing John's condition, and John kept his distance from Edd for the next several days. But it was the last time John beat up on his younger brother.

Edd sang around the house, in the fields, and walking along the road. W. D. taught him how to cut hair, and young Edd would go down to the local store, set up a soft drink crate, and cut hair for some extra money. He sang while he was down at the store, too. Soon, he began playing at neighborhood gatherings, house parties, and square dances. He learned that when he sang, people took notice and gave him compliments; it was easy to get some money and get the attention of girls if you were a singer.

Bill Westbrooks was a struggling singer who had landed a job with the Hunt Brothers Furniture Store in Dyersburg, Tennessee. Part of the job involved appearing on a radio program sponsored by the store and traveling around on a small flatbed truck to sing and advertise the store. Soon Westbrooks moved to Jackson, where the Hunt Brothers had opened another furniture store. The store sponsored a radio program for Westbrooks and also provided a truck to travel around on and sing to advertise the furniture store.

Because Edd Arnold was attracted to music, he came and listened to Bill Westbrooks sing, and he hung out at the radio station in Jackson where Westbrooks performed. According to Westbrooks, he first met Arnold when "I went to a homecoming—a gathering out kind of near his home. . . . We started calling him Smiling Eddy Arnold. You could hear him laugh above five hundred people. . . . Directly he come to where I was by the sound truck and we got to talking—and so I told him we was fixing to have a talent show. Hunt Brothers was fixing to have it on Sunday afternoon. Anybody from anywhere around there could appear on our broadcast. And we was going to run it for thirteen weeks. And the one that won out on the top got to be on the program— for free. . . . I asked him, 'Eddy, don't you want to enter this talent contest?' . . . and he said, 'Yeah, Bill, I believe I would.' . . . And so Eddy was on the talent show—but Eddy didn't win. But anyway, I said, 'Eddy, I'd like to have you work with me.' And he said he'd like to work with me 'cause him and his mother and his brother John . . . were pretty poor. He kind of wanted to get out of that country, and plowing them mules. He was getting tired of them mules!"

On the radio program, Arnold appeared with Bill and Vera Westbrooks, Al Gobel, Jimmy Allen, Speedy McNatt, Val Morris, Buddy Tucker, and Angelina Palozola. Rollin Sullivan and Gabe Tucker played for Westbrooks on WTJS in Jackson (although not at the same time as Arnold), and Westbrooks gave Sullivan the name Oscar because he couldn't remember Rollin. The nickname stuck.

At that time Arnold sang Gene Autry songs such as "That Silver-Haired Daddy of Mine." They worked "the kerosene circuits" where they would go to a schoolhouse, charge 10 or 15 cents for admission, and play for the farmers. Arnold didn't make much money, but at least he was on the radio. By 1936, radio was mass entertainment in the United States, and families sat around their home sets in the evening and listened to President Roosevelt's Fireside Chats, the drama and comedy shows, and the big bands coming out of New York and Chicago with their network feeds. Since the radio stations were broadcast over the AM band, and the radio waves could bounce off the ionosphere, even people living way out in the country could pick up a number of radio programs. And that's how country music was heard—coming from Chicago over WLS on the *National Barn Dance*, from WSM's *Grand Ole Opry* in Nashville, and from other barn dances in neighboring states. Arnold listened and soaked it all in.

In addition to his job on the radio, Arnold landed a job with the Smith Funeral Home driving the hearse, which also served as the ambulance. The city didn't have an ambulance service, so a funeral home usually had an ambulance, which answered emergency calls. That was how Arnold learned the proper way to pick up an injured person with the least amount of pain or damage and get the person to a hospital.

Arnold slept at the funeral home. He was near when an emergency call came in; also, he helped the funeral home when a pallbearer was needed.

The Westbrooks group did well on WTJS and late in 1937 went over to Memphis where they had a spot on WMPS. But after two weeks, the station's management decided the band's services weren't needed—so they were fired. Apparently, the station owner was mad at the station manager and fired the manager and everyone he had hired—which included the band. Westbrooks went back to Jackson, but Arnold and McNatt decided to try their luck in St. Louis. "I had a sister, two half brothers, and two uncles in St. Louis," remembers Arnold, "so we took off." They took the train over and moved in with Patty Bruns, Arnold's sister, at 23 Euclid Avenue. They arrived on January 16, 1938.

Arnold and McNatt then made the rounds at the radio stations, auditioning for a job. At KWK, located in the Chase Hotel, they landed an early morning program, *The Early Birds*. Billing themselves the Tennessee Harmony Lads, Arnold and McNatt performed. There wasn't a regular sponsor, so the duo had to sell spots. The radio station was a good advertising medium; Arnold and McNatt went to clubs, offered to play, then plugged their appearances on the air to attract a crowd. They played some rough joints; at one place, a customer poured a beer down

Speedy McNatt and Eddy Arnold, "The Tennessee Harmony Lads," in St. Louis.

the hole in Eddy Arnold's guitar. It made him mad, but he kept playing; after all, singing was better than farming.

Arnold and McNatt averaged $1.50 to $2.50 for a performance; their biggest take was $10 for an out-of-town picnic. As their income increased, they moved out of the Bruns's home into a one-room apartment in a building at the corner of Union and Laclede, with the bathroom located down the hall.

Arnold and McNatt did pretty well in St. Louis. There Eddy Arnold developed into a singer, and both young men studied music on the side. Arnold remembers practicing reading music so he could read off sheet music. The big bands dominated radio programming, and musicians were required to read. For a country artist who played by ear, it would be a step up to be able to read music. Also, most musicians unions wouldn't allow country performers to join, and some even instituted a test where the applicant had to be able to read and write music before being allowed to join. Knowing how to read and write music was a status symbol for a musician as well as a possible necessity for radio jobs because you had to be in the union in order to be on the network and hit the big time. So Arnold set about learning. He also took six vocal lessons in St. Louis.

The hard work paid off; the duo moved over to KXOK, which was owned by the newspaper, the *Star-Times*. Things were so good that at the end of 1938, Arnold bought his first car, a 1932 coupe.

> ➤ *He had a winning, pleasant demeanor and wasn't easily ruffled or disturbed, even when that drunk poured a beer down his guitar.*

By the time Eddy Arnold turned twenty-one years old, he had come a long way. He had achieved his first dream of singing on the radio, and he was doing so well that he was making a pretty good living at it.

His talent, as well as his basic nature, was winning friends and fans because he knew how to meet people. Eddy Arnold was determined to the point of stubbornness that he was going to make it. He had a winning, pleasant demeanor and wasn't easily ruffled or disturbed, even when that drunk poured a beer down his guitar. He had maturity beyond his years and innate intelligence. His mind absorbed all that was going on around him, and he read the newspapers and kept up with current events; he was a quick learner and deep thinker. He let decisions brew within him and didn't make many false moves. After two years in St. Louis he felt it was time to move on but wasn't entirely sure where his next step would be. However, he had become a seasoned entertainer, knew he wanted a crack at the big time, and felt he was ready for it.

3

With the Golden West Cowboys

Sometime in late 1939, Eddy Arnold was driving his 1932 coupe from St. Louis to his hometown of Henderson to visit his mother. It was around nine in the morning, and the car radio was tuned into WSM, the powerful 50,000-watt station from Nashville, Tennessee, that broadcast the *Grand Ole Opry* every Saturday night. *Opry* star Pee Wee King had a morning program on the station, and Arnold was listening to it. He had met King for a brief handshake back around 1936 while he was performing on the Jackson radio station, and he had followed King's career. He knew King had a singer named Jack Skaggs as a regular, but that day he did not hear Skaggs.

Arnold wondered if King was looking for a male vocalist, and when Arnold returned to St. Louis, he sent a handwritten letter and a picture to King in Nashville asking if King would consider him as a male vocalist. King's manager (and father-in-law) J. L. Frank replied to Arnold and requested a transcription. Since that was before the era of tape, all recordings were made on transcriptions, a thin disk that looked much like a record. Arnold talked with KXOK Program Director Blaine Coldwell, who recorded one for Arnold at KXOK, and the singer sent it off.

Frank and King listened, liked what they heard, and sent for Arnold. Hired for $15 a week, Arnold convinced Frank and King to hire Speedy McNatt as well, and the two became members of the Golden West Cowboys.

It was an opportune time to be on the *Grand Ole Opry*. In January 1939, the Opry attracted a major sponsor, Prince Albert Smoking Tobacco, through the Esty Agency; in October, through the efforts of

Dick Marvin, a key executive of Esty, the *Opry* went on the NBC network on Saturday nights with a thirty-minute segment sponsored by Prince Albert. The *Opry* was organized and run by George D. Hay, "the Solemn Ole Judge." Other key executives at WSM were Program Manager Jack Stapp, who had joined the station in 1939 after a stint with CBS in New York, and Harry Stone, who was general manager for the station.

The time in Nashville on the *Grand Ole Opry* was short-lived for young Eddy Arnold; he performed with the Golden West Cowboys starting in January 1940, and the group played in and around Nashville throughout most of the spring. Then the group moved to Louisville, where they performed on WHAS on a daily show at 9:00 A.M. sponsored by Dr. Caldwell's Syrup of Pepsin. It was a time of professional growth for Eddy Arnold and the first time he toured extensively and played major vaudeville houses in front of large audiences. And it was the first time he saw the role of a manager and how the business of country music worked.

> ➤ *The* Opry *was organized and run by George D. Hay, "the Solemn Ole Judge."*

The key figure behind the career of the Golden West Cowboys was J. L. Frank, one of the most powerful executives in early country music. He had been the manager and booking agent for Gene Autry and Smiley Burnette when Autry was in Chicago appearing on the WLS *Barn Dance*. In fact, Frank had gotten Autry on the WLS program and then used the exposure to get Autry personal appearances. In 1932, Frank and Autry hired Pee Wee King's band to accompany them on tour (Autry's band was in an automobile accident and could not perform); later Pee Wee King performed with Autry on WLS and then in Louisville at WHAS when Autry moved there.

Autry went to Hollywood in 1934 to become a singing cowboy star. However, J. L. Frank remained in the Midwest, managing the Golden West Cowboys, a group he created and that was later headed by Pee Wee King. Frank also promoted live country music shows, one of the first men in the nation to do so.

When Eddy Arnold joined the Golden West Cowboys, he joined a well-organized group that would influence his career. First, Pee Wee King and the Golden West Cowboys were not a traditional hillbilly group. They came out of vaudeville and theaters in the Midwest; their organization was based more on the big band model where a group had an owner and a manager, and the musicians had different roles. Second, the Golden West Cowboys were the first *Opry* group to have a manager, which meant the group was not so dependent on—or obligated to—the WSM executives for advice, guidance, commitments, or career decisions.

Musically, they were smooth and more pop sounding than the traditional string bands such as the McGee Brothers, Missouri Mountaineers, the Delmore Brothers, or Uncle Dave Macon. Visually, they eschewed the bib overall look of mountain folk for the western apparel of the singing cowboy; furthermore, they were sharp dressers and presented an attractive image.

Pee Wee King was an unlikely *Opry* star if you believe the traditional story about the *Opry* wanting to represent only true Southern folk music. He was born Frank Julius Anthony Kuczynski in Milwaukee, Wisconsin, and grew up in Abrams, near Green Bay, Wisconsin. He learned the accordion and joined his father's polka band, then struck out on his own at fifteen after taking the name King from his idol, big band leader Wayne King. His first group was the Farm Hands, organized around 1932; he then formed the King's Jesters, which played mostly western music, heavily influenced by the western music heard on WLS's *Barn Dances* by singer Gene Autry.

King met J. L. Frank in 1932 when Autry's band, the Range Riders, were involved in a car accident in Wisconsin while on tour. Frank and Autry heard King's band performing on the radio while they were getting their car repaired at a service station, and Frank called and asked if the group could help Autry fill in the scheduled date. King agreed; later, in the early fall of 1932, King was hired for Autry's Range Riders full time to play accordion. He appeared with Autry on WLS in Chicago for about a year, then moved with Autry and J. L. Frank to Louisville, Kentucky, where Autry had obtained a position on WHAS for a show.

When Autry was performing in Louisville, there were three band members named Frank, so Frankie King became Pee Wee, with the name given to him by either J. L. Frank or Autry. Autry had been trying to get into the movies and in 1934 made his first appearance in a Hollywood western, Ken Maynard's *In Old Santa Fe.* In 1935, he left Louisville and moved to Hollywood to begin his career as a singing cowboy.

In the summer of 1935, Pee Wee King and J. L. Frank moved to Louisville where King joined Frankie More's Log Cabin Boys on WHAS. The following year, J. L. Frank organized a group called the Golden West Cowboys, put Pee Wee in charge, and found a sponsor,

Eddy Arnold visits Pee Wee King and the Golden West Cowboys in 1946, after he had left the group. From left to right, Pete Pyle, Roy Wiggins, Pee Wee King, Hal Smith, unknown member, Becky Barfield, and Arnold and Chuck Wiggins.

Crazy Water Crystals, a laxative company, for a show on WHAS. During personal appearances, the Golden West Cowboys were sometimes teamed with a group from KNOX in Knoxville, Roy Acuff and his Crazy Tennesseans.

By 1937, the Golden West Cowboys consisted of Pee Wee King on accordion; Abner Simms on fiddle; Milton Estes on banjo; Curley Rhodes on bass; Curley's sister, Texas Daisy, on vocals; and Cowboy Jack Skaggs on guitar. The group auditioned for David Stone, Harry Stone, and engineer Percy White for the *Opry*. The group was hired and on June 4, 1937, made its *Opry* debut, although J. L. Frank made Archie Campbell, then going under the name Art Bell, the head of the group when it first joined the *Opry*. Pee Wee King had to insist that his band members be allowed to join the musicians union; at first the union objected, but with King's persistence, the union relented and King's Golden West Cowboys were among the first musicians with a country music group to become members of the union, which gave them access to network exposure.

The Golden West Cowboys were not the first *Opry* group to dress in western clothes (that honor belongs to Zeke Clements), but they dressed well and brought the cowboy image to the *Opry*. They even went to Hollywood in 1938 and appeared in Gene Autry's movie, *Gold Mine in the Sky* (billed as J. L. Frank's Golden West Cowboys).

> ➤ *By July 29, 1940, shortly after Eddy Arnold left Nashville for Louisville, the* Opry *was on forty stations and reached all the way to the West Coast.*

During his time with the Golden West Cowboys, Eddy Arnold joined Texas Daisy as the group's main vocalist. Arnold, Pee Wee King, Milton Estes, and Curley Rhodes did group numbers of Sons of the Pioneers songs as well as love songs. The Golden West Cowboys added fiddler Redd Stewart in 1940 in Louisville. King's group spent about a year in Louisville, then moved back to Nashville in July 1941 and rejoined the *Grand Ole Opry*.

It had been a great learning experience for Eddy Arnold as a professional. But it was also important for Eddy Arnold's personal life. While in Louisville, Arnold had met Sally Gayhart, who worked at the Woolworth store at the lunch counter. Eddy met her after she had been in the audience for one of the Golden West Cowboy shows. She stopped him and asked him for an autograph; he was happy to oblige, but quickly realized she didn't have a pen or paper.

Pretty young Sally Gayhart was from LaGrange, Kentucky, just outside Louisville, and came to the city after her father died. At the time, she was dating a boy who played piano at the radio station—which was why she was in the radio audience when she met Eddy. The two began dating between Arnold's appearances and continued until Arnold and the Golden West Cowboys moved back to Nashville.

By July 29, 1940, shortly after Eddy Arnold left Nashville for Louisville, the *Opry* was on forty stations and reached all the way to the West Coast. During that year, Hollywood became enamored with the *Opry* and shot a movie, *The Grand Ole Opry*, which starred Roy Acuff and Uncle Dave Macon. The movie company was Republic, known for its B western and singing cowboy movies where Gene Autry and Roy Rogers rode the studio ranges.

In the summer of 1941 (probably mid to late July) the Golden West Cowboys moved back to Nashville and the *Grand Ole Opry*. Fiddler Redd Stewart was drafted soon after they moved; King hired Chuck Wiggins and Shorty Boyd who performed trio numbers with him while Eddy Arnold sang two songs solo during shows.

Within weeks after the Golden West Cowboys moved back to Nashville, J. L. Frank met with Dick Marvin, the executive at the Esty Agency responsible for purchasing radio advertising, and Harry Stone, general manager of WSM, over lunch. On that August day, Frank, Stone, and Marvin agreed to pull together a Camel Caravan to be sponsored by the R. J. Reynolds Company through the Esty Agency. Since Frank was the manager of the Golden West Cowboys, that group would perform. Stone committed to the agency that the *Opry* would not have any competing tobacco sponsors and agreed to work with *Opry* members—waiving the requirement that each *Opry* act had to be back in Nashville every Saturday night for the weekly broadcast. That allowed King's group to tour constantly from November 1941 until December 1942.

The Camel Caravan was originally a popular radio show hosted by Vaughn Monroe. When the touring show was organized, the Esty Agency decided to have groups from Hollywood, New York, and Nashville on the road. Since R. J. Reynolds had long been a sponsor for the *Grand Ole Opry*, it was in a position to contract the *Opry* to provide performers for the patriotic tour. The Camel Caravans played at military bases all over the United States and were a mixture of business and patriotism.

The tour would carry a patriotic theme—all military personnel in uniform would get into the concerts free and many concerts would be held on military bases—and during the show cigarette girls would pass out free samples of Camel cigarettes to military personnel in the audience.

King's group consisted of himself on accordion, Redd Stewart on fiddle, singer and guitarist San Antonio Rose, and singer/emcee Eddy Arnold. In addition to King's group, other performers included comedienne Minnie Pearl, eighteen-year-old pop vocalist Kay Carlisle, dancer Dollie Dearman, a trio of girl singers (Mary Dinwiddie, Evelyn Wilson, and Alcyone Bate Beasley), and four female dancers known as the Camelettes. Master of ceremonies for the show was *Opry* regular Ford Rush, although Arnold emceed King's segment. Others who performed on the shows during the nineteen-month tour were Chuck

Eddy and Sally Arnold.

Wiggins (Cowboy Joe), Joe Zinkan, Gene Widner, and Curley Rhodes (Cicero the Comedian).

Eddy Arnold moved into a three-room house on Dickerson Road when he came back to Nashville. He could see he was making headway in his career: only two years before he was in St. Louis with Speedy McNatt on a radio station; now he was touring with a top name group and appearing on major radio shows. Life in Nashville was bound to be looking up: he was back on the *Grand Ole Opry*, with its network connections, and about to embark on a national tour with the Camel Caravan. But he was in love with a girl back in Louisville, Kentucky, and missing her nearly drove him crazy.

While appearing in Charlotte, North Carolina, Arnold went to a pay phone and called Sally long distance and proposed to her; she said she would think about it. Soon she accepted, and in November, she came to Nashville and the two were married on November 28, 1941. Right after the marriage, Arnold left his wife in a small apartment and took off for Panama with the Camel Caravan. "It wasn't really fair to Sally," he remembers. "As soon as we got married, I left." But he'd married the girl of his dreams, and life looked good. It wasn't until after they were married that Sally learned she had been earning more at her job at Woolworth's soda counter than Eddy Arnold was making as a performer.

On Sunday, December 7, 1941—only nine days after Eddy and Sally were married—the Camel Caravan from the *Grand Ole Opry* was in San Antonio, Texas, to perform at Kelly Field, Randolph Field, and Fort Sam Houston. In an auditorium during an afternoon show, the announcer broke into their performance with the news that the American naval base at Pearl Harbor had been bombed by the Japanese. Later that evening the troupe sat and listened to President Roosevelt tell the nation that the date would live "in infamy" and that war was being declared on Japan.

A few days later the United States declared war on Germany as well. And so 1941 ended with the United States part of World War II, embarked on a mission that would change the country and the world.

4

Nashville before World War II

In 1939, the Great Depression still hung over America. There were still 8 million unemployed in the nation of 131.6 million people. Prices were low, but that was deceiving, since salaries were also low and money was scarce.

At the beginning of 1939, you could buy a good used car for around $500 (or less!). The well-dressed executives at WSM could purchase a tailored suit for $18.95 with top-of-the-line wing tip shoes for $5. Newspaper ads touted off-the-rack suits for $14.96 to $17.95 with topcoats costing around $20. Shirts cost from $1 to $1.65, sweaters $1.95 to $3.95, and pants $1.95 to $3.95.

A young couple setting up a household could purchase a three-piece bedroom suite for $39.50 or a rocking chair for $3.89—with credit terms of 25 cents down and 25 cents a week. A fifty-piece kitchen set—including a cabinet, silverware, and glassware—could be purchased for $39.95. For dinner, roast beef cost 15 cents a pound, a round steak cost 29 cents a pound, potatoes were 5 cents a pound, and red snapper was extravagant and expensive at 30 cents a pound. For the bathroom or outhouse, toilet paper was 4 cents a roll.

Nashville was surrounded by farms at that time. If a farmer needed overalls, he would have to pay 87 cents for them; if his wife needed a flannel nightgown, that would be 47 cents. Although those prices sound unreasonably cheap, the plain fact is that most farmers earned less than $100 a year.

The year before, in 1938, President Roosevelt had stated that the South was the nation's top economic problem, putting the entire nation at risk with its severe conditions. The annual wage in the South was around $865, compared to $1,291 in the rest of the nation.

Between January and October 1939, when major changes were happening at the *Opry*, there were also earthshaking changes in the world at large. Newspaper headlines throughout the year talked about Hitler and the war developing in Europe. The year before, Germany had annexed Austria; on March 15, the German army had entered Prague and quickly destroyed Czechoslovakia.

On the home front, President Franklin Roosevelt was still creating jobs and work with his various federal programs, although Congress was concerned about deficit spending. On January 30, 1939, the Tennessee Valley Authority won a victory in the United States Supreme Court, which ruled the TVA was constitutional. The suit had been brought by the Tennessee Electric Power Company, which argued the federal government could not compete against private enterprise. The Tennessee Valley Authority would play a pivotal role in bringing electricity to one of the poorest regions of the country, and helped carry electricity to rural areas in Tennessee.

The marvels of electricity were being advertised to the nation at large. On April 30, 1939, the New York World's Fair opened. It was the last great World's Fair, held at a time when a World's Fair allowed people to see all the modern advances in science and technology. It introduced television to America, and President Roosevelt became the first president to appear on TV with an appearance from the World's Fair. However, not many people watched the event on TV; there were fewer than four hundred sets in all of the United States.

The Fair was lit gloriously and called "The World of Tomorrow." The message was that the World of Tomorrow would be brightly lit, no longer a slave to the sun for light. But this World of Tomorrow was mostly confined to cities. In 1935, only two out of one hundred farms in the middle Tennessee region had electricity. Private utility companies refused to wire rural areas, arguing it was cost prohibitive and farmers wouldn't pay their bills. In 1937, Congress passed the Rural Electric Act, which required companies to wire rural areas.

On September 1, 1939, Hitler invaded Poland, bringing on a declaration of war from Great Britain and France. The United States declared its neutrality, and there were cries from the country to "keep us out of war." At the time the *Opry* began its network broadcasts, it had been about six weeks since Hitler had invaded Poland.

Radio had come of age during the 1930s, and WSM and the *Grand Ole Opry* were in the right place at the right time. By the end of the decade there was an average of 6.6 soaps on every day; popular shows included *Burns and Allen, Our Gal Sunday, Search for Tomorrow, The Jack Benny Show, The Shadow,* and *Captain Midnight.*

> ➤ *WSM had received 50,000-watt clear channel status in 1932. It had the maximum power allotted to American radio stations.*

WSM had received 50,000-watt clear channel status in 1932. It had the maximum power allotted to American radio stations with no other stations on its spot on the dial. Nashville was situated in a geographically advantageous location; virtually anyone within a two-hundred-mile radius could easily pick up the *Grand Ole Opry* just by tuning the AM radio to 650.

The *Opry*'s success depended on its being carried on AM radio, whose waves bounced off the ionosphere at night, enabling listeners hundreds of miles away to tune into the broadcast. If the *Opry* had been on FM, the signal would have been cleaner and clearer, but it would have been limited to Nashville and the immediate area. Instead, the cracking, popping sound of AM radio airwaves carried the *Opry* over much of the United States and even into Canada.

At the same time there were major changes at the *Grand Ole Opry,* there were changes in the music world at large that would have a direct effect on *Opry* performers and country music in general. Those changes affected publishers and songwriters.

In 1939, the American Society of Composers, Authors, and Publishers (ASCAP) decided to raise the fees charged to radio stations for the right to play its songs. This performance rights organization, founded in 1914, was the force that made songwriting a profitable profession because it licensed songs for play; that is, by paying ASCAP, a club, radio station, or concert hall could perform any song it wished while ASCAP collected the money and distributed it to its songwriters and publishers. For twenty-five years, it was virtually the only game in town, and the years of having a monopoly had bred arrogance in its ranks and resentment outside the fold.

The attempt to dramatically increase the fees in 1939 led to a countermove by broadcasters, who first banned all ASCAP songs from the airwaves and then formed a new performance rights organization, Broadcast Music, Inc. (BMI), which opened its doors on April 1, 1940.

The possibility of country music songwriters earning significant money from their songs changed dramatically on January 1, 1940, when a ten-month radio boycott of ASCAP songs began. *Opry* performers had to find songs that were public domain or else write their own. Pee Wee King's group in Louisville stopped using "Night Time in Nevada," their regular theme song, and began using the "No Name Waltz," a tune composed by fiddler Redd Stewart. Later, Stewart and Pee Wee King took that basic melody and added lyrics to produce "Tennessee Waltz."

By April 1, 1940, BMI had officially opened its first office in New York and let it be known the organization would sign up songs from anyone—there was no requirement that a songwriter had to be "elected" by its current members, which was the requirement at ASCAP. That's why most early country music songs are registered with BMI, which built a great deal of its early success on country music. But the benefits ran down a two-way street; for the first time, country music songwriters and publishers had access to a performance rights organization that would collect money for them for public performances. As country music was increasingly played on radio, there was a way for country songwriters to get paid for the exposure. And that brought big bucks into country music's songwriting and publishing coffers.

The call to arms was strong; American antiwar sentiment practically evaporated after Pearl Harbor and, a few days later, Germany declared war against the United States. Thousands of young men signed up for the armed forces, and those who didn't sign up knew they would soon be drafted. Indeed, 75 percent of young American men born between 1918 and 1927 would serve in World War II. Although the draft induced many to serve, the intense feelings of patriotism and the belief that Hitler must be defeated in order for the world to be safe were paramount in the country. So bond drives, rationing, and victory gardens began to affect the country. Entertainers also felt the call to serve—some at home and some abroad.

At Melody Ranch in Hollywood was Gene Autry, the most popular singing cowboy during the 1930s. The success of the singing cowboys meant employment for a number of songwriters who had to come up with songs for Autry and the other singing cowboys who followed, such as Tex Ritter and Roy Rogers. Autry generally required five to eight songs for each of his movies and always insisted on quality songs. One of the best songwriters for supplying Autry material was Fred

Rose, a pop songwriter who had written hits such as "Deed I Do," "Red Hot Mama," and "Honest and Truly" during the 1920s. Rose had moved to Nashville in 1933 to appear on WSM on an afternoon show, *The Freddie Rose Song Shop*; while in Nashville he had married.

Rose moved to Hollywood in 1938 to work on the Gene Autry movie *Gold Mine in the Sky*. He stayed and worked on a number of Autry movies, writing "Be Honest with Me" and other songs for Autry. But in the summer of 1942, Autry entered the armed forces as a pilot, and Rose moved back to Nashville because his wife wanted to return home. Rose was popular at WSM and quickly landed an afternoon show on the radio station. Roy Acuff also approached him about starting a publishing company because Acuff wanted to keep the rights to his songs (he reasoned that "if the New York and Chicago publishers wanted to buy them, they must be worth something") and because the songbook business was extremely profitable but also a burden—he needed someone to handle that part of his business.

Fred Rose was in a unique position. He knew the people at WSM and the *Opry*, he had learned about the huge market for country music—and the money involved—through his work with Autry and the singing cowboys in the movies, and he was a pop songwriter who came to Nashville as country music was changing from folk-based music into major commercial music. Rose would play a major role here, introducing the pop song format with country topics to replace the folk song format. That had already been done with western music, most of which was composed by Tin Pan Alley writers who used pop song structures with western themes. Fred Rose would take that same process to Nashville and apply it to Southern-based country music.

In January 1943, another national sponsor bought time on the *Opry*. The Ralston Purina Company, maker of feed for farm livestock, purchased a thirty-minute segment, called the "Purina Grand Ole Opry," which was broadcast over the NBC network in the South and Southwest. It was another step in the direction of making the *Opry* a national show.

During the war years, the *Opry* would continue to hold performances. By October 1943, it was on 125 stations on NBC's national network. In addition, transcriptions were sent out all over the country and put on Armed Forces Radio.

A huge influx of servicemen swept through Nashville. The South was chosen for the site of a number of armed services training camps because of the large amounts of cheap, undeveloped land that could be turned into bases and because of the mild climate.

In Nashville the Aviation Manufacturing Corporation of California (later AVCO) established an airplane manufacturing plant, Vultee Aircraft, in 1939; the plant opened in May 1941 and employed seven thousand workers. The Nashville Bridge Company, on the Cumberland River in East Nashville, built submarine chasers and mine sweepers for the navy; the Kerrigan Iron Works made pontoons; Allen Manufacturing manufactured stoves for the armed services; the Tennessee Enamel Company manufactured shell and torpedo parts; the DuPont plant made parachutes; General Shoe manufactured military footwear; Werthan Bag manufactured sandbags; and Phillips & Buttorff made pontoons. Military airplanes were manufactured by Tennessee Aircraft while military uniforms were made by Washington Manufacturing, Southern Manufacturing, and the O'Bryan Brothers. A hospital for wounded soldiers, Thayer General, was built in Nashville; it would treat thirteen thousand soldiers. On Thompson Lane an Army Air Classification Center was constructed that classified numerous recruits for the flying services; later it served as a hospital and then a demobilization center.

> *During the war years, the* Opry *would continue to hold performances. By October 1943, it was on 125 stations on NBC's national network.*

In Clarksville, just west of Nashville, Camp Campbell was constructed in the summer of 1941; it joined Camp Forrest in Tullahoma and the Smyrna Air Field as military training bases just outside Nashville.

On weekends Nashville was filled with servicemen with weekend passes; during 1942, more than 1 million soldiers visited the city, and many of them went to see the *Grand Ole Opry*. Jack Stapp left WSM to serve in London, and some of the musicians and performers also left—but a number of key performers stayed home and kept performing. *Opry* performers and National Life and Accident Insurance salesmen were engaged in war bond drives, which raised a good deal of money and contributed to positive public relations for country music and Nashville.

5

Striking Out on His Own

The Camel Caravan Tour of *Opry* performers ended at Christmas 1942; the troupe had traveled more than fifty thousand miles, performing 175 shows in 19 states at 68 army camps, hospitals, air fields, and naval and marine bases. In March 1942, it left the United States and performed in the Panama Canal Zone.

When it was all over, the Camel Caravan had done as much as anything to spread country music throughout the country to servicemen. It had also done a great deal for Eddy Arnold, who gained a wealth of experience and national exposure.

Most *Opry* performers were tied to the Saturday night *Opry* shows, and that prohibited *Opry* acts from extensive touring. Even though *Opry* performers played shows during the week, they could never venture too far away because they had to be back in Nashville on Saturday night. The performers on the Camel Caravan had no such restrictions; Eddy Arnold experienced extensive touring during 1942 and performed before a wide variety of audiences—not just for those who had heard him on the *Opry*. Also, although the *Opry*'s Camel Caravan had *Opry* members, it wasn't strictly a "country music" show in the style of the mountaineer image and sound of Roy Acuff. King's group was more pop sounding, and the diverse audiences on the tour demanded a style of music beyond the traditional string band sound.

There were some memorable adventures along the way. Troupe members were stranded in Guatemala for about a week—and had to idle away each day, not knowing when they would be able to return. Finally, they got back to Texas and Eddy Arnold had to hitch a ride

Harry Stone.

on the back of a truck, braced against the freezing air all the way back to Nashville. But the tour was a heady experience for the young singer, who became more worldly wise with the traveling and meeting a large cross section of people, from dignitaries to conscripts.

The Camel Caravan performances also brought Eddy Arnold to the attention of some key executives and decision makers. WSM General Manager Harry Stone sometimes visited the shows, and he was impressed by Arnold's smooth vocals. He was also impressed by Arnold's stage introductions and the fact the singer was an ambitious, levelheaded young man. Stone and Arnold had struck up conversations during the Camel Caravan tour and gotten to know each other a bit. In Nashville after the tour ended and the Golden West Cowboys were back on the *Opry*, Arnold went into Stone's office one day in December. He told Stone he wanted to pursue a solo career and asked if Stone could use him in that capacity. Stone looked at Arnold and said, "I don't see why not." Eddy Arnold then submitted his resignation to Pee Wee King.

➤ *The Tennessee Plowboy was a name given to Eddy Arnold by Judge George D. Hay.*

Harry Stone hired Eddy Arnold for a variety of musical jobs at WSM in 1943, made him a member of the *Grand Ole Opry*, and gave him several daytime radio shows during the week where Arnold performed with just his guitar. In the fall, Arnold formed his first band, the Tennessee Plowboys consisting of longtime buddy Speedy McNatt on fiddle, Roy Wiggins on steel guitar, Gabe Tucker on bass, and Herbert "Butterball" Paige on electric take-off or lead guitar.

The Tennessee Plowboy was a name given to Eddy Arnold by Judge George D. Hay back when most performers had a handle with which to advertise themselves; Roy Acuff was the Smoky Mountain Boy, and Uncle Dave Macon was the Dixie Dewdrop. And so Arnold became the Tennessee Plowboy—an accurate name for billing him at the time.

> *Throughout 1943 and 1944, Eddy Arnold stayed busy performing on WSM during the weekdays, on the* Grand Ole Opry *on Saturday nights, and on personal appearances throughout the South.*

Throughout 1943 and 1944, Eddy Arnold stayed busy performing on WSM during the weekdays, on the *Grand Ole Opry* on Saturday nights, and on personal appearances throughout the South. The *Opry* sent out a number of tent shows in the Southeast where several performers would set up a tent near the edge of town, put up posters and alert the media, and hope a crowd showed up to buy tickets. Generally, a single performer undertook the financial risk of buying (or leasing) a large tent, having promotional materials drawn up, and paying the other performers. The *Opry* collected a 15 percent commission from ticket sales in exchange for use of its name.

Eddy Arnold performed on a tent show tour organized by Jam Up and Honey, two blackface comedians. During a tent show performance in Arkansas, advertising executive Charles Brown watched Eddy Arnold and was impressed with his voice and stage demeanor.

The Ralston Purina Company had begun advertising on WSM's *Grand Ole Opry* in January 1943; advertising executives Charles and Bill Brown, in charge of the account at the Gardner Advertising Company in St. Louis, soon broke off and formed their own agency, the Brown Brothers, with the Purina account. Charles Brown decided to make Eddy Arnold the star or host of the "Checkerboard Square" segment of the *Opry*. There was some grumbling among the *Opry* troupe when Arnold obtained the plum spot; some muttered he was "too young" or "inexperienced" for such a slot while others felt that because they were seasoned, loyal *Opry* performers, it was "their turn" and they should have been given the spot. Arnold didn't say much; he just went about his business of hosting the show—but he heard the whispers and felt the envy.

Eddy and Sally Arnold at their apartment in Madison, Tennessee.

The Brown Brothers then began to sponsor a one-hour show from the Andrew Jackson Hotel with a large cast, a big band led by Owen Bradley, and Eddy Arnold as the host. It was a mammoth job, but the daily show, broadcast over the Mutual Network, lasted about a year.

During 1944, Eddy and Sally Arnold moved into a house on Branch Avenue off Gallatin Road in Madison, about seven miles from downtown Nashville. Arnold's mother often lived with them; she would stay with Eddy and Sally awhile, then go to St. Louis to stay with her daughter, then go to Jackson, Tennessee, to stay with son W. D., who owned the Library Barber Shop. In June 1944, she received a telegram at Eddy's house that her son, John, had died during the D-Day invasion. John, a member of a division of paratroopers, lost his life on the second day of the invasion (June 7) and was buried in France. By that time Eddy and John had become close with the boyhood fights a thing of the past. The death of his brother caused Eddy Arnold once again to face a family tragedy—and it hurt.

Things were hopping in Chicago during the spring and summer of 1944. The American Federation of Musicians held a convention and reelected James Caesar Petrillo as president, the Republicans held their convention in June and nominated Thomas Dewey, and the Democrats held their convention in mid-July and renominated Franklin Roosevelt for a fourth term. The Democratic Convention was dull except for the decision about a vice-presidential nominee; after Roosevelt's current vice president, Henry Wallace, and his first choice, Supreme Court Justice William O. Douglas, were rejected, he settled on a little-known senator from Missouri named Harry S. Truman.

Harry Stone, head of WSM, one of NBC's major affiliates, had plenty of reasons to be in Chicago that spring and summer. During one trip, he had dinner with Chicago music publisher Fred Forster, who owned Forster Music (ASCAP) and Adams, Vee, and Abbott (BMI) located at 216 South Wabash Avenue. Since Forster and other Chicago publishers controlled the copyrights to a number of country songs, it behooved Stone, whose station carried the *Grand Ole Opry*, to keep good relations.

By then Eddy Arnold had made a name for himself in country music through his appearances on the *Opry* as host of the Purina segment. He had toured with the Camel Caravan and was on some *Opry* tent shows. Insiders could see his star rising; most knew he was someone to watch.

During the dinner with Forster, Harry Stone talked to the Chicago publisher about Eddy Arnold and told him Arnold was looking for a recording contract. Forster had heard Arnold on the radio and told Stone he would recommend Arnold to his friend, Frank Walker, head of A & R (Artist and Repertoire) for Victor Records, "when you feel the boy is ready." Stone replied, "He's ready right now."

That led Forster to call Walker long-distance in New York, and Walker replied that Forster's recommendation was good enough—he would send Arnold a contract. So Walker wired Arnold a message that he wanted him to become a Victor artist. That was good news for Arnold, who had auditioned for Art Satherley at Columbia and an A & R rep from Decca—and been turned down by both. Now he was being signed to a label unseen and unheard.

He also signed with Forster's publishing company. Arnold had been trying his hand at writing songs since he branched off on his own. During 1944, he had written a number of songs with Wally Fowler and J. Graydon Hall, which were published by Fowler. Fowler put out a songbook with a number of the songs, which Arnold sold at personal appearances. Country artists have always depended on merchandise sold at concerts—anything from songbooks to T-shirts—to provide an income. During the 1940s, the major source of merchandising revenue came from songbooks, which the publisher would print and then either sell to the artist, who would resell them for a markup, or provide them to the artist who would receive a commission for selling them. Eddy Arnold had his picture on the cover of the songbook from Fowler, and his fans bought it as a souvenir as well as to learn the songs.

Fred Forster, who did not have any children, took Arnold under his wing and eventually developed a fatherlike relationship with the young singer. When Forster first called Arnold, he told the singer that he should expect a contract from Victor and, when it arrived, he should send it to Forster's attorney to look over. Arnold did so, and Forster's lawyer made some suggestions; the initial royalty rate was half a cent for each record sold.

But Arnold's joy was tempered with disappointment. In 1942, the president of the musicians union (the American Federation of Musicians or AFM), James Caesar Petrillo, called a strike to begin August 1. In May, Petrillo announced the decision to strike, so most labels stockpiled recordings before the strike; that didn't help Arnold, who didn't have a recording contract before the strike.

The central issue for the strike, announced at the AFM's annual convention, was the provision of a Performance Trust Fund to provide money for musicians out of work. The demand came about because of the rising popularity of recordings and the threat to put musicians out of business if radio played records instead of hiring musicians to perform live. Additionally, Petrillo wanted more money and better working conditions for musicians—a key demand in most labor strikes. The labor leader held firm for fifteen months, despite pleas from President Roosevelt not to strike. However, there was a capitulation because musicians were allowed to make transcriptions for V-Disks to be sent to soldiers overseas; the proviso was that V-Disks could not be sold and had to be destroyed once soldiers finished listening. V-Disks were recordings produced by the Army to be sent overseas for entertainment for soldiers, allowing them to hear the top acts of the day when they were far from home.

From August 1, 1942, until December 1944, the strike brought the recording industry to a halt, although Victor tried to make recordings in Cuba and Mexico. Then in the fall of 1943, Decca capitulated

Eddy Arnold with Minnie Pearl—two members of the Camel Caravan.

to the union; however, Victor and Columbia continued to hold out until the next year when they began to run out of stockpiled recordings, and releases by a cappella groups proved not to be commercial. Finally, Victor and Columbia reached an agreement with the union, and the strike ended. Frank Walker wired Arnold to go into a radio station immediately to make some recordings. Victor had a lot of recording to catch up on, so the studios in New York and Chicago were booked solid. Besides, Eddy Arnold was a new, unknown act; he was not a priority.

During 1944, Eddy Arnold had been frustrated at his lack of opportunity for recording. He would hear an a cappella record—some singers did them to work around the musicians strike—and think, *Could I do that?* It was embarrassing to have to answer the question: "Do you have a record out yet?" Eddy Arnold wanted a record out so bad he could taste it; he felt the musicians strike attacked him personally, that life was slipping away and he couldn't salvage his big opportunity.

After Arnold had signed with Forster, the publisher sent him a song to consider singing: "Cattle Call." The song, written by Tex Owens, had been recorded by Owens, and numerous other singers had sung it; Arnold remembers he first heard it in St. Louis when a cowboy singer did it on the radio. But Fred Rose had rewritten the original song, putting a bridge into the song, and rewritten the lyrics to make it more commercial. Rose never took credit for it; one story says he did it as a favor for Fred Forster, an old friend, but other sources have noted that Owens never liked Rose's changes and refused to share songwriting credit on the song.

The yodel in the song fit Arnold's voice perfectly, and crowds loved it whenever he sang it. Soon, Eddy Arnold was using it as his theme song on the *Opry* and on his personal appearances.

On December 4, 1944, Arnold took musicians Gabe Tucker, Speedy McNatt, Roy Wiggins, and Butterball Paige into WSM radio Studio B with engineer Percy White to record four songs. The songs were "Mother's Prayer," "Mommy Please Stay Home with Me," "Cattle Call," and "Each Minute Seems a Million Years." When the session was finished, the masters were sent to New York. This was the first studio recording session by a major label in Nashville.

6

The War Years

In January 1945, Eddy Arnold's first single, "Mommy Please Stay Home with Me" backed with "Mother's Prayer," was released on Bluebird, Victor's budget label. The single is a story song about a young boy whose mother goes out and parties, even though the child pleads, "Please stay home with me." A number of women worked during World War II—about 20 million women, or one-third of the 60 million domestic workforce—and the song addressed an underlying concern that women were losing their commitment to motherhood and connection to their children and family because they were out in the world. The mother in the song is a wayward woman, who prefers enjoying the bright lights and good times of a party to staying home with her child; the end result is the death of her child after she returns from a night of drinking to find him "in raging pain and nearing death." The child dies with the words, "Please, Mommy, please stay home with me," on his lips.

The final verse concludes with a warning to mothers: "don't neglect your duty" and don't "ignore your baby's pleading." In many ways the song was prophetic because its message would resonate throughout the rest of the century.

The story of the record business during World War II was a fight for shellac. Because of wartime rationing and shortages, it was difficult to get shellac to press records, and the government had imposed controls on the amount of shellac that labels could use—and how many records could be pressed. Victor saved big pressing runs for proven artists such as Perry Como and Vaughn Monroe. For a brandnew act such as Eddy Arnold, the single run was it. The result was that after 85,000 copies were sold, no more Eddy Arnold records were pressed.

Arnold's second record, "Each Minute Seems a Million Years" backed with "Cattle Call," came out in June 1945, and sold enough to chart, with the A side rising to number five. "Each Minute Seems a Million Years" is at a brisk tempo with a fiddle and Roy Wiggins's distinctive steel guitar as the lyrics tell of a longing for a love that has gone. "Cattle Call," which Arnold was using as his theme song, begins with Arnold strumming his guitar, then sounding the distinctive yodel. The bridge sections, one that begins with "He rides in the sun" and the other that begins "He's brown as a berry" where the song moves to the "four" chord, were Fred Rose's contribution.

On July 9, 1945, Arnold went back into the WSM radio studio for his next recording session and recorded "Did You See My Daddy Over There," "Many Tears Ago," "I Walk Alone," and "You Must Walk the Line." The first release, again on Bluebird, from this session was "Did You See My Daddy Over There," backed with "I Walk Alone." "Did You See My Daddy Over There" is a World War II story song that tells of a boy stopping soldiers who have come back from the war and asking about his dad. "I Walk Alone" is a song of faithfulness with the singer telling his love that when they're apart, he is still true.

The recording session took up four hours in a very busy life. Every Saturday night Arnold appeared on the *Grand Ole Opry* on the Purina segment, and during the week he toured, performing wherever he could. Many of the shows were in tents with other *Opry* performers while other performances were in schoolhouses, town halls, or wherever else he could get a booking.

Eddy Arnold was also building relationships with the label personnel. At that point, Victor sold records through its warehouse distribution system. The warehouses stocked RCA products—phonographs as well as records—and shipped them to stores. Arnold got to know the managers of each of the warehouses and developed a relationship with each of them. When he had a new record coming out, he would call them and chat, telling them about the record. In turn, they would be more inclined to stock a record from an artist who extended the personal touch. On his personal appearances, Arnold would be sure to stop by the warehouses and meet the managers and employees, then go to record stores and sign autographs and visit with store employees.

Eddy Arnold, with his instinctive feel for the business of music, laid the groundwork for his records to sell. In many ways he was his own best salesman; his records were consistently available for consumers to purchase. As a result, all of the records sold well on the discount Bluebird label and caught the attention of Victor executives in New York.

> ➤ *A number of* Opry *acts organized tent shows—it was a good way to earn extra income—and the Jam Up and Honey show featured Minnie Pearl as well as singer Eddy Arnold.*

By the end of 1945, Eddy Arnold had a lot going for him. He was on the *Grand Ole Opry* every Saturday night, which was beamed to thousands across the country. He hosted his own fifteen-minute segment of the *Opry*, which allowed him to show off his considerable skills as a master of ceremonies. Next, he had some records that sold well enough for the top brass at Victor to take notice. Finally, he had a manager, Tom Parker, who was a genius at promoting acts and would guide his career outside the *Opry* power structure.

Eddy Arnold had gotten to know Tom Parker in the fall of 1944 when Parker was the advance man for the tent show organized by the comedy team of Jam Up and Honey. The tent shows, organized by *Opry* members, took country acts to audiences who could not travel because of wartime restrictions on gas and tires. A number of *Opry* acts organized tent shows—it was a good way to earn extra income—and the Jam Up and Honey show featured Minnie Pearl as well as singer Eddy Arnold.

The job of an advance man was to let people know a show was coming to town and then make sure a crowd showed up to buy tickets. Tom Parker was a genius in that area, perhaps one of the best advance men that show business has ever known. He was good at going into a town, notifying the newspapers, getting posters printed and distributed, and creating excitement for the coming show. And he did it with little or no money for promotion.

People who knew Colonel Tom Parker (the title is honorary and came first from Louisiana Governor Jimmie Davis, a former country music singer, and later from Tennessee Governor Frank Clement after Parker had become Arnold's manager) always say something to the effect, "Well, you know, Parker was an old carny." The explanation—he was a "carny"—means he had a connection to the traveling carnivals and circuses before World War II. It was a world filled with magic—the appeal of an exotic group of traveling performers who played all over the country and brought joy and excitement to audiences whose lives were brightened by the arrival of entertainers in their area.

In the carnival world, Parker learned the ropes of advancing shows. In addition to coverage from newspapers and posters, Parker learned how to pay off politicians and town officials and, as radio in the rural South became more popular, to deal with radio disc jockeys in order to get a crowd for the circus.

To be a good advance man and promoter, you had to be a fast talker and Parker mastered the art; also, he developed the ambition to be the biggest promoter in America. He settled in Tampa, Florida, because that was where most of the traveling circuses and carnivals spent the winter, and around 1935 married Marie Mott, a divorcee with a ten-year-old son.

> *Tom Parker was a genius perhaps one of the best advance men that show business has ever known.*

Parker was a man for hire to any show that needed an advance man or PR person; that was how he became acquainted with Gene Austin, the crooner who had a huge hit in the mid-1920s with "My Blue Heaven." In 1939, when Parker and Austin met, the singer was playing small gigs in the South; Parker convinced Austin to hire him as his booking agent, and soon Austin was getting numerous dates in small towns with good-sized crowds.

Parker elected to stay in Tampa when Austin wanted to move to Nashville in the early 1940s; there Parker was hired to head the Tampa Humane Society and raise funds for the group. Parker soon had the Humane Society financially self-supporting; additionally, he convinced merchants to donate pet food and got lots of press coverage from lovable puppies and kittens being adopted by cute girls and boys.

Parker had worked with country music acts who came to Tampa for concerts at the National Guard armory since 1941; there he worked for J. L. Frank, Roy Acuff, Bill Monroe, and others, promoting concerts. Acuff was so impressed with Parker's success in promoting concerts that he reportedly invited him to work at the *Grand Ole Opry* in Nashville, but Parker turned him down and stayed in Tampa.

That was where Parker was in the fall of 1944 when the Jam Up and Honey tent show, featuring singer Eddy Arnold, toured Florida

Eddy Arnold at an airport with, left to right, an unknown man, manager Tom Parker, and Roy Wiggins.

and other Southern states. Arnold was also impressed by Parker's effectiveness at organizing, promoting, and advancing shows, and since he did not have his own manager (the two most influential music executives in Arnold's life had other obligations; Harry Stone worked for WSM while J. L. Frank managed Pee Wee King's Golden West Cowboys), he entered a handshake agreement with Tom Parker for management.

Every performer longs to find someone who totally believes in the performer's talent, who is competent in handling the demanding day-to-day aspects of live performances—booking the hall, promoting the concert, making sure an audience shows up—so the performer can just appear and do his show. Furthermore, the artist needs someone who will dedicate his life to promoting the artist and his or her career, someone whose thoughts and activities are constantly focused on making the singer a star. Eddy Arnold found that person in Tom Parker.

Parker had an old Studebaker with a trailer hooked behind with "Eddy Arnold The Tennessee Plowboy" in foot-high letters on the back and sides. Assisting Parker were his brother-in-law, Bitsy Mott, and Bevo Bevis, who had first worked for Parker at the Tampa animal shelter. The team would spend all their time promoting the concerts and career of Eddy Arnold.

Arnold couldn't have asked for a better manager. There is an apocryphal story that Parker once purchased a hot plate and some chickens so the chickens would "dance" while Arnold performed, thus classifying the act as an agricultural event and avoiding the $25 entertainment tax whenever they played. The story has been passed around for years—but it is not true.

However, Parker was shrewd and made sure things went well for his act. Once, in Houston, the manager of a venue told Parker that songbooks and other merchandise couldn't be sold during the show without paying a commission to the venue manager. Parker replied they didn't pay commissions, so the venue manager forbade the sale of any merchandise. When the manager asked about intermission, Parker replied there would be none—and the manager panicked because he would be unable to sell all the hamburgers and hot dogs he had cooked to sell during the intermission. Finally, the manager said, "You can sell your songbooks," and Parker smiled serenely.

Another time, in Chattanooga, Parker and Arnold played for a promoter who was notorious for not paying the act. So Parker and Arnold got together before the show, and Parker told Arnold not to perform until Parker waved his hand. Then Parker went to the promoter and said, "You know, my acts are kinda funny. They won't play until I wave my hand. And I won't wave my hand until I'm paid." The promoter then paid, Parker stepped out and waved to Arnold, and the performance went ahead.

Tom Parker was audacious enough to demand top dollar for his act when other country acts were underpaid (Arnold was receiving $500 a week for his Purina radio show, *The Checkerboard Jamboree*, when other artists were working for next to nothing), and he never let up in his efforts to get Arnold in the public spotlight.

Parker was so dedicated to his artist that one day Arnold told him he should take some time off or get a hobby. Parker looked Arnold in the eye and replied, "You're my hobby." That was a big reason for the success of Eddy Arnold at the beginning of 1945 when his first record was released: he had Tom Parker doing everything humanly possible as a manager, booking agent, and promoter to get him out in front of the public and make him a star. No artist could ask for more than Tom Parker gave Eddy Arnold.

Eddy Arnold in a backstage dressing room.

Arnold was traveling with a four-piece band, and during his show, like all country shows at the time, the audience expected some comedy. The skits, generally old vaudeville and minstrel show routines recycled, were done by mandolin player Rollin Sullivan and bass player Lloyd George. Sullivan had picked up the nickname Oscar from Bill Westbrooks back during the Jackson, Tennessee, days, but George didn't have a nickname. Then one day, while Eddy Arnold was at the counter checking the group into a hotel, the woman at the counter yelled to someone on the stairs with some laundry, "Lonzo!" Arnold cracked up; he loved the name and decided that George and Sullivan should be Lonzo and Oscar.

Eddy Arnold's first two sessions for Victor were held at the WSM radio studios. They were both done for Bluebird, the discount label that sold records for 35 cents each. The top or Black label sold for 50 cents each; that label was limited to the pop acts and top sellers. However, with Arnold's records selling so well, Victor executives decided he should be released on the Black label because they would receive more money from each record sold.

Sometime in early fall 1945, Eddy Arnold received a phone call from Steve Sholes who was in charge of country and blues recordings (then called hillbilly and race records) for Victor. Sholes, a big, heavy man with a high-pitched voice, said to Arnold, "We think we can make you a star. How about recording in Chicago?" Arnold agreed immediately, and a session was set for November 21, 1945, at the Victor Studio in Chicago.

Sholes, whose father worked for Victor in Camden, New Jersey, started work with the firm in 1929, just after he graduated from high school. During his college days at Rutgers University, Sholes worked for the firm part-time, and after his college graduation in 1935 went to work full-time, first in the factory storeroom of the radio department and then in the sales department.

Sholes had played saxophone and clarinet in local bands during the big band era, and this musical background served him well when he decided to move to the record department from the radio department in 1936, taking a $25 a week cut in pay in order to listen to test pressings of recording sessions and assure quality control. In July 1943, Sholes joined the armed services, where he worked in New York with the V-Disk program. Since Victor was one of the major manufacturers of V-Disks, Sholes kept in close contact with the label. Also, Sholes produced some sessions for the V-Disks and gained valuable studio experience as a producer.

When he rejoined Victor after his discharge from the army in July 1945, he was put in charge of hillbilly and race music—not a high honor for a New York record man at the time. The power and prestige at a label were in the pop music division; for most executives, being put in charge of hillbilly and race music was an insult and demotion. It was the bottom rung for most A & R men; however, a few A & R men developed a respect for the music and performers in the fields and brought integrity to the sessions. Steve Sholes was a rare man—he developed a love and respect for the people in country music as well as the music itself. His first success in the field was Eddy Arnold.

Eddy Arnold and Sholes met for the first time in Chicago the night before the session. Arnold always came to his sessions well prepared, with his band fully rehearsed so they could complete four songs in a three-hour session. Sholes would send Arnold some songs to consider, and Arnold would find other songs. It was a mutual give-and-take between producer and artist with Sholes wanting Arnold to feel comfortable with the songs and Arnold needing some outside input into songs and the sessions.

With his band that consisted of Dempsey Watts on bass, Roy Wiggins on steel guitar, Rollin Sullivan on electric mandolin, Butterball Paige on guitar, and Speedy McNatt on violin, Arnold recorded four songs, "(I'll Have to) Live and Learn," "Be Sure There's No Mistake," "I Couldn't Believe It Was True," and "I Talk to Myself About

You." It would be the beginning of the Eddy Arnold–Steve Sholes team that would grow close personally and professionally.

As 1945 drew to a close, Eddy Arnold was still known for his radio appearances more than his recording sales, although his sales had been strong and promising. But Steve Sholes knew he had an artist who was not only talented with an appealing pop-type voice, but also serious, ambitious, and willing to work hard on his career in a determined, businesslike manner.

On the personal side, 1945 provided two major milestones in the lives of Eddy and Sally Arnold. They bought their first home, a four-bedroom house in Madison, and their daughter Jo Ann was born on December 17. Not only was Eddy Arnold a rising star in country music, he was a proud papa and successful family man as well.

7

Nashville at the End of World War II

On April 12, 1945, Eddy Arnold was driving to Paducah, Kentucky, on his way to a personal appearance when he heard on the radio that President Franklin Roosevelt had died. The news stunned him; for the past twelve years—ever since he was a fourteen-year-old schoolboy living on a farm in Chester County, Tennessee—Franklin Roosevelt had been president of the United States. Since that time, Arnold had left the farm, had lived in Jackson, St. Louis, Nashville, and Louisville, and had begun singing on the radio. He had gone from a farm boy singing in the fields with a dream to sing on the radio to a young man earning his living singing country music. In short, he had gone from being a "nobody" to being on the cusp of becoming a "star" in country music. Just as it affected most other Americans, the news of Roosevelt's death was devastating to him. Still, the show must go on, so Eddy Arnold performed that night in Paducah.

Less than a month later, on May 7, 1945, the Allies captured Berlin and declared victory in Europe; they then turned their attention to the Pacific. In August the United States dropped two atomic bombs on Japan, effectively ending the war in that part of the world. On that August day when the news came over the radio, Eddy Arnold was in Charleston, West Virginia. The end of the war meant no more gas coupons or gas rationing; Arnold pulled into a service station and asked the attendant to fill 'er up—and paid with cash instead of coupons.

The war lasted four years. Servicemen were anxious to get back home, and the home folks were anxious to have them back. The war had effectively ended the unemployment problems of the country. In 1940, the unemployment rate was 14 percent; in 1943, it was 1.9 percent. During the war, 16.3 million Americans served in the military, a stark contrast to 1939 when only 335,000 people were in the armed services. By mid-1945, about 18 percent of the workforce, or about 12.1 million, were in the armed services.

Immense changes in the country had occurred during the four years the United States was actively engaged in World War II. In 1940, more than 20 percent of Americans still lived on farms and less than 33 percent of the farms had electricity while only 10 percent had flush toilets. More than 50 percent of all households didn't have a refrigerator, about 30 percent didn't have inside running water (in rural areas it was 60 percent of whites and more than 95 percent of blacks), and 58 percent of households lacked central heating. Most Americans (56 percent) rented their housing.

The shift away from farms and small towns and toward big cities and factory work changed the working life of most Americans. Until the 1930s, the typical workweek for men in manufacturing was about fifty hours; by the end of the war a forty-hour workweek had been established, and workers worked five days instead of six. There were fewer farmworkers (between 1940 and 1944, the number of farmworkers dropped by 16 percent), but food production was up by 20 percent, primarily because of the increased number of tractors and other mechanical devices on farms.

Approximately 27 million Americans moved during World War II, about 40 percent to serve in the military and the rest primarily to obtain work in war plants or for the government. Since the population of the United States in 1940 was 132 million, about 20 percent of the population shifted during the war.

During the twenty-five-year period 1920–45, the country was linked by radio. In 1920, there were virtually no radio sets in the United States; by 1929, there were 12 million sets. That number continued to increase throughout the 1930s and World War II until by the end of the war about 90 percent of American households had a radio set.

In 1940, only about 25 percent of all Americans had a high school diploma, and about 5 percent had a college degree. The average Southerner earned less than $1,000 a year; only 7.8 million Americans made enough money to pay taxes. By the end of 1945, the number that paid taxes had increased to nearly 50 million out of a population that had grown to 140 million.

At the beginning of the war, most Americans were poor; after the draft was instituted in the summer of 1940, about 20 percent of the young men were declared unfit because of malnutrition or other problems caused by poor living conditions. For many young American men, their service in the armed forces was the first time they had regular meals, good housing, and a secure job. For some Southern conscripts, it was the first time they had worn shoes or clothes that were new or didn't have holes. The country was poor as well; some of the first draftees trained with wooden guns.

> *For some Southern conscripts, it was the first time they had worn shoes or clothes that were new or didn't have holes. The country was poor as well; some of the first draftees trained with wooden guns.*

During the war, the United States was transformed into a powerful, productive, wealthy nation. Prior to the war, unemployment stood at 14 percent, and many of the nation's factories produced at limited capacity. But during the period of World War II, factories were transformed to produce almost 300,000 war planes, more than 100,000 tanks, 2.5 million trucks, almost 95,000 ships, and 44 billion rounds of small arms munitions.

The changes in America were immense and almost beyond comprehension, but a single example will vividly illustrate the extent of what happened. At the end of 1941, when World War II began, the United States Army owned 200,000 horses for its cavalry. In August 1945, the war effectively ended with an atomic blast from a bomb dropped by an airplane.

During the war years, 1941–45, things changed a great deal in Nashville and in the country music community; some of the changes would lay the groundwork for Nashville's becoming the Capital of Country Music, the city synonymous with country music.

The South, more than any other region, benefited from World War II. Most of the new training camps for the army were in the South. Approximately half of all those serving in the armed forces during the war—about 6 million young men—spent time at a Southern base and were exposed to the South for the first time in their lives. While those outside the South came into the region for the first time during the war, many residents of the South left the region for work in defense or defense-related plants in the North and the West. California gained more than 1 million residents during the war while northern cities also had population growth, much of it from South- erners moving north. Those who came into the South often heard country music for the first time; those leaving the South carried their taste for country music with them. All the war-related movement led to the spread of country music throughout the nation.

The United States had been defined by regions before the war; people tended to define themselves as Southerners or Westerners. But during the war, the patriotism at home and the efforts of the armed services caused Americans to see themselves more as Americans and blur the differences in ethnic, racial, or regional backgrounds. Outside the country foreigners did not see a Yank or a Southerner or a West- erner; they saw an American. Americans also became more aware of the differences within their own country, and that tended to enhance their view of themselves as Americans and helped them enjoy the idea of diversity rather than see diversity as divisive.

On Saturday night, December 8, 1945, exactly four years after the United States officially entered World War II, the *Grand Ole Opry* was broadcast live from the Ryman Auditorium on Fifth Avenue in Nashville. At noon that Saturday there had been a one-hour matinee featuring *Opry* acts; that night the radio listings noted the times for the performers: at 6:00 was Wally Fowler; at 6:15 Pee Wee King and Lew Childre performed; at 6:45 Paul Howard and Minnie Pearl were on; at 7:00 Ernest Tubb entertained; at 7:30 it was the Golden West Cowboys; at 7:45 it was Ol' Times and Lew Childre; at 8:00 it was Eddy Arnold; at 8:15 Uncle Dave Macon performed; and throughout the rest of the evening in the fifteen-minute segments that structured *Opry* performances were Clyde Moody, Roy Acuff, the Duke of Pa- ducah, Bill Monroe, Curly Fox and Texas Ruby and, closing the show, the Fruit Jar Drinkers.

By that time Nashville had been the place for several recording sessions by major labels; the WSM radio studios had first recorded Eddy Arnold for Victor on December 4, 1944, and there were other recording facilities, basically connected with radio stations. There were some major publishing companies, led by Acuff-Rose (whose founder, Fred Rose, had enticed his son from his first marriage, Wesley, to leave his job as an accountant for Standard Oil in Chicago and move to Nashville as general manager of the publishing company), and recording label executives were increasingly coming to Nashville to look for talent and record them.

Also, *Billboard*, the major music trade magazine, had begun a chart on country (then called folk) recordings. It showed the "Most Played Juke Box" recordings, and they were "It's Been So Long, Darling" by Ernest Tubb, "Sioux City Sue" by Dick Thomas, "You Two-Timed Me One Time Too Often" by Tex Ritter, "With Tears in My Eyes" by Wesley Tuttle, "Silver Dew on the Blue Grass Tonight" by Bob Wills and the Texas Playboys, "Shame on You" by Red Foley, "Honestly" by Dick Thomas, and "You Will Have to Pay" by Tex Ritter.

The top pop songs on December 8, 1945, were "It's Been a Long, Long Time" by Bing Crosby, "Clickety Click" by Sammy Kaye, "It's Been a Long, Long Time" by Harry James, "I'll Buy That Dream" by Dick Haymes and Helen Forrest, "I Can't Begin to Tell You" by Bing Crosby and Carmen Cava, "Waitin' for the Train to Come In" by Peggy Lee, and "It Might as Well Have Been Spring" by Dick Haymes, Paul Weston, and Margaret Whiting. Network radio was king and the top radio programs included those by Bob Hope, *Fibber McGee and Molly*, *Lux Radio Theatre*, Walter Winchell, Edgar Bergen, Jack Benny, *Mr. D. A.*, Fred Allen, Abbott and Costello, Screen Guild, *Take It or Leave It*, *Kraft Music Hall,* Eddie Cantor, Jack Haley, the Aldrich Family, *The Shadow*, *One Man's Family*, and the *Family Hour.*

In terms of country music in general, the biggest song to come out of the war was "There's a Star Spangled Banner Waving Somewhere" by Elton Britt. The song was incredibly popular after its release in mid-1942, and it put country music on the pop charts. Country songs were recorded by a number of artists, including the premier pop singer, Bing Crosby. Crosby's hits with songs such as "Pistol Packin' Mama" and "New San Antonio Rose" made country music widely accepted and acceptable in the pop music world. And that, in turn, gave country artists a boost.

The major changes in country music in Nashville were all connected to the *Opry*. The war had caused the country to be united by radio, and WSM emerged as a major radio station. The *Opry* was a major performance outlet with a network program; that attracted advertising agencies with New York connections and the money to promote tours. The *Opry*, through Jim Denny, had organized its booking agency to capitalize on the demand for live country music shows after the war.

Musically, Roy Acuff was the major star on the *Opry* through the war years, and he presented the mountaineer image. Acuff's star

Eddy Arnold with Gene Autry.

power came from the fact that he hosted the *Prince Albert Show* over the NBC network each Saturday night. But other musical stars such as Ernest Tubb, who had joined in 1943 and who represented the Texas honky-tonk sound with his hit "Walking the Floor Over You," were ascending at the *Opry*.

At the end of 1942, Ernest Tubb was a hot commodity in demand on records and for personal appearances. He decided to leave Texas, and had to choose between Hollywood (which he initially favored because of the possibility of future movie work) or Nashville, home of the *Grand Ole Opry*. The pendulum swung in Nashville's direction because of J. L. Frank, whose solid reputation for booking country acts and promoting concerts was firmly established through his work with Gene Autry and Pee Wee King's Golden West Cowboys. Frank called Tubb in December 1942, when the singer was in Birmingham for an appearance, and invited him to perform on the *Opry*. Tubb agreed and on January 16, 1943, made his debut at the War Memorial Auditorium in a guest spot that was beamed out over the NBC network. The formal invitation to join the *Opry* was then extended to Tubb, who accepted.

During World War II, Tubb recorded "Soldier's Last Letter," a song written by Redd Stewart, Pee Wee King's fiddle player, who was then serving in the army; Stewart sent the song to J. L. Frank, who gave it to Tubb. Also during the war, Tubb recorded "Tomorrow Never Comes," "Careless Darlin'," "It's Been So Long, Darling," and "There's a Little Bit of Everything in Texas." By 1945 he was appearing regularly on the *Opry*.

Clearly, by 1945 the *Opry* was expanding from the sound of acoustic string bands to include the various tastes of its listening audience. Even Bill Monroe, who had a traditional string band lineup, was changing in music and sound.

In 1939, Monroe and his group had gone to Nashville to audition for Judge Hay, Harry Stone, and David Stone for the *Opry*; he became a member of the *Opry* in the fall of that year. Meanwhile, Monroe had begun to hone his sound, which was a basic string band sound, but played in overdrive. Monroe's group played their music fast and, though he did not have a drummer, with a beat. He changed members as he worked on his music and, by the end of 1945, had assembled what many consider the best bluegrass group of all time: Lester Flatt on guitar and vocals, Chubby Wise on fiddle, Cedric Rainwater (real name Howard Watts) on bass, and Earl Scruggs on banjo. Monroe's music had begun to be called bluegrass after the name of his group, and the addition of Scruggs, with his unique style of three-fingered picking, defined the sound of bluegrass from that point on. Thus by the end of 1945, bluegrass music was named, defined, and sent out into the world.

The hiring of Bill Monroe represented the taste of Judge Hay, but the hiring of Ernest Tubb, Pee Wee King's Golden West Cowboys, and Eddy Arnold represented the vision and taste of Jack Stapp and Harry Stone, who saw the need for the *Opry* to expand beyond its initial barn dance sound into something more commercial to a diverse audience, as well as appealing to advertisers who wanted to reach a large market.

Roy Acuff was the biggest star of the *Opry* and held the coveted network spot each week. But Bill Monroe with his hard-driving sound that evolved to become bluegrass, Ernest Tubb with his Texas honky-tonk sound, and Eddy Arnold with his smooth countrypolitan sound were also important members of the *Opry* at the end of 1945.

All of those men would play a key role in the future of country music, although at times it seemed that they were leading the industry in four different directions.

Actually, in terms of *national* acceptance, country music was headed in a fifth direction that was not represented on the *Opry*. Western swing bands led by Bob Wills and Spade Cooley dominated country music record sales at the end of World War II. It was really a country music version of big band music—the Jazz Age meets hillbilly culture—and dominated the country market from the West Coast.

> ➤ *At the beginning of 1946, country music from Nashville was national on the NBC radio network because of the* Opry *shows sponsored by Prince Albert Tobacco and Ralston Purina.*

At the beginning of 1946, country music from Nashville was national on the NBC radio network because of the *Opry* shows sponsored by Prince Albert Tobacco and Ralston Purina. But with the success of the *Opry* came some dissatisfaction.

In April Roy Acuff left the *Grand Ole Opry* and the *Prince Albert Show*. Acuff was frustrated because of the *Opry*'s requirement that he be back every Saturday night to perform on the show. Saturday nights were the biggest nights for personal appearances, and Acuff's popularity kept him in constant demand for appearances—at much higher fees than the *Opry* paid. So Acuff went to the West Coast to tour and appear in movies. He was replaced by Red Foley, a smooth-voiced singer who had been on the *Opry*'s major competitor, the *National Barn Dance* on WLS out of Chicago.

Red Foley was more popular with *Opry* audiences than with *Opry* members when he started the *Prince Albert* segment. *Opry* regulars coveted the spot vacated by Acuff, and many resented it going to an "outsider." But the WSM brass knew Foley had network experience; furthermore, the Esty executives wanted Foley, and they got him. Foley represented the smooth sound of a country crooner who could be popular with city audiences as well as rural customers.

Another important addition to Nashville and country music came in September 1946 when Acuff-Rose signed a songwriter, Hank Williams, to their publishing company. Fred Rose soon obtained a recording contract for him with a small label, Sterling. Hank's first recording session occurred on December 11, 1946, when he did "Wealth Won't Save Your Soul," "Calling You," "Never Again," and "When God Comes and Gathers His Jewels" backed by the Willis Brothers, then known as the Oklahoma Wranglers. But when the year ended, Hank Williams was still living and performing in Montgomery, Alabama. The following year he signed with MGM Records, headed by Frank Walker, who left Victor at the end of the war to start the new label backed by the movie company.

8

The Hits Begin and a Star Is Born

For Eddy Arnold, the year 1946 began with the release of "I Talk to Myself About You" backed with "Live and Learn." Neither song charted in *Billboard*, although sales were impressive. Arnold's sessions were scheduled so he would have four records—or eight songs—released a year. His next session in 1946 occurred on March 20 in Chicago. Arnold brought Lloyd George on bass, Owen Bradley on piano, Speedy McNatt on violin, Rollin Sullivan on electric mandolin, Johnny Sullivan (Rollin's brother who had been in the navy during the war) on guitar, and Roy Wiggins on steel guitar. It would be Owen Bradley's first recording session as a musician, and Arnold added him to give some "bottom" to the session since, at that time, country sessions did not have drums on them.

During the session in RCA's Studio A, the group recorded four hours—from 1:45 until 5:45 in the afternoon—and got down six songs. Those songs were "All Alone in This World without You" by Vic McAlpin, Owen Bradley, and Betty Wade; "Can't Win, Can't Place, Can't Show" by Paul Westmoreland; "What Is Life without Love?" by Vic McAlpin, Owen Bradley, and Arnold; "That's How Much I Love You" by Wally Fowler, Graydon Hall, and Arnold; "Why Didn't You Take That Too" by Shep Sessions and Mel Butler; and "Chained to a Memory" by Jenny Lou Carson.

The session marked a turning point in Arnold's recording career because it was the first after he had signed an agreement with Hill and Range Publishing Company. The publishing company gave Arnold a monthly check; in exchange, he listened to the songs they brought him, and when he found an unpublished song, they received the publishing. The advantage was that Hill and Range eased the burden of finding songs; they brought him good material. For the session two songs, "Can't Win, Can't Place, Can't Show" and "Chained to a Memory," were Hill and Range songs.

The first release from the session was "Can't Win, Can't Place, Can't Show" backed with "All Alone in This World Without You."

> ➤ *No longer was Arnold just a popular* Grand Ole Opry *artist; he was a major national recording artist.*

"Can't Win, Can't Place, Can't Show" is an up-tempo number with the message that life is a long, hard race. There is a jazzy fiddle and some jazzy guitar runs with some female vocalists in the background. "All Alone in This World Without You" is a medium tempo love song that would be Eddy Arnold's second record to chart in *Billboard*. It entered the charts on July 13, 1946, and rose to the number seven position. The difference in the recording and Arnold's previous one was that it was on the Victor label, not Bluebird. The reason was record company economics. Bluebird was a budget label, selling for 35 cents for each record; Arnold's records were selling in such numbers that Victor wanted them on the Black label, which sold for 50 cents. If a record sold 100,000 units on Bluebird, it grossed $35,000; if it sold the same amount for Victor, it grossed $50,000—a sizable difference.

The next song released from the Chicago session would be the song that really launched Eddy Arnold as a country music star. "That's How Much I Love You" is a sprightly number, full of wit and wisdom, as the singer tells his sweetheart in clever terms how much he loves her, using phrases such as "If you were a horse fly and I an old gray mare, I'd stand and let you bite me and never move a hair."

"That's How Much I Love You" was released in September, entered the *Billboard* charts on October 12, and rose to number two—but its popularity caused the major change in Eddy Arnold's career to that point. No longer was Arnold just a popular *Grand Ole Opry* artist; he was a major national recording artist whose appeal and success went beyond the boundaries of the *Opry*'s listening audience.

Eddy Arnold recorded his first session in New York on September 24, 1946, at RCA's Studio Number One, with John Sullivan on guitar, Eddie McMullen on steel guitar, Rollin Sullivan on mandolin, Speedy McNatt on violin, Lloyd George on bass, and Harold Spierer on piano. Roy Wiggins had left Arnold and joined Red Foley briefly before returning to Arnold, so the steel guitar sound is a little different, more Hawaiian.

In the four-and-a-half-hour session that began at 1:30 in the afternoon he recorded four songs: "What a Fool I Was" by Bob Miller; "Easy Rockin' Chair" by Fred Rose; "To My Sorrow" by Vic McAlpin; and "It's a Sin" by Fred Rose and Zeb Turner. But before any songs from the session were released, Arnold released "That's How Much I Love You" and then "What Is Life Without Love?" which was released on a red 78 disk in March 1947.

"What Is Life Without Love?" has philosophical lyrics about the meaning of life, and on the first line Arnold slips into a falsetto; it would become his first number one record. His second number one was "It's a Sin" backed with "I Couldn't Believe It Was True." It would be a double-sided hit with "I Couldn't Believe It Was True" rising to number four on the charts.

Throughout 1946, Eddy Arnold made some major strides in his career. He toured a great deal, performing with other *Opry* acts such as Rod Brasfield, was the star of the *Opry House Matinee* on Saturday afternoons, and had a songbook out, published by Adams Vee and Abbott. Arnold's second songbook, *Eddy Arnold's Radio Favorites*, contained twenty songs, including "Many Tears Ago," "Each Minute Seems a Million Years," "I Walk Alone," "All Alone in This World," and "Be Sure There's No Mistake." Pictures of Arnold in the songbook were a further enticement for fans to purchase it.

On Saturday nights Eddy Arnold appeared on the *Opry* in the prime 8:00–8:15 P.M. segment sponsored by Purina; additionally, Arnold appeared in the 11:00–11:15 segment sponsored by the *Eddy Arnold Songbook*. The other major star who hosted a national segment was Red Foley, who had the *Prince Albert Show*. Despite the *Opry*'s intention to present the image of one big happy family, there was a good deal of grumbling among *Opry* members that the two men had the plum spots.

Still, there couldn't be too much obvious grumbling at the *Opry*. First, the show was the major national showcase for country music because it reached such a large audience. Next, the sponsors made the final decision on who would host their portion, and nobody argues with money. If Prince Albert or Purina wanted a certain artist, there was nothing other artists could do about it, no matter how much they felt they deserved the spot. It was out of their—and the *Opry's*—hands.

But a look at Eddy Arnold and Red Foley hosting the two major *Opry* segments says a lot about the future of commercial country music after World War II. First, both were, in many ways, pop-type singers, much smoother than the harsher sound of honky-tonk or traditional country acts. Next, both men were good emcees, in line with network emcees who could introduce acts and make smooth transitions from one song, or one act, to another. Finally, the advertisers wanted to reach the broadest possible audience and, since they had the power of the purse, could make demands on who they felt would reach that audience most effectively. Although it has been much overlooked, the plain fact is that advertisers have directed the future of country music as much as any producer, songwriter, music executive, or artist because the advertisers made the decision about who to back for major network exposure.

In addition to Purina and Prince Albert, other major advertisers on the *Opry* included Crazy Water Crystals, R.C. Cola, the *Southern Agriculturalist*, Wallrite, Cherokee Mills, the *Eddy Arnold Songbook*, the *Ernest Tubb Songbook*, Safkil, Weatherhouse, and Michigan Bulb.

Joining Eddy Arnold and Red Foley on the *Opry* were Pee Wee King and the Golden West Cowboys, Minnie Pearl, the Duke of Paducah (Benjamin "Whitey" Ford), the Oak Ridge Quartet, the Old Hickory Singers, Uncle Dave Macon, Jam Up and Honey, Bill Monroe and His Blue Grass Boys, Curly Fox, Texas Ruby and the Fox Hunters (which featured guitarist Grady Martin), the Cackle Sisters, Rod Brasfield, Paul Howard and His Arkansas Cotton Pickers, the Crook Brothers, Oscar Stone and His Possum Hunters, Lew Childre, Paul Womack and His Gully Jumpers, Clyde Moody, Robert Lunn, the Bailes Brothers, Wally Fowler and His Georgia Clodhoppers, the Happy Valley Boys, Ernest Tubb and His Texas Troubadours, Grandpappy Wilderson and His Fruit Jar Drinkers, Kirk McGee, Lazy Jim Day, Bradley Kincaid, Lonzo and Oscar, Lulu Belle, and, accompanying Red Foley, a young guitarist named Chester Atkins. They were joined by announcers Jud Collins, Ernie Keller, Grant Turner, Louie Buck, and David Cobb.

It was a strong cast of the best group of country music talent assembled by any radio station in the United States. It was also a variety show that kept people entertained no matter what their taste in country music with string bands, comedians, honky-tonkers, and old vaudeville performers all taking a turn on the stage.

By the end of the year Eddy Arnold had joined the top recording artists of the year in country music with his hits "Chained to a Memory" and "That's How Much I Love You." The entry of Arnold as a top recording artist, along with other *Opry* acts Red Foley, Bill Monroe, and Ernest Tubb, indicated the future direction for country music. More and more, it was no longer good enough for country performers to be great live performers on stage; they would also need to have hit records. The *Opry's* cast reflected that fact as they began to demand artists have recording contracts and hit recordings as criteria for joining the *Opry* cast in the years after World War II.

Other top recording artists in country music outside Nashville were Rosalie Allen, Gene Autry, Bill Boyd, Elton Britt, Bill Carlisle, Spade Cooley, Cowboy Copas, Ted Daffan, the Delmore Brothers, Al Dexter, the Hoosier Hot Shots, Zeke Manners, Hank Penny, Tex Ritter, Texas Jim Robertson, Floyd Tillman, Merle Travis, and Wesley Tuttle.

During 1946, three engineers from WSM, Aaron Shelton, Carl Jenkins, and George Reynolds, had begun Castle Recording Studio at the WSM radio studios. The following year they moved to the Tulane Hotel on Church Street—only a block away from the WSM studios in the National Life building. Although most of the work was done for local commercials, the studio would mark the beginning of the Nashville recording industry.

Its "beginning" can be traced to January 1947, when Francis Craig and His Orchestra, who performed regularly at the Andrew Jackson Hotel in downtown Nashville across the street from WSM, recorded "Near You." The song was done for Bullet Records, founded by Jim Bulleit (Bullet), who had headed the Opry Artists Bureau before World War II. "Near You" was an enormous success, a pop hit that sold 3 million records, and the next year Milton Berle adopted it as the theme song for his TV variety show, the *Texaco Star Theater.*

In August 1947, Paul Cohen from Decca Records came to Nashville and recorded sessions with Ernest Tubb and other country artists at Castle, and that began the move toward New York A & R men using Nashville as a recording center for country acts. The Nashville sessions replaced the old policy of field recordings whereby New York recording executives and engineers traveled from city to city recording artists. It also solved the problem of scheduling

Eddy Arnold with Steve Sholes.

country performers in the major labels' recording studios in New York, Chicago, and Los Angeles. After World War II the recording industry was booming—in 1947, $214.7 million worth of records would be sold at retail—and the labels' studios were booked for the pop acts based in New York, Chicago, and Los Angeles. Country acts could be relegated to "other" studios; it would be much easier if they didn't come to the major cities to record. So Nashville, because of Castle Studio and the large number of top country acts on the *Opry*, began to emerge as a place for country artists to record.

Eddy Arnold became a superstar in 1947. The impetus was "That's How Much I Love You," which came out in September 1946 and launched him as a major record seller, selling 750,000 units. That record, combined with Arnold's appearances on the *Grand Ole Opry* in a network segment, his touring, and his businesslike approach to his career, brought him into 1947 as a major country act. More giant hits would follow.

On May 18, 1947, Arnold went into RCA's Chicago studio and recorded nine songs, including "I'll Hold You in My Heart (Till I Can Hold You in My Arms)" and "Bouquet of Roses." The two songs were recorded back-to-back during the 4:30 to 7:45 session after an hour break in the afternoon. "I'll Hold You in My Heart" was released first—in August—and quickly rose to number one on the country charts, staying there for forty-six weeks and crossing over to the pop charts, where it rose to number twenty-two.

"Bouquet of Roses" was released as the B side of "Texarkana Baby." After the A side became a hit, the jukebox operators flipped it over, and "Bouquet of Roses" became a huge hit.

Eddy Arnold left no doubt he was a country music superstar. He had been unsure of his position with the company, fearing that he would be dropped from the label, but on a trip to New York in August 1947, Steve Sholes told him that Jim Murray, who headed Victor's record division, wanted to meet him. Arnold was apprehensive; his first comment was, "What's he want to meet me for?" Sholes replied, "He just wants to meet you." Arnold wondered, *Are they going to cancel my contract?*

When Arnold entered Jim Murray's office, the executive stood up and greeted Arnold with a handshake, then offered him a cigar, which Arnold declined. Then Murray said, "Every Monday morning I see those sales figures come across my desk. Those are tremendous figures. I wanted to know what you looked like." That was the first Eddy Arnold knew about the Monday morning sales reports. But it let him know that he was an important part of Victor Records.

Under the management of Tom Parker, Arnold placed a number of advertisements touting his career. In the February 8 issue of *Billboard* an ad for "What Is Life Without Love?" backed with "Be Sure There's No Mistake" quotes Arnold saying, "Here's my latest record, Folks! I'm kind of proud of this record because I reckon both sides will be hits. They're the kind of songs that always make the real foldin' money in the jukes. But don't take my word for it. Give a listen and see for yourself."

A *Billboard* review of this record states,

> A sweet-singing cowboy, Eddie [sic] Arnold pipes it
> expressively for both of these torch ballads with the
> strong support of his Tennessee Plowboys keeping the
> spin thoroughly rhythmic. Particularly tuneful is "What's
> Life Without Love?" and it's torch appeal for "Be Sure

There's No Mistake" as he warns his love that she is
breaking his lonely heart.

His show included his band, with Roy Wiggins, Rod Brasfield,
the Oklahoma Wranglers, Johnny and Jack, and Miss Lillie Belle.
Lonzo and Oscar had left; their recording of "I'm My Own Grandpa"
was so successful that they struck out on
their own.

➤ *In November*
1947, Arnold
began a period
of fifty-three
consecutive
weeks when he
had the number
one record in
country music.
First, "I'll Hold
You in My
Heart" hit
number one.

In November 1947, Arnold began a
period of fifty-three consecutive weeks when
he had the number one record in country
music. First, "I'll Hold You in My Heart" hit
number one; when it dropped out of that
slot, it was replaced by "Anytime," then
"Texarkana Baby," "Bouquet of Roses," "Just a
Little Lovin'," and "A Heart Full of Love (for
a Handful of Kisses)."

In addition to the hit records the biggest
thing that happened to Eddy Arnold in 1947
was the beginning of a weekly half-hour
radio show broadcast over the Mutual Network at midday. *The Checkerboard Jamboree*
was sponsored by Ralston Purina and put
together by the Brown Brothers. The show
began on November 17, 1947, and was broadcast live from the Princess Theater in Nashville.
There were actually two shows sponsored by Ralston Purina broadcast
back-to-back; Eddy Arnold hosted one, and Ernest Tubb hosted the
other. Both performers received national network exposure outside
the *Opry.*

Not only was Eddy Arnold heating up in 1947, country music in
general was popular. In April, *Billboard*'s "American Folk Tunes"
column noted that Arnold and his band had been booked by the Jolly
Joyce Theatrical Agency into a concert in Akron, Ohio, at the armory:

With the swing stars and name bands finding fertile fields
in the concert and classical halls, there is no reason . . .
why the Western singing and instrumental names can't
duplicate the feat as well. . . . Pointing out that many of

the Western names enjoy a bigger following away from metropolitan centers than the big name bands, Joyce feels that the time has arrived for the Western names to tackle the concert field. With interest in folk music and in folk entertainers at its highest peak, Joyce asserts that a whole vast new field in the concert sphere is ready to receive the Western names.

Out on the road, Eddy Arnold was proving to be a major concert draw. In Columbia, Ohio, he drew 4,000; in Akron, 4,000; at Dayton, 1,500. And at the Sleepy Hollow Ranch in Quakerston, Pennsylvania, on a Sunday afternoon in August, 11,000 fans came to see him. In Philadelphia, 3,000 fans came to see him, and the gate receipts were $5,000.

Eddy Arnold had already performed before large crowds at fairs and civic or municipal auditoriums, but there was a trend emerging where major cities outside the South booked country artists and attracted large crowds. Perhaps the biggest concert that year was in New York, when Ernest Tubb took an *Opry* troupe that included Minnie Pearl and Judge George D. Hay to Carnegie Hall.

The second biggest concert occurred a few weeks later, on October 31, when Eddy Arnold headlined a country concert at Constitution Hall in Washington, D.C. That led to an article in *Time* about Arnold. In the article, which came out during the last week of 1947, the reporter asked Arnold about the "Plowboy" sobriquet and whether it fit. Arnold replied, "Boy, I sure did plow. That's why I wanted to learn to play that guitar, so I wouldn't have to keep plowin' all my life."

Eddy Arnold had vivid memories of the 1942–44 musicians strike when he could not begin his recording career; he vowed not to be caught flat-footed again. Throughout 1947, there were rumblings of another musicians strike, called again by James Caesar Petrillo. During his August session in New York, Arnold recorded sixteen songs over two days, including "The Prisoner's Song," "Rockin' Alone," "It Makes No Difference Now," "Will the Circle Be Unbroken," "Molly Darling," "Seven Years with the Wrong Woman," "I'm Thinking Tonight of My Blue Eyes," and "Who at My Door Is Standing" on August 19 and "Texarkana Baby," "Anytime," and "I've Got a Lifetime to Forget" on the twentieth. Then on December 17, Arnold went to New York again for an all-day session that produced "A Heart

Full of Love (for a Handful of Kisses)," "Just a Little Lovin' (Will Go a Long, Long Way)," "You Know How Talk Gets Around," "There's No Wings on My Angel," and eight others.

The New York sessions in August and December added another player to Arnold's recording work: Charlie Grean. Grean was an A & R man for Victor and a studio bass player; he would help Sholes during the sessions.

The move to stockpile recordings proved fortuitous—the recording ban lasted almost the entire year of 1948 before it was resolved in December 1948. Thus the major record labels couldn't record during 1948, and artists who had the foresight to stockpile recordings had a decided edge over the rest of the field. In country music that artist was Eddy Arnold.

9

The Top Selling Singer in Country Music

In 1948, Eddy Arnold dominated the country music field like no other artist has before or since. During the entire year, he held the number one record on the charts every single week except two.

The year began with a cover story on Eddy Arnold in *The Cash Box*, a major trade magazine. It was announced that he had sold 2.7 million records in 1947—more than the entire pop division at Victor, although he didn't know it at the time. He did know it was his first taste of big money, and he bought a new four-bedroom house in Madison.

In January, Arnold appeared on a number of network radio shows: the *RCA Victor Show* and *Sunday Down South* on NBC; *We, the People* and the *Western Theater from Hollywood* on CBS; the *Spike Jones Show*, *Hayloft Hoedown*, the *Paul Whiteman Show*, and the *Breakfast Club*, all on ABC; *Luncheon at Sardi's* on the Mutual Network; and *Hospitality Times*, which was a transcription.

In addition to the appearances on major network radio shows, the biggest exposure for Eddy Arnold in 1948 was the beginning of a daily fifteen-minute radio show broadcast over the Mutual Network during the noon hour. *The Checkerboard Jamboree* was sponsored by Ralston Purina and put together by the Brown Brothers. The show originated live at the Andrew Jackson Hotel every weekday. Arnold was host and emcee; others on the show were the Willis Brothers or

Oklahoma Wranglers. The Brown Brothers brought the group to Nashville from Kansas City, where they had a radio show. They became Eddy Arnold's band (along with Roy Wiggins) and toured with him.

Each show began with Arnold's theme song, "Cattle Call," where he sang the yodeling section. Owen Bradley, a WSM musician and local big band leader, was arranger for the show and wrote commercials. Bradley had impressed the Brown Brothers by his musical ability, his knack for organizing musicians, his cheerful enthusiasm toward making music, and his unique ability to be a big band guy and, at the same time, be able to respect and work with country musicians.

> ➤ *In 1948, Eddy Arnold dominated the country music field like no other artist has before or since.*

Arnold's daily show for Purina was broadcast on more than three hundred stations Monday through Friday at 12:45. The fifteen-minute show gave him national exposure, and his connection to the Brown Brothers and the Ralston Purina company also meant a network spot on the *Grand Ole Opry* every Saturday at 8:00 P.M. The show allowed him to promote his latest release on Victor; each single had a built-in promotional push and a way to be heard.

In February he was on the cover of *Barn Dance* magazine and was quoted as saying, "Everybody was always for me. They all thought I was pretty good, I reckon."

He was getting rave reviews in the media, and an appearance in Fort Worth in March generated three articles. Jack Gordon's article "Eddy Arnold, Former Plow Boy, Is Visitor" for the *Fort Worth Press* noted that Arnold was wearing "a dark maroon sports shirt, sharply tailored plaid trousers, fancy socks, and leisure-type shoes" during his interview in his hotel suite. The writer observed that Arnold was "blond and handsome, he looked like a movie glamor boy snatched from the University of California campus."

Gordon also reported that Arnold was earning $1,500 a night on tour—top dollar. Plans were under way for Arnold to do a movie, but the Hollywood producers wanted it to be a singing cowboy picture. Arnold's manager, Tom Parker, stated, "They want to make a movie cowboy out of Eddy. We want none of that. There are too many phony cowboys already. Eddy isn't a cowboy. He is a plain country boy." During his show, Arnold had sung "Now Is the Hour" and commented, "I'd sing more tunes like that, but my country fans wouldn't accept them."

Fighting the perceived notion that because he was a country singer he was some sort of cowboy, Arnold tried to set the record straight: "I'm a country boy, not a cowboy." He told Gina Bumpass of the *Fort Worth Star-Telegram,* "I enjoy hearing people say I should sing popular tunes, too, but I never will. I want to keep the fans I've already made and take my songs to those who've never enjoyed folk music before."

Ida Belle Hicks wrote in the *Fort Worth Star-Telegram,*

> Arnold, the show's star, is as plain as the songs he sings and as uncomplicated. He knows what he wants but he has no fancy ideas about changing his way of life. Success startled him more than a little, but now that he is tops among the folk song singers he wants to stay there just as he is. Switching style or going on to so-called better things are [sic] not for him.

On his show Arnold was singing "I Walk Alone," "Anytime," "I'll Hold You in My Heart," "It's a Sin," "Molly Darling," "That's How Much I Love You," "Cattle Call," and "What Is Life without Love?"

A review in the *Richmond Times-Dispatch* from a concert in March was glowing:

> The crowd was far from satiated when Arnold finally bowed out after a warm and friendly curtain speech and a promise to come back soon. His hold on the audience is nothing less than magnetic. For the first time in many a moon, a Mosque crowd stayed put until the show actually was over. We've seen symphony concert audiences display less courtesy and less inclination to wait for expected encores.

During his personal appearances, Arnold scheduled a two-hour show, although his portion generally lasted about half an hour. In the first hour, the Oklahoma Wranglers performed, then Annie Lou and Danny, then Brother Slim Williams, who performed in blackface and added "a touch of spice and variety with his old-time sermon on love, politics, and anything else that he happens to think of." The Richmond review concluded, "The Eddy Arnold show is clean, well-paced and just what the hillbilly fans ordered." Arnold didn't perform in clubs—it was mostly coliseums or armories.

Country music in the late 1940s was attracting attention from the national media. The April 1948 issue of *Mademoiselle* featured the article "Country Music Goes to Town":

> The decentralization of backwoods ballads was also
> helped along by the war. Industrial workers from the
> South carried their ditties cross country into the aircraft
> plants and shipyards of the Pacific coast. Service men
> from the hillbilly districts toted guitars and laments of-
> and-for home from camp to camp. When they weren't
> sounding off on their own they had the radio in the USO
> turned up volume-high for "There's a Star-Spangled Ban-
> ner Waving Somewhere" [the] unofficial hillbilly theme of
> the armed forces. . . . Radio, actually, has been the most
> important factor in the mass production and consumption
> of country music. The forefathers of our current hillbilly
> and Western singers had to travel by mule and wagon to
> get to where the people were. . . . But day in and day out
> country people have become accustomed to getting their
> music over the air. . . . The triple simplicity of rhythm,
> melody and lyric, the expression of moral and sentimental
> values all but universally accepted in the United States
> are in truth making hillbilly music really popular.

On May 15, Eddy Arnold celebrated his thirtieth birthday at the Hotel El Rancho Vegas in Las Vegas with a dinner party. Among the guests was actor Robert Mitchum. Two days later, on May 17, Arnold opened a record shop in Murfreesboro, Tennessee, about forty miles from downtown Nashville.

In the 1940s, purchasing country music records was difficult because it was hard to find them. A number of country artists, led by Ernest Tubb, attempted to rectify that by opening their own record stores. Tubb was the pioneer and also the most successful; his store was located on Broadway, just across the street from the Ryman Auditorium. He arranged to have a *Midnight Jamboree* broadcast over WSM every Saturday night after the *Opry* was finished, which used *Opry* artists. Tubb sold a number of records through mail order, advertising his store on the *Opry* and *Midnight Jamboree*.

Eddy Arnold decided to open his own record store in Murfreesboro in 1948. In April the town of Murfreesboro turned out for a parade and a Welcome Eddy Arnold Day. It was another example of Eddy Arnold looking for investments outside his performing career.

Arnold was the first country artist to successfully play Las Vegas. In 1948, he appeared at the Hotel El Rancho Vegas, and at the end of his engagement, hotel owner Bernard H. Van Der Steen published a congratulatory telegram stating,

> My sincere thanks and congratulations to your Tennessee Plowboy, Eddy Arnold. During his entire engagement at the Hotel El Rancho Vegas he sang his beautiful American folk songs to a top capacity house. He has proven a new theory in our entertainment policy that his folk songs are very much accepted by the Las Vegas public as entertainment. His presentation is sincere and humble and through this he made many friends on and off stage. During the past year he has proven our best find and has done top capacity business. My sincere thanks and may Hotel El Rancho Vegas soon have the pleasure of a return engagement.

That was high cotton for a country singer in the 1940s.

By the end of May, Eddy Arnold had the top four songs in the nation: "Anytime," "What a Fool I Was," "Texarkana Baby," and "Bouquet of Roses" with "I'll Hold You in My Heart" at number nine.

On July 22, Eddy Arnold played Hope, Arkansas, and a reviewer captured the mood of the show:

> Everyone from the Colonel's Lady to Rosie O'Grady was at the Court House last night to hear the Eddy Arnold Hillbilly Jamboree. They came in Cadillacs, Buicks, Model T's, trucks and wagons. They sat on benches, in cars, on cars and in trees. Half of the crowd was standing. No one seemed to get tired and from the whistles, cheers, and applause everyone was well satisfied. The only comment of displeasure was "it wasn't long enough."

The reporter noted,

> To meet Eddy and talk with him, it is easy to see why he has been able to gain such popularity and keep it so long. He graciously autographed pictures and books for an hour after the show. Eddy is a very straightforward young man with a pleasing personality. The success he has gained

has not changed him from the generous hearted lad he
was while still a plowboy in west Tennessee. . . . He takes
pride in singing the simple songs that anyone can understand and which most people appreciate. Eddy likes to
sing. His profession wasn't chosen because it would fur-
nish him a good living, although it is doing that due to
his popularity, but because singing means something to
him. "Unless I like a song," Eddy said, "I never sing it no
matter how many requests there are for it. I like to feel
the sentiments in the songs I sing, and when I don't like a
song, I can't put a thing into it to make it live."

The reporter added that Arnold is "never away from home more
than 10 to 12 days a month." Arnold went to Arkansas to help the
political campaign of Vernon Whitten for Congress. After the concert
Arnold was quoted as saying, "My being with Mr. Whitten is purely
friendship. The political side of it does not interest me except that I'd
like to see Vernon elected."

There were mob scenes at some of his personal appearances, and
a headline in the Bradenton, Florida, newspaper proclaimed, "Eddy
Arnold Halts Traffic in Bradenton." During an August appearance in
the town, Arnold "literally stopped traffic in Bradenton yesterday
afternoon while making several personal appearances in the city."
The August tour of Florida lasted ten days and was done in a used
Studebaker Land Cruiser. He wore a Stetson hat, which advertised
that "All Well Dressed Men Wear Hats." The demand was so great
that in Tampa he did five shows one Sunday, at 2:00, 4:00, 6:00, 8:00,
and 10:00 P.M.

Eddy Arnold made his last appearance as a member of the *Grand
Ole Opry* on September 11, 1948. It was difficult for him to say goodbye, and in some ways, he did not want to leave. But there was some
friction as well. First, the *Opry* demanded he pay it 15 percent of all
the money he made on personal appearances; the *Opry*'s officials reasoned that people came to see him because of his connection to the
Opry, so they were entitled to a commission. Tom Parker wanted
Arnold to leave because the singer was at the height of his popularity and he could get more bookings—and make more money—if he
was not required to be back at the *Opry* every Saturday night.

The advantage of the *Opry* was the exposure it provided its
artists; there were network shows and the *Opry* itself reached a large
number of people. Without the *Opry*, most performers would not

Eddy Arnold on his Mutual Network show.

have national radio exposure, which was essential for an artist's success. In 1946, Roy Acuff had left the *Opry* to take advantage of the demand for bookings. But Acuff soon returned to the *Opry* because he could not be successful without it; the demand for bookings soon decreased without the *Opry* exposure.

But Eddy Arnold had a daily show over the Mutual Network, so he would still have network exposure. Also, a network show on CBS wanted him.

In the spring of 1948, the Brown Brothers Agency had negotiated with William Paley, head of CBS, for a show, *Hometown Reunion*, which would be aired on Saturday nights—prime time for a country artist. The show would feature the Duke of Paducah, a cast of thirty singers, the Willis Brothers, Annie Lou and Danny, Donna Jean, Paul Link and the Hometown Band and Choir. Starring on that show would be Eddy Arnold. *Hometown Reunion* premiered on September 18, the week after Arnold's last appearance on the *Opry*, so Arnold didn't miss a beat in terms of Saturday night network exposure.

There were other conflicts with WSM during the year. Tom Parker convinced Ralston Purina to sponsor a weekly half-hour transcribed show. The Brown Brothers wanted it to run on WSM on Saturday nights, but WSM refused, so Purina decided to put it on rival station WLAC. When WSM commercial manager Irving Waugh found out the deal, he said he would program a half-hour show against it. That move led Ralston Purina to agree to run the show on WSM on Fridays if WSM would put on a show before and after to help build an audience. WSM agreed in order to keep Eddy Arnold off the competition. Thus the *Friday Night Frolics*, starring *Opry* performers, began on WSM in 1948.

After Eddy Arnold left the *Opry*, the radio show knew it needed a smooth-voiced singer, so officials hired George Morgan to replace Arnold. Relations were strained but cordial, and Arnold didn't want to burn any bridges; he still appeared on the *Opry* now and then after he left, and at the end of the year, he appeared on the Prince Albert portion of the *Opry*.

At the end of 1948, Eddy Arnold had dominated the year's top-selling records with "Bouquet of Roses," "Anytime," "Just a Little Lovin'," "Texarkana Baby," "My Daddy Is Only a Picture," "I'll Hold You in My Heart," "A Heart Full of Love," "Then I Turned and Walked Slowly Away," and "What a Fool I Was." In second place was the artist who pushed him out of the number one position twice that year, Jimmy Wakely, with "One Has My Name, The Other Has My

Heart" and "I Love You So Much It Hurts." Other top country artists that year were Hank Thompson, Carson Robison, Moon Mullican, and T. Texas Tyler, followed by Tex Williams, Cowboy Copas, Ernest Tubb, Pee Wee King, Sons of the Pioneers, Red Foley, Tex Ritter, Roy Rogers, Floyd Tillman, Bob Wills, and Gene Autry, whose recording of "Here Comes Santa Claus" ended up on the country charts. In addition to Arnold's records, other top songs of the year included "I'm My Own Grandpa" by Lonzo and Oscar, "Tennessee Waltz" by Pee Wee King, "Humpty Dumpty Heart," "Life Gets Tee-Just, Don't It," and "Tennessee Saturday Night."

> *He vowed to invest his money in something he knew something about: land. At least you can see land, walk on it, and touch it.*

Eddy Arnold was always a careful man with his money, but knew he couldn't just hide it under a mattress. In his first investment, for a vibrating mattress, he lost $35,000. After that he vowed to invest his money in something he knew something about: land. At least you can *see* land, walk on it, and touch it. And since God quit making land but keeps making people, the value of land is bound to rise. In 1948, Arnold bought his first piece of land for an investment. Located on Gallatin Road at the corner of two major streets, the lot looked shaggy with its weeds, but it had a prime location. Arnold purchased it for $12,500.

His political convictions were also taking shape that year during the election campaigns of Harry Truman and Thomas E. Dewey. Some may ponder whether a person's liberalism or conservatism is shaped by family and society or by genes. Are people born liberals or conservatives? Eddy Arnold's father was a dyed-in-the-wool Democrat who lived most of his life under Republican presidents (Abraham Lincoln, Andrew Johnson, Ulysses S. Grant, Rutherford B. Hayes, James Garfield, Chester Arthur, Benjamin Harrison, William McKinley, Theodore Roosevelt, William Howard Taft, Warren G. Harding, Calvin Coolidge, and Herbert Hoover). Eddy Arnold's father lived under only three Democratic presidents: James Buchanan (who was president when Will Arnold was born), Grover Cleveland, and Woodrow Wilson.

Will Arnold came of age when no true Southerner could be a Republican because that was the party of Abraham Lincoln, who had waged war on the South. As a young man, he lived during the corrupt Grant administration and saw the heyday of the robber barons and the Gilded Age as well as the idealism of Woodrow Wilson. Eddy Arnold remembers his father was a staunch Democrat but also remembers his father's sister, Eddy's aunt Nannie, who would regularly come over to the Arnold household and argue politics with his father.

Eddy Arnold was born when Wilson was president, and he came of age during Franklin Roosevelt's administration and somehow *wanted* to be a Democrat like his father. But he just didn't lean that way. Arnold didn't like Roosevelt's run for third and fourth terms, although he tended to admire the president while in office. He disliked Harry Truman's administration, and during the Democratic Convention when Truman was nominated, Arnold listened to the radio while Hubert Humphrey, then mayor of Minneapolis, gave a convention speech. "Hearing Hubert Humphrey's speech at the Democratic Convention made me a Republican," says Arnold. Although he was still not registered to vote, he somehow knew deep inside that his beliefs fit the Republican party.

10

Life at the Top

L ife was going great for Eddy Arnold at the end of 1948, but it was going to get even better. On January 2, 1949, his son, Richard Edward Arnold Jr., was born—and Eddy Arnold was the proud papa of two children. Arnold purchased a policy from the Life and Casualty Insurance Company to assure his son an education. He had also purchased a policy for his daughter; the policies would mature when they were eighteen and make sure they could attend college, whether Eddy Arnold was still selling records or not. Arnold also purchased a life insurance policy from New York Life—and paid all the policies in full. It was the way he always liked to do business, paying cash in full for everything he bought.

In the first issue of *Variety* in 1949, Tom Parker placed an ad that stated, "Eddy Arnold and I regret that we have no available personal appearance dates for the season of 1949." That was certainly true—no other country artist was in as great a demand as Eddy Arnold—but it was also something of a ruse. Parker knew the ad would get the attention of the music industry and it did; it also prodded some concert promoters to call requesting dates, and if the dates were particularly lucrative, a spot in Arnold's schedule might be "found" to accommodate the request.

Arnold's personal appearances were quite profitable; an ad in *Billboard* naming cities and the amount grossed from ticket sales included Fort Worth, $8,323; Dallas, $6,245; Oklahoma City, $7,612; Washington, D.C., $9,280; Jacksonville, Florida, $6,120; Tampa, $4,278; Norfolk, $7,330; Roanoke, $2,555; Richmond, $3,923; Raleigh, $2,730; Little Rock, $4,309; Monroe, Louisiana, $1,881; and

Atlanta (one week), $13,000. In every city except Atlanta, the top price for a concert ticket to see Eddy Arnold was $1.

Network radio appearances for Arnold in 1949 included the *RCA Victor Show*; the *Spike Jones Show* (three times); the *Paul Whiteman Show*; *Don McNeill's Breakfast Club*; *We, the People*; *Command Performances*; *Luncheon at Sardi's*; the *Western Hit Review*; and the Prince Albert segment on the *Grand Ole Opry*. In addition, he was featured on *The March of Time* and continued to host *The Checkerboard Jamboree* each weekday over the Mutual Network. No other country artist got as much national exposure in the late 1940s or early 1950s as Eddy Arnold. The network appearances allowed Arnold to transcend the world of country music, and his record sales reflected those of a top-selling pop artist.

> ➤ *In 1949, Eddy Arnold was a heartthrob.*

In 1949, Eddy Arnold was a heartthrob. An article from Oklahoma City pointed out, "The voice has put Eddy across. But his looks haven't hurt him in his stage appearance. Six feet tall, with sandy blond hair, Eddy has a face that is good looking without being pretty. Women call him handsome, but he is still rugged enough for the men."

An article in the *Houston Post* by Betty Betz, titled "Arnold Gets Marriage Bids in Mail," quoted Arnold: "Ah gets a dozen marriage proposals in the mail every week from teen-age girls. Could you please tell 'em ah already got a beyootiful wife at home in Tennessee?"

Obviously, the media couldn't resist a dig at Eddy Arnold or country music, despite the success of both. Arnold never spoke like that, and he wasn't a hayseed; painting him as one reflected a media bias against Southerners and country music. Indeed, Arnold always went out of his way to set himself apart from the old hillbilly stereotypes.

In 1949, Bea Terry wrote "Folk Music and Its Folks." She stated that Arnold "does not care to be classified as a hillbilly singer and tells me he is just a country-boy-singer." She continued, "The popular singer does not wear the regular cowboy apparel, either. On stage he wears slacks and a sports shirt, and he does not wear boots. He wears a white hat but it is not one of those wide brim westerns. Off stage, he wears suits with semi-dress or sport shirts."

The marketing strategy for Arnold was to release four records a year, or eight songs. (That was before the era of long-playing albums, which had only been introduced to American consumers the year before.) Each would achieve maximum sales before the next was released. Other acts released a large number of disks each year (sometimes as many as twenty-four). According to an article in *Variety* at the end of the year, "Arnold himself is the kingpin of the hillbilly artists on disks. . . . It's not unusual for Arnold to reach into the 1,000,000 copy class. He's had more disks that did go over that figure than any singer or band on Victor." Using this marketing strategy, most of Arnold's records sold more than 1 million copies each, and by the end of 1949, he had sold more than 9 million records.

Arnold released an album *To Mother* in time for Mother's Day 1949. The album included six songs: "That Wonderful Mother of Mine," "M-O-T-H-E-R," "Bring Your Roses to Her Now," "I Wish I Had a Girl Like You, Mother," "I Wouldn't Trade the Silver in My Mother's Hair," and "My Mother's Sweet Voice." "I did it for my mother," he said.

Eddy Arnold went to Hollywood in June 1949 and filmed two movies. On the way out he stopped for a two-week engagement in Las Vegas. Negotiations had begun the year before when Hollywood approached Arnold about starring as a singing cowboy in a movie. Discussing his movie career, Arnold said, "When those movie producers came to me, they wanted me to put on a ten-gallon hat, leather chaps, a pair of six-guns, and be a Texas cowboy singing star in the horse operas. But I didn't believe that I knew anything about horse operas, and I finally convinced them of that, thank goodness."

Once he was on the movie set, publicity swirled about his desire to get back home. The *Detroit News* published Harold Hefferman's article, "Studio Nips Flight of Lonely Balladeer":

> No singer has ever leaped from obscurity to fame with
> such speed, and Columbia considers it engineered a
> smart coup in landing him for his first movie. It's admit-
> tedly no great shakes as celluloid drama but should
> serve its central purpose—a showcase for the man his
> millions of followers know today only through the
> sound of radio and records. He's come a long way in
> three short years and the fantastic Hollywood scene isn't
> helping him lick that feeling of bewilderment. . . . "I just
> dunno how it all happened," replied Eddy when we
> asked him to sum up his success story. "All I can say is
> I'm plenty scared right now. I gotta go into a scene with

that girl over there and, boy, the butterflies are playin'
ping pong with my stomach."

Another writer reported, "Eddy Arnold . . . was so homesick for
his family in Nashville that he brought his bags, packed, to the studio yesterday to pose for his still pictures for *Feudin' Rhythm*, and
left for the airport the moment Bob Coburn, head of the still department, said 'that's all.'" The story had some elements of the truth but
missed a central point; yes, Eddy Arnold loved Nashville and wanted
to get back to his family, and yes, he brought his packed bags to the
photo session, but Arnold was a busy man, much in demand, and he
needed to get back to his other obligations on radio and personal
appearances. In fact, time was so tight that Arnold had begun flying
to his personal appearances in a DC-3. Ever mindful of the financial
advantages of company tie-ins, an ad proclaimed, "For dependable
air transportation the Eddy Arnold Show uses Capitol Airways,
Nashville, TN."

One of those obligations involved work with his sponsors. As
host of *The Checkerboard Jamboree* and spokesman for Purina, Eddy
Arnold made a number of personal appearances on behalf of the company, promoting its line of farm feed products. In 1949, the company
ran a contest for Mike and Ike, two pigs who competed for weight
gain. One was fed Purina Hog Ration; the other received straight
grain. A number of feed stores competed, and the winner was the
Gross Feed Store. The singer went from store to store, judging the
hogs; he also did remote broadcasts of his daily noon show from
various stores.

Television was in its infancy but was already making its presence felt. Regular television programming was introduced to
America in 1947, and the following year was the first full year of
network programming. On September 15, 1949, Eddy Arnold made
his first appearance on network TV when he appeared on Milton
Berle's show.

Back home, Eddy Arnold appeared at a free concert sponsored by
the local newspaper on August 21. The performance at Nashville's Centennial Park drew an estimated thirty thousand. In September, Arnold
bought a 107-acre farm just south of Nashville in Brentwood. The farm
had been a working farm, and the former owner threw in two mules and
some farm equipment with the purchase. When Arnold left town for
some personal appearances, his wife lost no time in selling the mules.

His concert appearances continually drew large crowds and rave reviews. Here is one from Chicago:

> Swooners and boppers, beware! Judging by last night's crowd at the Coliseum any vocalist who hopes to keep his public better hurry on down and get himself a ten-gallon hat and some yodelling lessons. The menace to the moaners comes in the form of a young man named Eddy Arnold—subtitled the "Tennessee Plowboy"—who last night packed the Coliseum with close to 5,000 raving fans. The boy with the talented tonsils received just about the most caterwauling ovation that ever tickled an entrepreneur's ear. One girl actually fainted, and had to be carried out by a constable.

Another article disclosed that he "now gets upwards of $1,000 a night." In truth, he was often getting $1,500 per appearance and a portion of the gate receipts.

At the end of the year, he remained busy. In October, he spent a week in Colorado Springs making some short promotional films for the Purina Company. On November 9, he was on the cover of *Billboard*, and in December, he made a guest appearance on the *Perry Como Chesterfield Supper Club*. During the Christmas season, he released his first Christmas record, "C-H-R-I-S-T-M-A-S" backed with "Will Santa Come to Shanty Town."

RCA was promoting its new bit of technology, the 45 rpm vinyl single, and Eddy Arnold pitched in to help. An ad in *Billboard* at the end of 1949 pictured Arnold with his family and a record player; it bore the caption, "Home is Where the '45' is says Eddy Arnold. 45 rpm is an important part of our family life!"

It was a good time for country music in general. Writing for the *American Weekly* in February 1949, Jack Stone let his article title "Millions in Music—Hillbillies in Clover" sum up the scene: "Hillbilly songs account for about 15 percent of music biz, an estimated $30 million worth [which] allows hillbilly singers themselves to flaunt hand-tooled leather belts, Fifth Avenue flannel shirts, and drive high-priced cars." Arnold's "Bouquet of Roses" "outsold most pop records," and "200 record companies [turned] out an average of 100 hillbilly songs a week." Also, two former country music performers, W. Lee "Pappy" O'Daniel (Texas) and Jimmie Davis (Louisiana), were governors.

Explaining country music's success after World War II, Stone continued.

> Once confined to the South and Southwest, [country music] has spread all over the country. What skyrocketed hillbilly music? Radio, mainly. The war, too. Northern boys in Southern camps brought back the hillbillies' melodic tales of hard times and good times, of poverty and pathos, of crop woes and personal tragedy, of bright happiness. Southern boys in Northern camps were hillbilly emissaries. Population shifts helped also. The notion that hillbilly singers are Broadway dudes affecting rural identity is false. Those who make the grade come from small towns, learned their homely warbling at their grandma's knee. Imposters have a tough go of it, for the hillbilly-loving public can spot a phony a mile off. In popular music the song's the thing. In hillbilly, it's the performer who sells. There was the case of the hillbilly crooner who, in his first experience with a squalling adolescent girl, mistook her adoration for derision and apologized to his listeners: "I reckon that was pretty bad, but shucks, you don't have to yell at me."

For the most part, the national media (especially from New York) treated country music rather condescendingly, writing in a smarmy, cutesy vein that put down the music as it told of its success in record sales and income generated from personal appearances.

An article from *Time* in 1941 about the hit song "New San Antonio Rose," written by western swing legend Bob Wills and recorded by Bing Crosby, illustrates the tone: "This song, 'New San Antonio Rose,' may baffle or even irritate fastidious rhetoricians, and its tune is strictly golden bantam. Yet last week Decca Records reported that in January alone the song had sold 84,500 disks."

In 1943, that same magazine headlined an article "Bull Market in Corn" where it stated, "Almost any simple soul might write hillbilly words and the composition of hillbilly music has always been regarded by Tin Pan Alley as a variety of unskilled labor."

Life published an article in 1943 that discussed the immensely popular country song "Pistol Packin' Mama" during the war; it described the song as a "raucous little item" and "obnoxious." Elaborating on the record by Al Dexter, the article said that the song "is naive, folksy, and almost completely devoid of meaning.

Its melodic line is simple and its lyric rowdy and, of course, monotonously tautological" before concluding that the record "promised to become even more of a national earache than it is at the moment."

"Hillbilly Boom" by Maurice Zolotow in a 1944 *Saturday Evening Post* cited the sales figures of "Pistol Packin' Mama," "which prove that hillbilly music has come into its own." The writer noted that other million sellers during the same time included country songs such as "There's a Star-Spangled Banner Waving Somewhere" by Elton Britt and "No Letter Today" by Ted Daffan and His Texans. "On the road, hillbilly troupes will consistently outdraw legitimate Broadway plays, symphony concerts, sophisticated comedians, and beautiful dancing girls," and Roy Acuff would draw large crowds where others, like Betty Grable and Bob Hope, "would only succeed in drawing boll weevils." In an attempt to show a little respect for the diversity of country music, Zolotow concluded, "Although all hillbilly music sounds monotonously alike to the urban eardrum, it includes many types of music."

An article in *Billboard* in 1944 about the success of country music in New York held that New Yorkers' "newly developed interest in bucolic bounce is said to stem from demands of transient war workers and servicemen for hoe-down hi-de-ho" and described the music as "ridge-runner rumbas." It discussed the "sorghum and sow-belly sentiment" in the music and the fact that "city slickers, who first sneered at the corn, are now ordering it as a steady diet." The article ended, "It appears that 'Turkey in the Straw' is beginning to pay off in sliced white meat."

"Whoop-and-Holler Opera" appeared in *Collier's* in 1946. Doron K. Antrim began, "There's a moanin' and a wailin' throughout the land as the resurgent hillbillies whang away at their doleful tales of love and woe." Country music was "the epidemic of corn" sweeping the country, and country musicians were "barefoot fiddlers who couldn't read a note but who could raise a voice on endless tunes, especially with the aid of corn liquor."

In 1948, the *Christian Science Monitor* ran "Hillbilly Phenomenon" in which Robert Scherman wrote, "Cowboy music is paying off in a big way. In the past year its chief exponent, the hillbilly singer, has been the biggest money maker in show business." During country shows, audiences were said to "whoop, stomp, jump, and generally raise the roof" while the band consisted of "an ill-tuned fiddle, a couple of raspy guitars, perhaps a bass fiddle, and a delicate little instrument known as the steel guitar, from which there can be coaxed anything from the croak of a bullfrog to the clang of a cowbell."

"Corn of Plenty" appeared in *Newsweek* in 1949: "The corn is as high as an elephant's eye—and so are the profits." The article continued that "while the rest of the music business remained in its chronic fluttery state, the hillbilly output remained fairly constant. But the demand for it has multiplied fivefold since the war. This week the industry was still moving in concentric circles and nothing was dependable—except hillbilly music." The article gave some grudging respect, stating, "Once a specialty product marketed in the Deep South, it now has a nationwide sales field," before concluding, "It would seem that all a singer needs is a hoedown fiddle, a steel guitar, a mandolin, and a new inflection in his voice—and he's set for the bonanza."

> ➤ *WSM and the* Grand Ole Opry *also received national attention for their success with country music.*

WSM and the *Grand Ole Opry* also received national attention for their success with country music. An article in the October 26, 1949, edition of *Variety* was headlined "Fort Knox No Longer Has Exclusive on Pot of Gold; WSM, Nashville, Talent Corners a Good Chunk of It": "WSM has been going about its job of cornering the hillbilly market. In the process it has made a lot of people rich, has given the recording business a sizeable hypo when most needed, and has established WSM's distinctive role in the broadcasting and musical pattern of the nation." The article went on to note that the *Opry* was a 125 person unit; that WSM grossed about $600,000 a year with approximately two-thirds of that from the *Opry*; and that WSM programmed six hours of the *Opry* every Saturday night. The article reported that R. J. Reynolds, sponsor of the Prince Albert segment of the *Opry*, had an exclusive agreement that prevented anyone except local sponsors from sponsoring the *Opry*.

WSM also produced *Sunday Down South* featuring Snooky Lanson, Beasley Smith—the WSM orchestra leader who had composed "That Lucky Old Sun"—and a cast of 45. The article pointed out that WSM had 230 employees and that 200 were "talent."

In addition to the income from radio, the *Opry* grossed $640,000 a year on barnstorming units (with an average ticket price of 80 cents) and made $275,000 from *Opry* shows at the Ryman with ticket prices set at 30 and 60 cents. The *Opry* received international exposure in 1949 when it was chosen by the War Department for a series of performances at European military bases.

> ➤ *"Fort Knox No Longer Has Exclusive on Pot of Gold; WSM, Nashville, Talent Corners a Good Chunk of It."*

Writers also pointed out that Nashville had more than just country talent on the *Opry*; there had been broadcasts from the Hermitage Hotel featuring Dinah Shore, Kitty Kallen, Kay Arme, Jerry Sullivan, and James Melton; and the Castle Recording Studio, run by three WSM engineers, "is perhaps the busiest auxiliary plant in the U.S.; that's where the boys groove out the profits for Decca, Columbia, Capital, Victor, London, etc."

Eddy Arnold was asked his views on the national success of country music as well. They appeared in *National Jamboree* magazine:

> Well, it's like this. . . .When the war started, millions of young guys in every state in the union were thrown together in barracks, training camps and on the battle-fronts. Kids from New York's East Side mingled with guys from Broken Bow, Oklahoma, Kimball, South Dakota, or Dallas, Texas. You could go down a chow line and pick a guy from almost every state. These kids worked together, fought together and they played together too. The kid from Manhattan listened to the Texans tell about roping a steer, or the Nebraskan telling how large the corn grows out there. They began to exchange ideas and it was at this point that the kid, born and bred in the big city, heard folk music for the first time.

At the end of 1949, the major labels for country music were Victor, Capitol, King, MGM, Decca, and Columbia. In terms of stars, Victor had Eddy Arnold, Pee Wee King, Texas Jim Robertson, and the Sons of the Pioneers; Capitol had Hank Thompson, Jimmy Wakely, Tex Williams, and Tex Ritter; King, owned by Syd Nathan in Cincinnati, had Moon Mullican and Cowboy Copas; MGM had Hank Williams and Carson Robison; Decca had Red Foley and Ernest Tubb; 4 Star had T. Texas Tyler; and Columbia had Floyd Tillman, Roy Acuff, Ted Daffan, and Gene Autry.

11

In the Movies

Eddy Arnold's movies were released in January 1950. In *Feudin' Rhythm*, Ace Lucky (Kirby Grant) has a radio program that is ready to go on TV. Eddy Arnold, playing himself, is a singer on *The Ace Lucky Show* on KXIW. He has a son, Bobby, who has been adopted by Mr. and Mrs. Upperworth—but Bobby doesn't know that Arnold is his father.

There are three concurrent plots. Bobby is a raging terror who wreaks havoc on the radio show's cast and crew and has immunity because he is Mrs. Upperworth's son. The other plot involves Mrs. Upperworth's attempts to transform the show into "her" show featuring drama and high culture when it goes on television; this is justified because she is the financial backer. The final "plot" is Mrs. Upperworth's attempt to fire Arnold from the cast to get him away from Bobby before Bobby finds out Arnold is his real father.

Eddy Arnold sings "Cattle Call," "You Know How Talk Gets Around," "Nearest Thing to Heaven," and "There's No Wings on My Angel." The movie falls into slapstick as Mrs. Upperworth's set collapses on TV during a failed kidnap attempt, and the crew of *The Ace Lucky Show* has to come to the rescue. The basic theme is that country music might not be high culture, but it's what the friends and neighbors want.

The other movie, *Hoedown*, features Jock Mahoney as Stoney Rhodes, a handsome but none-too-bright cowboy movie actor, who is dropped by his studio while in Smoky Falls, Tennessee. Broke and without a friend, the actor learns the tour was financed with $10,000 put up by his mother, who mortgaged her home in an effort to save Stoney's career. A pretty young reporter, sent to write a sob story on

Eddy Arnold with the cast of Feudin' Rhythm.

the actor's quick rise and fall, runs out of gas on the way to the interview and stops for help at a farm belonging to Eddy Arnold (playing
himself). It just so happens the singer is preparing for a hoedown.

Eddy's cousin, Carolina Cotton, falls for Stoney, and Eddy, under
the mistaken impression that it is Stoney's voice he heard singing the
songs in his movies, wires an agent to sign him as a new western
singer. While driving to the farm, the agent, Sam (Fred Sears), is held
up by bank robbers. On the day of the hoedown everyone discovers
that Stoney can't sing a note. (He had tried to tell them that his movie
songs had been dubbed, but in the general hubbub he wasn't heard.)
The identity of the bank robbers is revealed when they try to steal
the $2,000 paid by the audience to see the benefit. A wild battle fol-
lows with Stoney against the outlaws and getting much the worst of
it until Carolina kisses him and declares her love for him. Thus
inspired, he goes berserk and overwhelms the heavies, recovering

I'M THROWING RICE
(AT THE GIRL THAT I LOVE)
Words and Music by STEVE NELSON, ED NELSON, Jr., and EDDY ARNOLD

$100,000 they had taken from a nearby bank. As a result of his hero-
ism, Stoney receives eight movie offers along with a big reward. Furthermore, he realizes he is in love with Carolina Cotton. While all
this is going on, Eddy Arnold and Vera, the reporter, have quietly
fallen for each other, so the picture ends with a romantic scene. In the
movie Arnold sings "Just a Little Lovin'," "I'm Throwing Rice," and
"Bouquet of Roses."

Despite Arnold's and Tom Parker's attempts to have Eddy
Arnold *not* appear in a cowboy movie, both were essentially B westerns. Arnold wore his Stetson hat, but it wasn't a cowboy hat; it was
almost a cross between a fedora and a western-style hat. Also, he
wore a sports coat and slacks and didn't have a horse. But the rest of
the cast dressed as cowboys, rode horses, shot guns and, despite
some cars in the movie, staged some shoot-em-up chase scenes with
cowboys and horses.

Eddy Arnold did not have a chance to see the movies before they
were released. He first saw them in a small movie theater near his
home in Madison. He didn't particularly like what he saw, and he
remained embarrassed by the pictures. They were "cheapies," as he
put it, made to capitalize on his fame, and the acting was rather
wooden while the story lines were far-fetched and hokum. Still, they
gave him more exposure, and his popularity was so great that the
movies were profitable.

On January 26, Arnold went to Durham, North Carolina, for the
grand opening of the Liggett and Myers Tobacco Company manufacturing plant. Liggett and Myers's Chesterfield brand sponsored a
major radio show hosted by Perry Como on NBC. At the dedication
were Perry Como, Arthur Godfrey, and Bob Hope. All appeared at the
radio program broadcast from the event. It was a major network
appearance for Arnold, as was his guest appearance on Arthur Godfrey's television show that same month. He also appeared on Perry
Como's radio and TV shows in April.

He continued to tour, and during May, he was on a Texas tour
with Jam Up and Honey, Professor Gabe Tucker, Annie Lou and the
Oklahoma Wranglers, and Little Roy Wiggins. In August he performed
a free concert in Nashville at Centennial Park before fifteen thousand
people in the pouring rain. The songs he sang included "Take Me in
Your Arms and Hold Me"; "Enclosed, One Broken Heart"; "Why
Should I Cry?"; "I'm Throwing Rice"; "Cattle Call"; "Cuddle Buggin'
Baby"; "Anytime"; and a medley of some of his other hits.

Left to right: Perry Como, Bob Hope, unknown man, Arthur Godfrey, and Eddy Arnold at opening of Liggett and Myers manufacturing plant.

In terms of making money, 1947 through 1953 were banner years for Eddy Arnold. In 1948, he made $250,000 in record sale royalties alone. By January 1950, the *Eddy Arnold Song Book*, which sold for 50 cents, had sold about 85,000 a year since its release. Arnold also merchandised a guitar-shaped pin for 50 cents. It was said that he received an average of five thousand fan letters each week. And at a time when the average income was around $3,000 a year, Eddy Arnold reportedly made more than $250,000 during 1950. Of course, he had to pay 90 percent of his income to the IRS.

The business side was good, although there were a few setbacks. In August, he closed his record shop and gave $5,000 worth of records to the Tennessee Industrial School to distribute to Davidson County orphanages; that move liquidated his stock and eased his losses with a tax break.

He was beginning to see some tangible rewards for his success. During 1950, he purchased another farm in Brentwood, just south of Nashville, and in July he moved into a new home. But there were some personal setbacks as well. On Sunday, September 24, his mother died in St. Louis. She was seventy-six and had spent her final years living at various times with her children. In July while visiting Patty, she had suffered a heart attack.

> ➤ *The life of an entertainer is one of continuing demands.*

She left a large family; in addition to her children with Will Arnold (Eddy, W. D., and Patty), there were two sons from her first marriage—R. C. and Ernest Engel—and the children from Will Arnold's first family. The funeral was held in Henderson, where she was buried in the Methodist cemetery.

The life of an entertainer is one of continuing demands. No matter what happens in his personal life, a performer is expected to take the stage with a smile, entertain his fans, and meet the obligations of fame. Shortly after the loss of his mother, Eddy Arnold was back on the road as well as doing his radio show and television appearances.

The day before his mother died, *The Eddy Arnold Show*, a half-hour show on NBC, debuted. Sponsored by Purina, it ran on Saturday nights. The show was actually *The Checkerboard Jamboree* extended fifteen minutes. Eddy Arnold had become so popular that the decision was made to rename the show for its host.

He had moved into the ranks of the top-selling artists of all time and was recognized for that achievement. In August 1950, executives announced that Eddy Arnold had sold 12 million records for RCA Victor in five years; by the end of the year, that figure had increased to 14 million. Also by the end of the year, Eddy Arnold was heard on more than 1,500 radio stations each week. Among his shows was *Robin Hood's Eddy Arnold Show*, sponsored by a flour company. He was on 300 stations on the Mutual Network sponsored by Purina, receiving $500 a week for that show. During 1950, he had appeared as a guest on six network shows (radio and TV) sponsored by Chesterfield, including those hosted by Perry Como and Arthur Godfrey. He had appeared on Milton Berle's TV show and *The Big Show* hosted by Tallulah Bankhead, which was the last "big" production for network radio. For the Christmas season, he released his second Christmas single, "White Christmas" backed with "Santa Claus Is Coming to Town."

There were some changes in the Nashville music community; Harry Stone, who lost some key struggles in the corridors of power at

WSM, resigned in October 1950 (the reason given was health). Arnold came to the rescue of his old friend, putting him on the payroll during the difficult time and paying his moving expenses when Stone relocated to Phoenix, Arizona, to run a television station there.

By 1951, Arnold had moved from being just a country artist to a major American artist. In January he headed to Houston for a twelve-day appearance that earned him $15,000. He bought a western outfit for the appearances at the Houston Fat Stock Show—which was the only event where he wore cowboy garb when he performed. Then he spent two weeks on *The $64 Question*, made three appearances on Perry Como's network show, and recorded his own radio program for the Mutual Network each Saturday afternoon. He did some promotions for the Treasury Department that were heard on almost 1,500 radio stations. His current single, "Lovebug Itch," was moving up the charts.

In July 1951, Eddy Arnold moved his office from the Third National Building in Nashville to Brentwood, a subdivision just outside Nashville in Williamson County, near his home. Arnold would keep his office in Brentwood for the rest of his career.

With his career in high gear, Arnold had hit records in 1951 with "There's Been a Change in Me," "May the Good Lord Bless and Keep You," "Kentucky Waltz," "I Wanna Play House with You," "Something Old, Something New," "Somebody's Been Beating My Time," and "Heart Strings." All were top ten records. In 1952, he continued his string of hits with "Bundle of Southern Sunshine," "Call Her Your Sweetheart," "Easy on the Eyes," "A Full Time Job," "Older and Bolder," and "I'd Trade All of My Tomorrows (for Just One Yesterday)."

In July 1952, he announced he would not renew his contract with Hill and Range, with whom he had first signed in 1948. Hill and Range had brought him a lot of great songs, such as "Bouquet of Roses," but they wanted him to record a number of other songs he didn't want to record—and he was tired of the pressure. Plus, the money they paid him wasn't as important, and he realized he wasn't really a songwriter—he was a singer and wanted to concentrate on doing his best at singing.

Also in July 1951, he hosted *The Chesterfield Show* on the CBS TV network as a summer replacement for Perry Como. Filmed in New York, the show was fifteen minutes, airing at 7:45 P.M. (Eastern) on Monday, Wednesday, and Friday. The show ran through the summer, until the end of August. The success of the show led to more important media exposure: his picture on the cover of *TV Guide* on August 8 and an article featuring him on August 23.

> ➤ *"I'll Hold You in My Heart."*

A concert review from Texarkana noted that after singing "Call Her Your Sweetheart" and "Easy on the Eyes," he performed "Texarkana Baby," "which sent a flock of high school girls in the audience clear out of this world. The sighs coming from the high school crowd were reminiscent of Frank Sinatra's early days." Arnold then sang "Cattle Call," which

> went over big with the crowds. . . . As Arnold started to leave the stage set up in the arena, the fans went wild—they wouldn't let him go. So the country boy from Tennessee came back to do a medley of old time folk favorites, "Molly Darlin'," "I'm Sending You a Big Bouquet of Roses," and "I'll Hold You in My Heart." After concluding the show with "There's Been a Change in Me," Arnold left the arena to a resounding round of applause and cheers.

The article also reported that Arnold "visited polio patients at St. Michael's Hospital" where he sang "Smoky the Bear" and "The Horse in Striped Pajamas."

In addition to his regular concerts, Eddy Arnold opened at the Hotel Sahara in Las Vegas on May 5, 1951.

Although Eddy Arnold had an active interest in current events, being an avid newspaper and magazine reader (he read Time cover to cover each week), he had never really been excited about a presidential race until 1952 when World War II hero Dwight Eisenhower ran. On November 3, 1952, along with Roy Acuff, he sang at a giant Jamboree for Eisenhower at the Ryman Auditorium. He also placed a $200 bet with Ernest Tubb, a die-hard Roosevelt Democrat, that Eisenhower would beat Adlai Stevenson; right after the election Ernest Tubb wrote out a check for $200 to Eddy Arnold to settle the bet. Arnold put it in his top middle desk drawer and never cashed it.

He had become an active citizen as well as a recording artist and took part in charity shows: he headed the American Cancer

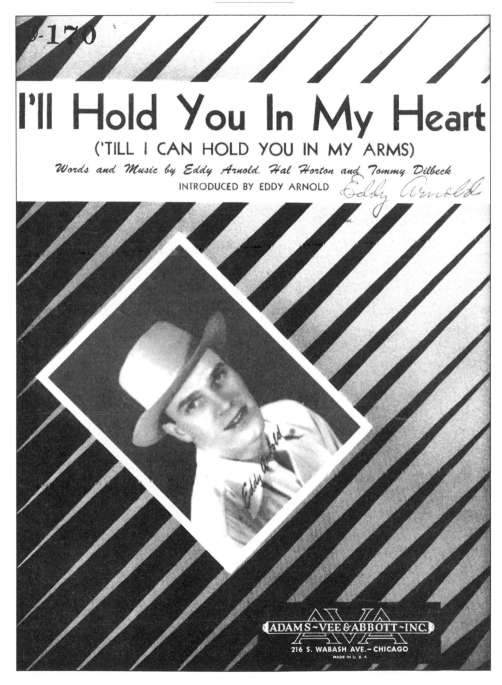

Society drive, and he did a series of shows for victims of a tornado in Fayetteville, Tennessee.

In a 1952 interview, Arnold described his recordings as "kind of on the fence. They're not pop, but they're not quite as hillbilly as some of the others. I do a lot of ballads and novelties. A lot of my songs go into the popular field later on—'Anytime' went pop last year, but my record of it sold 650,000 copies in 1948."

In 1952, he had his own network television show, *The Eddy Arnold Show*, as a summer replacement for Dinah Shore's show. The fifteen-minute show appeared on the CBS network on Tuesdays and Thursdays in prime time from Chicago's Studebaker Theater.

Country music on TV was getting some attention, as indicated by the *Oakland Tribune*:

> The boys with the string ties, guitars and cornball jokes are madder than all get-out over the way TV has been giving them the high-toned brush-off. They point to the fact that local TV outlets in many cities have Western, hillbilly or country-type programs which net higher popularity ratings than many of the so-called slick type or big time shows. Western melody-makers in this neck of the woods are getting particularly cantankerous over their lot in the video scene. Cliffie Stone, a pudgy sagebrush maestro who conducts the "Hometown Jamboree" here every Saturday night, is drafting a petition this week to present to the Academy of Television Arts and Sciences.
>
> [Stone complained that television executives] "continue to look down on us. . . . And when they do give one of us a tumble, they want to change our style, which would make it no longer a Western show. It's the informal atmosphere that gives the proper rollicking pitch to a hillbilly soiree. But a legitimate TV producer shrinks back in abject fear when a Western star explains that 'he don't need no writer feller or director.' There's an ironic but true axiom that a Western melange loses its charm with the fans if the corn is distilled out of it."

In July 1951, the great journalist Ralph J. Gleason wrote in the *San Francisco Chronicle*,

> The Western field, which has shot to such popularity since the war, is a strange mixture of simple singers, pseudo cowboys who never rode a horse, and Arkansas

Eddy Arnold visiting Cincinnati disc jockey Nelson King at radio station WCKY.

fiddlers from Arizona. It's rife with jealousy; most of the stars being quite touchy about whether they are "folk singers" or "Western singers" and they themselves refer to other artists whom they dislike as "hillbillies." But one and all, they hold Eddy Arnold in awe. . . . For one thing, Arnold is pretty generally credited with having a major part in the boom of Western Music. He has a good, homely, unpretentious voice and it manages to sound as authentically folksy as a sunbonnet and a corn-cob pipe. On the other hand, he tries to make his songs more than just simple laments, but he never departs far enough from his formula of just plain singing to lose the quality of sincerity that has made him the best selling artist in the folk and Western field for several years.

Eddy Arnold with his mother on the album cover of his album, To Mother.

Gleason went on,

> Eddy Arnold attributes one reason for the sudden popu-
> larity of what he calls "country music" to the big shift in
> population during the war when people from the country
> moved to the city in droves to work in war plants and
> stayed. It wasn't that city people hadn't liked the music
> before, Eddy believes, it was "just that they hadn't been
> exposed to it. There's a feeling and a rhythm to country
> songs that grows on you," according to the Tennessee
> Plowboy. "And once it grows it stays. That explains my
> appearance on so many shows that have a wide audi-
> ence—like the Perry Como and Milton Berle TV shows.
> For another thing, I find records like my 'Love Bug Itch'
> and 'I Wanna Play House with You' being played more
> and more on big city stations. We country music people
> have moved into town—that's for sure."

Eddy Arnold and Tom Parker met in Arnold's attorney's office and dissolved their artist/manager relationship on September 4, 1953. Arnold had sent Parker a telegram informing him the relationship was terminated, and Arnold has always stated, "We were two different personalities." The *Pickin' and Singin' News* noted it was an "obvious clash of personalities between the unassuming, easy-going Arnold and the aggressive, energetic Parker." There were also some conflicts over business arrangements Parker had set up. After an initial period of awkwardness, Arnold and Parker resumed their friendship and occasionally did business together with Parker booking and promoting some of Arnold's dates through Jamboree Attractions, which Parker formed. Arnold's radio and TV bookings were done through the William Morris Agency.

> ➤ *"There's a feeling and a rhythm to country songs that grows on you. And once it grows it stays."*

The split with Tom Parker marked the end of the first period of Eddy Arnold's career, and it was an important milestone. The same month that Arnold split from Parker, he recorded a song that pointed to a new direction he wanted to take. On September 21, he went into the studio and recorded "I Really Don't Want to Know." The song had been brought to him during a Las Vegas performance by Julian Auberbach of Hill and Range. Auberbach played the demo acetate sung by songwriter Don Robertson, accompanying himself on piano, in Arnold's hotel room. Arnold listened and said, "That's the prettiest song I've ever heard. I'd sing that song if it hair-lipped grandma."

With that song Arnold could try the type of sound he had been thinking about. He recorded it without a fiddle or steel guitar, with two acoustic guitars and a male group backing him.

Eddy Arnold's recording of "I Really Don't Want to Know" marked a new direction musically for him, although his first efforts were tentative, not wanting to lose his fan base. His live shows were also changing a bit, a harbinger of things to come. Sometime in the mid-1950s in either Beaumont or Galveston, Texas, he told his band to take a short break during the show, and he performed some songs by himself with his acoustic guitar. Roy Wiggins was first insulted and then perplexed. "We could do any of his songs exactly like the record," he remembers. "So I didn't see why he didn't want us to play." Wiggins also remembers that the acoustic set came after they had been touring with Tex Ritter and Ritter had a section in the show when he dismissed his band and sat on a stool to do a rollicking version of "Rye Whiskey."

The acoustic set allowed Arnold to perform some extra songs in the show, do only bits and pieces of songs without having to do the whole song, and develop an intimacy with the audience. The audience loved it, and he began to incorporate the acoustic set as a regular part of his show; in time it would become the favorite part of his live performances for many fans.

12

A Decade at the Top

Billboard devoted a special issue to Eddy Arnold in January 1955. It was, in many ways, the apex of his career up to that point.

The special presented a number of articles about Eddy Arnold and his career. There was a discussion of his recordings written by Chick Crumpacker, RCA Victor's promotion man for country and western, and an article by Ben Park, the producer, director, and writer for the TV show *Eddy Arnold Time*. The half-hour show, shot on film at the Kling Studios in Chicago, featured Arnold singing a few songs, then a small story acted out, then a few more songs. Costars included Betty Johnson and the Jordanaires. The show was heavy on music with ten to eleven songs.

The show's executive producer was Joe Csida, and the musical director was Charlie Grean, who played bass and helped produce Arnold's records. The show was financed by Arnold, who was unable to find a sponsor. He ended up losing a good deal of money on it. Arnold, Csida, Grean, and Ed Burton had gone into business together the previous year, with Csida, who was formerly editor for *Billboard*, serving as Arnold's manager after the split with Tom Parker. In addition, Csida, Grean, and Burton owned two publishing companies, Trinity (BMI) and Towne Music (ASCAP).

The special commemorated Eddy Arnold's tenth anniversary with RCA, and an album, *An American Institution*, was released in conjunction with the special. RCA president Frank Folsom, in his article, noted that Arnold had sold 30 million records in his first ten years with the company: "This boy from the country has done more

Eddy Arnold with his children, Joanne and Dickie.

to bridge the gaps from 'way-out-yonder' to Broadway than most people realize."

The previous year Arnold had another string of top ten records, including "I Really Don't Want to Know," "My Everything," "This Is the Thanks I Get (for Loving You)," and "Hep Cat Baby." In 1955, he would have hits with "I've Been Thinking," "In Time," "Two Kinds of Love," "Cattle Call," "The Kentuckian Song," "That Do Make It Nice," "Just Call Me Lonesome," "The Richest Man (in the World)," and "I Walked Alone Last Night." Arnold's remake of "Cattle Call" and "The Kentuckian Song" were recorded with orchestra leader Hugo Winterhalter and featured Arnold with a large, lush section of strings behind him.

> ➤ *Most of the major recording labels had offices in Nashville by 1955.*

Winterhalter had come to Nashville to Arnold's home to discuss working with the singer. The session that resulted brought some criticism from many in the country music community, who felt Arnold had sold out by recording with such a pop backing, but the recordings sold extremely well and Arnold felt the commercial success justified the new sound.

Arnold was determined to pursue the "new" sound. He put steel guitar player Roy Wiggins on a salary and then helped him set up a real estate business, with Arnold providing the financial backing. Guitarist Hank Garland had already left Arnold and become a top session player. Arnold also stopped his daily radio show sponsored by Purina that had been on the air since 1947. But after 1955, Arnold hit a dry spell in country music with only a few hits ("Trouble in Mind," "You Don't Know Me," and "Tennessee Stud") until 1962, when he had four top ten hits, before his career with the new sound took off into pop superstardom beginning in 1964.

The lull in his career of country music corresponded to the lull in the country music industry. Country music had been extremely successful during the decade after World War II, and Nashville had established itself as a major player in country music to the point that most of the major recording labels had offices in Nashville by 1955. A primary reason the labels had established offices in the city was the commercial success of country music out of Nashville, especially the tremendous success of Eddy Arnold. Not only did Eddy Arnold have great success selling records—thus bringing millions of dollars into RCA's coffers—but he also represented how successful country music could be when it joined forces with the corporate world.

Arnold was committed to his career, and he worked hard at it, promoting his records so that the distributors could sell them and giving a lot of time and attention to his recordings. While many artists did not learn a song until they were in the studio, Arnold always rehearsed his performances thoroughly before coming into the studio. At his home he had acquired a reel-to-reel tape recorder and set up a room where he would record himself doing prospective songs, working on the tempo and range, before he decided what to record.

In the *Billboard* special, Arnold's producer, Steve Sholes, discussed Arnold's method of recording and stated, "When the recording dates have been definitely set, Eddy accepts no bookings or heavy outside work for a two-week period prior to the sessions. He actually goes into training with plenty of sleep and all the other contributing factors to insure his health and strength for the forthcoming session." Indeed, Arnold usually recorded in the morning or afternoon when he was freshest so he could give his best performances.

He was also diligent in his concert appearances. Once, when Arnold was appearing in Fort Worth, he received a telephone call from western swing band legend Bob Wills. Wills wanted Arnold to go out drinking with him, but Arnold, who knew Wills's penchant for alcohol and tendency to go on a binge that could last several days, declined. "I had a show to do the next day," he remembers. "And I wanted to get plenty of rest for it and be in good condition."

This story not only illustrates Eddy Arnold's commitment to the fans who paid good money to see and hear him in concert, but it also shows why most critics and writers have avoided writing about him. Simply put, it is more interesting if an artist gets drunk, shoots up the town, misses the concert, or staggers through it, and careens self-destructively toward the next event. But for the folks who have paid money to see the performer in concert, it's a waste of time, effort, and money. Eddy Arnold always made sure that people who paid to see him got their money's worth.

Joe Csida, in the *Billboard* special, related that Arnold "is not quick to come to conclusions or make decisions. He thinks and studies and watches and analyzes every situation of any importance for a long time before he decides what his feeling or attitude or action will be. When he finally makes up his mind, his judgment is generally very firm, and he cannot easily be shaken in it." Ben Park described

The Eddy Arnold family on horseback.

Eddy Arnold as "relaxed, easy, warm, and honest." Both men captured essential elements of Arnold.

Eddy Arnold has always been the quintessential Southern gentleman in public. He is gracious, charming, considerate, and hospitable. In private, he is very determined, dogged, dedicated, and opinionated. He knows what's right for him—and he does it. In public, he strives to please and is genuinely interested in other people both professionally and personally; in private, he will not be pushed around. He does not make decisions quickly but mulls them over—often for a long time—before he comes to a conclusion. He is practical and pragmatic, yet also a romantic and dreamer.

Eddy Arnold always wanted to be successful commercially: "I wanted to sell a lot of records!" That comment and others led many to assume that money was more important to him than his music. Money was certainly important to him—he was always careful with his money, saved and invested it, and watched every penny as many who grew up poor in the Great Depression were prone to do. But he

valued his music greatly and demanded excellence both from himself
and from those working with him. He worked hard at his recordings
and performances with the result that both were top quality.

In terms of Eddy Arnold and the Nashville country music community, others often viewed him as "set apart" from country music.
True, he started in country music, and he is a country boy at heart,
but he always wanted to better himself, to be successful not just as an
artist but as a man, and he went to great lengths to educate himself
through travel, books, and listening to others.
He never matched the stereotype of the hard-
drinking, hell-raising country singer, and he
did all he could to distance himself from that
stereotype. "Drinking was never my favorite
sport," he says, and that kept him attending to
business when others were succumbing to the
bottle.

> *He always
wanted to better
himself, to be
successful not
just as an artist
but as a man,
and he went to
great lengths to
educate himself
through travel,
books, and
listening to
others.*

While other country singers might hang
out in bars, Arnold joined a country club;
while others might dress in flashy rhinestone
suits and buy chrome-covered Cadillacs,
Arnold wore slacks and a sports coat and
drove a Buick. While others might record
honky-tonk music aimed at the barroom jukebox, Arnold recorded ballads for people to listen to in their living rooms.

Because of his desire to broaden the
boundaries of country music, Arnold changed
his singing style. In his early recordings the
songs were generally up-tempo or medium
tempo, and he sang in a full-throated tenor. From the mid-1950s
onward he lowered the key to his songs (he rerecorded some of his
earlier hits two keys lower than the original recordings) and slowed
the tempo on numbers he previously did while searching for romantic ballads he could croon. His musical heroes had always been Bing
Crosby and Gene Autry, and he loved and admired them as much for
their singing style—easygoing, relaxed, and warm—as for the fact
that they were successful in the musical world as well as outside it.
Like Crosby and Autry, Arnold wanted to be a major recording artist,
but he also wanted to set a standard for success and achievement
outside the music business. The efforts paid off; he succeeded
beyond his wildest dreams.

Eddy Arnold with his young son, Dickie, on one of his farms.

In succeeding, Eddy Arnold changed the perceptions of those outside country music and the country music community itself. He changed the very definition of country music during his career.

Many have attempted to define country music in terms of lyrics ("simple, everyday stories"), music (through the folk roots, primarily from British folk songs), singing style (untrained, from the back of the throat), musical instruments (the steel guitar, fiddle), recordings (dominated by the acoustic rhythm guitar and sparse instrumentation), or quaint phrases ("three chords and the truth"). In actuality the core definition of country music must center on its being a *class* music. This class is working-class, blue-collar, originally Southern, and often described as white trash.

The term *white trash* is often applied liberally by those who dislike country music or who are outside the South; in fact, some people apply the term white trash to anyone who likes country music. The term is used much more selectively by those who like country music, those who are from the South, or those who work in the country music community. Even among the working class there is a pecking order, and although some may describe anyone they feel is "below" them economically or socially as white trash, the term generally fits the stereotypically uncultured, illiterate, uncouth, coarse individuals that people love to caricature when they look at people who love country music. Unfortunately, just enough of these kinds of folks exist—including a few country music artists—to forbid a total dismissal of this stereotype.

Eddy Arnold was not white trash by anybody's definition, and he always distanced himself from anything that smacked of this stereotype or image. Because he had dignity, self-respect, and a sense of honor, he raised the level of country music to the music of the middle class. In doing so, he represented a major trend in the United States in the decade after World War II.

13

Country Music's Growing Pains

The life story and music of Eddy Arnold reflect the shift in the United States from an agrarian to an urban nation during the post–World War II period. The United States recovered from the Great Depression—both mentally and fiscally—to become a powerful nation domestically and internationally. Country music moved from being regional music, confined mostly to the South (with the exception of the singing cowboys in the movies), to becoming national music, moving from a musical form on the fringes of American society to part of mainstream American popular music. Eddy Arnold played a major role in country music's rise to respectability in terms of image, status, and commercial success.

The year 1945 was the last year of World War II and a pivotal one for country music. American country music was dominated by western swing—particularly Bob Wills and Spade Cooley—and by West Coast country music. Of the top songs in 1945 only one, "It's Been So Long, Darling" by Ernest Tubb, was by a Nashville act. Indeed, 1946 would be a virtual repeat of 1945 with western swing still dominating country music. The top country music recording acts, Bob Wills and His Texas Playboys, Tex Ritter, Al Dexter, and Merle Travis, were all West Coast acts. While Nashville was important for its radio broadcasts of the *Grand Ole Opry* on WSM, it was not a recording center nor were its acts well known for their success on records. But all that was beginning to change, and a key person in the change was Eddy Arnold.

Nashville had all the musical elements that would guide the future of country music by the end of 1945. On the *Opry* was Bill Monroe with the Blue Grass Boys; by the end of 1945, his group

included Lester Flatt and Earl Scruggs, and the sound would define
bluegrass in the coming years. There was also Ernest Tubb, and his
Texas honky-tonk sound showed another direction country music
would take, especially into the 1950s as the hard-driving, barroom
sound virtually defined the sound of hard or traditional country for
the coming years. Hank Williams and Webb
Pierce later represented that traditional country music, which stayed close to its rural roots.

> ➤ *Nashville had*
> *all the musical*
> *elements that*
> *would guide the*
> *future of country*
> *music by the*
> *end of 1945.*

The star of the *Grand Ole Opry* was Roy
Acuff, whose mountain image fit with the
Opry's image of country music from folk roots
in the Southern area of the United States and
whose full-throated vocal sound was the
prime example of the country music singing
style. Uncle Dave Macon, with his vivid show-
manship and vaudeville background, connected country music to its folk and live
performance roots, but his sound and style
were already part of the past, although a past that would be treasured
and revisited time and again in the future.

Also on the *Opry* were Pee Wee King and his Golden West Cowboys, whose tight organization headed by manager J. L. Frank pioneered business practices in country music artist management and
bookings in the years to come and whose outfits—they dressed in
snappy cowboy clothes—would define the country music look after
the mountaineer image was shunned and discarded (except by Acuff)
after World War II.

And then there was Eddy Arnold, whose smooth vocal style—
reminiscent of a country Bing Crosby—would lead country music to
a more commercial sound and whose image pulled country music
away from the rural, hayseed image toward a more urban, urbane,
sophisticated look. Of all the acts on the *Opry* at the end of 1945,
Eddy Arnold would have the greatest impact on commercial country
music and the establishment of Nashville as the center for the country music industry in the following years. And Eddy Arnold, more
than any other single act of the period, would lead country music
into the mainstream of American popular music.

Since World War II, country music has proven itself to be commercially successful. In fact, even before World War II, going back
to Fiddlin' John Carson in Atlanta, to Vernon Dalhart in New York,
and through Jimmie Rodgers and the Carter Family as well as the

Eddy Arnold performing on his television show.

singing cowboys Gene Autry, Roy Rogers, and Tex Ritter, country music has done well as a business. The success led to major corporations recording and releasing this music. That, in turn, led to the possibility of broad exposure for the music—and access to the electronic media and distribution network that brings the product to the consumers.

But some country music has proven itself to be more commercial than others. Bluegrass, although it is vibrant, important music, has never been particularly commercial. Consequently, the field is dominated by small, independent labels that record and release the product; the major labels generally avoid it. The same fate has befallen western music since World War II; other than a few acts such as Gene Autry and the Sons of the Pioneers (who always transcended the genre and recorded songs that were not just western), this type of music is primarily recorded and released on small, independent labels. Even western swing, though reissued on major labels because it was originally recorded there, doesn't really have a place in contemporary country music. It was important in its day, but somehow its day passed.

What grew was commercial country music. And the leader of commercial country music was Eddy Arnold. Why is that significant? Because a much larger picture emerges when the commercial success of Eddy Arnold is examined in light of its impact on the decision of RCA Victor to set up a corporate office and recording studio in Nashville in 1955. And that led to the hiring of Chet Atkins and the unfolding of his career as a producer and executive.

The sales success of Arnold—as well as his exposure on network radio and TV—led to a change in the public perception of country music after World War II. First, it was acknowledged that country music had a commercial appeal, which helped assure its becoming part of mainstream American music.

Next, Eddy Arnold helped change the image of country music. Before World War II, the music was called *hillbilly*, a degrading term that signified backwoods bumpkins. Just prior to World War II, there were two distinct images for country—the singing cowboy and the musical mountaineer. But another image gradually evolved—that of a sophisticated singer who had a country background but assimilated the ways of the city. A singer who did not sing with a twang, who sang with violins instead of fiddles, and who dressed in tasteful sports coats and slacks (and later, tuxedos)—not cowboy hats, rhinestones, or dungarees. That was what Arnold did for country music—he moved it uptown and into the middle class.

Just as the country's population shifted from rural areas to urban areas, especially beginning in World War II, Eddy Arnold shifted country music—both musically and visually—from the rural, country image to one of the suburban gentleman who kept his down-home roots and rural values but acquired some city sophistication along the way.

That is the story of the generation that grew up in rural America during the depression and then got off the farm during World War II. They were proud of their heritage, but they wanted something more—they wanted respect, wanted to be part of mainstream America, and wanted to join the American middle class; in short, they wanted to be more worldly and less provincial. This is the story of Eddy Arnold's life as well as his music. He was moving up in the world—a country boy who was not a hick, someone who came from the farm but was not a rube, someone who sang country music but was not a hillbilly, and someone who had been in the hay fields but was not a hayseed.

Eddy Arnold was fortunate enough to come along at the time *Billboard* established its first country music charts in 1944, but his early success in the 1945–55 period occurred before the Recording Industry Association of America (RIAA) established its Gold and Platinum Record awards and the National Academy of Recording Arts and Sciences (NARAS) established the Grammy Awards, both in 1958. Although the phenomenal decade after World War II was, in many ways, the "Eddy Arnold Decade" in country music, the fact often goes unnoticed today because the awards from organizations that boosted popular music (the Grammys, the Country Music Association Awards) in the late 1950s and early 1960s were not in place during that period.

The story of country music from before World War II until the present time mirrors, in many ways, the story of the United States itself. Although the country had been changing from a rural, agricultural-based nation into an urban, industrial-based nation before World War II, the war certainly sped up the process and brought it to fruition. During the war, the population shifted from rural areas to cities, where defense plants were set up and workers were hired. It was not unusual for people from the South—still recovering from the Great Depression—to move to a major city during the war for jobs in defense or defense-related plants. In the services, Southerners were mixed with people from other parts of the country, so country music reached a wide variety of people. Also, American music became international music during World War II, primarily through the V-Disks sent out to servicemen and Armed Forces Radio. Country music left the South for good and became national music because Southern servicemen exposed others to country music in the armed forces and because Southerners moved out of the South in large numbers and fanned out across the country in search of defense-related jobs.

The city exerted a strong pull on rural Americans throughout the twentieth century. It was the place of bright lights—because the cities were wired for electricity before rural areas—and therefore people were not chained to the cycles of the seasons and daylight. In the city were action, excitement, and entertainment around the clock, and the city person was viewed as cosmopolitan—cultured, sophisticated, and worldly wise. The rural person was often viewed as a country bumpkin, a rube, a hayseed—all the uncool things nobody wanted to be. In the city were jobs, and for someone raised in the country doing farm work, it seemed that the jobs involved no work at all; it was easy money. So rural people moved to cities in large numbers throughout the twentieth century, particularly after the 1940s.

> Arnold openly embraced the middle-class values espoused after World War II, values that stressed getting along socially and joining in.

Rural people reacted to their move to the city in two ways. First, they wanted to keep some of their rural roots, so they planted gardens, read stories about idealized country life illustrated by Norman Rockwell with his idealized view of rural and small town life, and listened to country music. But rural people who moved to the city also wanted to get rid of the hayseed ways and acquire some sophistication, so they bought suits and ties, attended social functions, and attempted to join the middle class. The middle class is defined not only in terms of income, but also in values: the Protestant work ethic, independence, material possessions, and, increasingly, a ranch house in the suburbs.

Eddy Arnold was uniquely qualified to bridge the gap for those moving from the country to the city. He had rural roots; he grew up on a farm in Chester County, Tennessee, and knew hard work and hardship. His father died when he was eleven, and his family became sharecroppers on the farm they once owned. He grew up during the depression in the South, an area particularly hard hit. And he cut his teeth on country music after he left the farm, performing in a duo on radio stations in Memphis, St. Louis, and Louisville before moving to Nashville with Pee Wee King in 1940.

But Arnold also represented the acquired culture and sophistication of the city dweller. First, a performer acquires worldly ways through travel and the experience of meeting a wide variety of people. That was certainly not unique to Eddy Arnold, but he made the most of it. Next, his voice was smooth and pop sounding, like Bing Crosby's or Frank Sinatra's, rather than the harsh country sound of someone like Roy Acuff, Hank Williams, or Webb Pierce.

Next, Arnold openly embraced the middle-class values espoused after World War II, values that stressed getting along socially and joining in. He regularly visited radio stations, schmoozed with the movers and shakers, became comfortable socializing with strangers, and took care of business in a responsible, respectable way. He didn't show a

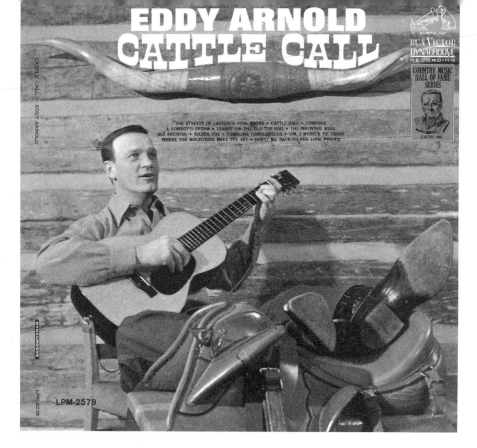

moody, self-absorbed, artistic temperament or dress outlandishly. Unlike some other country stars, he didn't deck himself out in rhinestones or build guitar-shaped swimming pools. His look was tasteful and understated; the upwardly mobile middle class could feel comfortable with him. Arnold accepted his audience; he did not challenge them. His audience responded by embracing him and buying his music; after all, Arnold's audience was too busy building careers and raising families after World War II to be challenged musically. It was a time of shoulder-to-the-grindstone hard work. Eddy Arnold and his music provided a sound track for that life.

In many ways, the story of country music is the story of a fight for respect. For a number of years country music and its performers were subject to stereotypical images of poor white trash. Those who loved the music were often embarrassed by their own tastes. They were both proud and ashamed—proud of their rural past and proud of their taste and connection with country music, but ashamed that the music was linked with so many negative cornpone images. The most important thing that Eddy Arnold did for country music was to give it respect. He carried country music into the world, and he didn't embarrass himself or the music.

In short, Eddy Arnold made people proud they were country music fans. And in a more general sense, he moved country music uptown, gave it self-respect and dignity. Arnold proved you didn't have to be a hillbilly to sing country music. Because of his commercial success—as well as the commercial success of country music in general—Eddy Arnold helped move country music into the American popular music mainstream. That led to country music becoming an accepted part of the corporate culture in the American entertainment industry by improving what corporate America looks at closest: the bottom line. By improving that bottom line, country music improved itself and became a major player in the world of music.

14

Rock 'n' Roll Arrives

A ll hell broke loose in 1956. That was when America discovered Elvis Presley, the singer who sold 10 million records and became the cultural symbol of teenage rebellion, the generation gap, the sexual revolution, juvenile delinquency, and a new individualism that swept young people into new attitudes and lifestyles.

Actually, it all started a bit earlier than that; musically, rhythm and blues thrived on small labels in the decade after World War II, the problem of juvenile delinquency was a national concern throughout most of the 1950s, and the previous year Bill Haley and the Comets had a number one song with "Rock Around the Clock," which was featured in the movie about juvenile delinquents, *Blackboard Jungle*. It's somewhat unfair to single out Elvis Presley as being responsible for the huge shift in the cultural life of America from the mid-1950s onward, but he was the central figure in the whole rock 'n' roll movement that energized the young generation in the fifties and threatened their parents.

On January 5, 1956, Elvis Presley came to the RCA Victor studios in Nashville on McGavock Street and recorded "Heartbreak Hotel," which would be his first number one record. Elvis had his first success in the South in late 1954 on Sun Records in Memphis, and like a steamroller, the momentum kept building throughout 1955. In November 1955, Elvis came to Nashville to the Country and Western Disc Jockeys Convention and agreed to a contract with RCA Victor. The man who signed him was Steve Sholes, Eddy Arnold's producer. The key to the deal was the Aberbach brothers, who owned Hill and Range Publishing Company (Eddy Arnold's former publishing company, which kicked in $15,000 to make the deal acceptable), and the catalyst was Eddy Arnold's former manager, Tom Parker. Parker would guide Elvis's career by relying on the same basic tactics he used when he was Arnold's manager: use the recording success with RCA Victor and money from publisher Hill and Range to build a career that would entice Hollywood to make him a movie star. And like Eddy Arnold, Elvis signed with the William Morris Agency to secure bookings on national television.

> *While the success of Elvis was the catalyst for the creation of the entire industry of rock 'n' roll, it almost killed country music.*

Parker had done it all before with Eddy Arnold; he took a country boy who appealed to the pop world and made him into a superstar, and his previous experience benefited Elvis. Parker also did for Elvis what he had done for Eddy Arnold: he gave him his total, undivided loyalty, commitment, and attention, and he worked tirelessly on his career.

While the success of Elvis was the catalyst for the creation of the entire industry of rock 'n' roll, it almost killed country music. Young singers, who might have gone into country music, were enticed into rock 'n' roll, and young audiences were swept up and wanted to see and hear young rock 'n' roll singers. The demand for country music nearly vanished overnight.

Substantive changes in the country music community in Nashville during 1956 altered the city and the industry permanently. Rock 'n' roll was only part of it, albeit a major part. First, there were the changes with radio.

Before 1940 most music heard on radio was performed live. That included the big network shows featuring the big bands and elaborate productions as well as the fifteen-minute broadcasts in the early morning when a country music group would sing some songs and advertise a product because a sponsor paid for the time. Radio listeners heard a variety of music and a variety of shows: big band, country music, soap operas, westerns, mysteries, comedies, and dramas.

The reasons for the live programs were fairly simple. The first twenty years of radio were characterized by that medium's experimentation and discovery that live shows worked well. Sponsors liked the human touch—being linked to performers who promoted their products. But there was another reason why live programs dominated

Eddy Arnold with, left to right, Elvis Presley, Frank Folsom, and Colonel Tom Parker.

radio: the record industry and the musicians union fought against the broadcast of records on the air.

The record companies fought radio airplay because they believed it hurt sales; they reasoned that listeners would not buy something they could get for free. So the record companies didn't want listeners to hear records for free. The musicians union fought the playing of records on the radio because it jeopardized a musician's livelihood; if records were played, then musicians would not be hired by radio stations, and thus musicians would be out of work.

Early country music on the radio was mostly live performances on fifteen- or thirty-minute shows. Early morning shows and shows during the noon hour were popular because, the reasoning went, that was when farmers listened. And farmers were perceived to be the audience for country music. If there was a show in the evening, it was probably on a Saturday night, and if it was a big show—lots of performers and lasting an hour or more—then it was called a *Barn Dance*. In fact, live country music—especially through the barn dances—was the primary outlet for country music on radio until around 1955.

In 1940, two significant things happened that would affect country music on radio. First, the Supreme Court let stand a lower court ruling that when someone purchased a recording, all property rights belonged to the buyer. When a disc jockey purchased a record, he was allowed to play it on the air. Although that did not protect the notion of intellectual property and, considered in the light of subsequent copyright questions, was a bad decision for the music business as a whole, it made radio airplay for records legal. That curbed the efforts of the record companies, who had marked their record labels "not for radio airplay" and hired a bevy of lawyers to enforce the ban on radio airplay.

The second thing that happened in 1940 was the election of James Caesar Petrillo from Chicago as head of the American Federation of Musicians. Petrillo ruled with an iron fist and campaigned vigorously to get records banned from the radio because they would displace musicians who earned their livelihood from live performances—often on the radio. Petrillo announced at the American Federation of Musicians annual convention in May 1942 that he would call a strike of all musicians on August 1, 1942. One of the things Petrillo fought was canned music.

Victor and Columbia were prepared to charge radio stations for their products in 1940 until the Supreme Court decision knocked that out of the question; Capitol Records, just formed at the end of 1941, took advantage of the situation and became the first label to distribute free promotional copies to radio stations for on-air play. Prior to that time, only music editors and record reviewers for print media were given free promotional recordings.

In 1946, the year after the war, 8 million records were sold; country music accounted for 13.2 percent of sales—topped only by popular with 50 percent and classical with 18.9 percent. The 550,000 jukeboxes, which before the war accounted for most of the sales of country records, now accounted for only about 10 percent of the total. Part of the reason for increased country record sales to consumers was the exposure country music was receiving on local radio shows and network shows, and through disk jockeys playing records on the radio.

World War II brought Americans together over the radio to hear news of the world. Also, people were employed because of the defense-based economy and were making money they could not spend because of the rationing of goods, the limited availability of consumer items, and the heavy encouragement of savings by the government through the war bond drives to finance the war. So there were pent-up savings and pent-up demand when the war ended in 1945; the result was that in 1946–47, a huge number of radio sets were sold. By the end of that two-year period, 93 percent of the American households owned a radio. But 1947 was also the beginning of the television revolution; just when radio was at the height of its popularity, TV would make its first inroads to replace it as the dominant medium in the United States.

There were changes at the network level for country music on radio after the war. NBC canceled the *National Barn Dance* on WLS in Chicago after star Red Foley left to join WSM and the *Grand Ole Opry*. Foley was replaced by Rex Allen, who left for Hollywood in 1949; then the WLS *National Barn Dance* moved to the ABC radio network but was canceled there after about a year.

By 1945, the *Boone County Jamboree* in Cincinnati had been renamed the *Midwestern Hayride*, and in 1948, it began to be featured on TV. The *Dixie Jamboree* on WBT in Charlotte appeared on the regional CBS network during World War II; it evolved into the *Carolina Hayride* and, from 1946, was broadcast over CBS on Saturday nights. The *Louisiana Hayride* was formed in 1948 on KWKH in Shreveport, Louisiana; the show and others appeared on CBS as *Saturday Night, Country Style* on a rotating basis.

The number of radio stations exploded after World War II. In 1946, the FCC licensed 500 new stations; in 1948, there were an additional 400. Disc jockeys became increasingly important because there was just not enough live talent to go around; also, playing records was easier and cheaper than hiring live talent. And records carried a wide variety of music—including country and rhythm and blues—which consumers wanted but could not get on network or big city radio stations. So small stations playing records by disc jockeys proliferated. The trend ran parallel to the trend of small, independent record labels recording country and rhythm and blues music. The major labels were locked into the pop sound that evolved from the big band era, with vocalists replacing the bandleaders as the stars, but still featuring a smooth, pop sound. The rough and raucous sounds of hillbilly and race music had found their outlet on jukeboxes prior to World War II, especially after Prohibition died in 1933 and bars became legal again.

In terms of technology, 1948 was a great leap forward; ABC went all tape, using the technology the Americans and Russians discovered in Berlin that had been developed by the Germans. Prior to that, recordings were done direct to disk; the Germans' Magnetophon, the forerunner to analog tape, revolutionized the recording industry. Also, in June 1948 Columbia Records premiered the 33 1/3 rpm record; in December, RCA brought forth the 45 rpm. The two new technologies on vinyl would eventually replace the old 78s. Radio was still the dominant mass medium in the United States; by the end of 1948, 94.3 percent of American families owned a set.

But there was virtually no music recorded in 1948 because of a strike called by James Caesar Petrillo, head of the AFM. The strike stopped new recordings from being made from January until December 1948. By the end of that period, most of the big bands had dissolved, effectively ending the big band era, although a few would regroup after 1948 and some would even survive into the 1960s.

The 1948 strike was Petrillo's last hurrah. The country had disliked his calling a strike during World War II, even after President Roosevelt had requested that he not do so. Further, some alleged he was a member of the Mafia, and Congress had accused him of being a racketeer. Finally, the Taft-Hartley Act, passed over President Harry Truman's veto in June 1947, limited the power of unions.

In the summer of 1947, Universal released *Something in the Wind*, where Deanna Durbin played a disc jockey working for a small radio station. As a promotion for the movie the firm created the National Association of Disc Jockeys—paying for eighty of the country's top disc jockeys to come to Chicago as part of the movie's premiere. But once in Chicago the deejays elected Barry Gray of New York to be president and organized themselves. The organization served as an example for country music broadcasters, who began their organization six years later.

On November 22, 1952, WSM invited about one hundred disc jockeys to come to town for a convention and *Grand Ole Opry* Birthday Celebration in honor of the *Opry's* twenty-seventh anniversary. About eighty showed up. The next year WSM President Jack DeWitt, Executive Assistant Irving Waugh, Artists Service Bureau Chief Jim Denny, Program Director Jack Stapp, and Publicity Director Bill McDaniel pulled out all stops and organized a major convention that attracted five hundred people—four hundred of them disc jockeys.

The convention began on November 21, 1953. Major labels were present—RCA Victor, Columbia, Decca, Capitol, and Mercury hosted events. *Billboard* gave out awards for top country talent—which would become a forerunner for major country music awards in the future—and BMI gave out its first country music songwriter awards.

The event would eventually shift to October and lead to the development of the Country Music Association, the CMA Awards, and a weeklong celebration for the business of country music. One of the first organizations to emerge from the event was the Country and Western Disc Jockeys Association.

The *Opry* saw this as a good business move. First, having all the country music businesspeople in town helped the Opry Artists Service Bureau, headed by Jim Denny, to make personal contacts with buyers of country talent. And the booking agency was making a lot of money by then.

At the meeting, Carl Haverlin, president of BMI, spoke. ASCAP, the major rival to BMI, would not license country music; the success of BMI stemmed in large part from the enormous amount of country music songs that it licensed. Further, the future success of BMI and the future success of country music were linked; if more stations played country music, then BMI could collect more money for country music songwriters and publishers—expanding the horizons of both BMI and the country music industry. Significantly, ASCAP was not present at the event, giving BMI an extra edge on the country music market.

The Country and Western Disc Jockeys Association would mark the beginning of a booster organization for country music. Although there was a close connection with the *Opry*—the *Opry*'s birthday was the reason for inviting everyone to Nashville—the organization operated independently of the *Opry*. Five years later the organization would evolve into the Country Music Association. But from 1953 to 1958, the Grand Ole Opry Birthday Celebration became the major convention for people involved in country music. All the foremost disk jockeys, talent bookers, and other businesspeople—as well as country artists—would come. It was a gathering of the tribes for country music and became a significant reason that Nashville served as a focal point for the *business* of country music.

Paul Ackerman wrote in *Billboard*,

> WSM is owned by the National Life & Accident Insurance Company, considered by many the fastest-growing insurance company in the world. Much of its success is attributed to the good will created by the "Grand Ole Opry" program and its talent. . . . The renowned "Grand Ole Opry" paves the way for the insurance company's salesman. It is an outstanding example of a far-sighted

public-service operation, producing very tangible economic benefits.

Ackerman also noted that "the country field was experiencing the greatest prosperity and vigor." In many ways, it was the peak for country music during the years the industry was dominated by the *Grand Ole Opry*. But in some ways, it also marked the beginning of the end. At the beginning of 1953, Hank Williams died; at the end of 1954, Fred Rose, head of Acuff-Rose Publishing, the first successful company independent of the *Opry*, would die.

15

Country Music Splits from Opry Domination

The recording industry in Nashville thrived during the decade after World War II because of local business, more than national recording sessions. The economy was booming, and businesses needed advertisements for radio. The recording studios provided them. There were also transcriptions to be made of the *Opry* and other shows and shipped across the country in an early version of syndicated programming. And publishing companies needed to demo songs and audition artists. The major labels came to provide an increasing amount of business for economic reasons: (1) it was cheaper to record the musicians in Nashville than send them to New York; (2) the musicians union charged a lesser rate in Nashville; and (3) a good group of versatile musicians was available at WSM (in the days of live radio shows a station had a number of musicians on its payroll or available for shows).

The "Nashville Sound" developed initially during this period because a handful of musicians played on the majority of sessions. They developed a way to do sessions by ear (without written arrangements) with head arrangements (done on the spot instead of worked out by an arranger beforehand) very quickly (they could record an average of at least one master recording per hour). Since labels had to make a profit, and since individual country recordings did not usually sell in huge numbers, it was good business to cut as many costs as possible during the production so that the release could recoup its money as quickly as possible.

That was how the publishers in Nashville found their niche. Publishers make the majority of their money from radio airplay through BMI and ASCAP, so Nashville publishers could earn a good income by the growing spread of country music on radio in the decade after World War II. And many of the country music publishers were based in Nashville, so the money came directly to them.

BMI was well aware of the importance of country music to its own growth as well as being aware of the amount of dollars dispersed to Nashville-based publishers. So in 1955, BMI named Frances Williams (now Preston) to open an office and sign up songwriters and take care of publishers. In 1955, business was great and getting better for country music in Nashville.

WSM was also making big money from advertising and its network connections while the *Opry* was making money from its advertising revenue as well as the admissions charged for its shows, which had expanded to include a Saturday afternoon performance. Beginning in 1947, when television first came into American homes, the engineers and executives at WSM watched the development of the new technology and its acceptance by large numbers of Americans. In 1954, WSM began a television affiliate that reaped immediate benefits. Plus, the insurance business continued to thrive.

So the country music industry did not thrive at the expense of National Life and Accident Insurance Company and WSM; rather, it thrived with them. And since the executives in each of the companies had their hands full with their own growth and development, it was easy to overlook the *Opry*—especially since the *Grand Ole Opry* was really only a show on Saturday. And besides, people like Jim Denny were over there taking care of all the operations at the *Opry* and dealing quickly and effectively with problems. It was a nice way to have your cake and eat it, too; the only problem was that the *Opry*—and those connected with it—was growing more powerful and popular than anyone in the insurance company or radio station realized. That created an inertia of sorts. The *Opry* kept getting bigger, and there was no way—or reason really—to check it or step back and rein it in. By 1955, the *Opry* was a giant locomotive chugging at high speed.

But there was an essential problem with the *Opry*'s domination of the country music industry in Nashville: a number of executives connected with the *Opry* had established their own businesses on the side and were reaping the financial benefits of the *Opry* connection. There was bickering among individuals, envy, and jealousy—mostly over outside income and personal power that transcended the corporation. All of that led to the most important memo in the history of country music.

The music industry has never really accepted the premise that there is such a thing as a conflict of interest. Thus the history of the commercial music industry is filled with examples of people working for a company but developing another related business on the side to fill a legitimate need and to earn extra income. As long as it didn't keep you from doing your job with the parent firm, according to the prevailing wisdom, then it was all right. Such was the situation at WSM and the *Opry* with employees forming publishing companies, promoting concerts, and building recording studios until WSM President Jack DeWitt wrote his memo.

In the memo dated August 2, 1955, he confronted his staff about their outside activities and told them that "it will be necessary to review all of these businesses, and in some cases require that they be terminated in the interest of harmony within our organization." DeWitt was concerned about the ethical questions of WSM employees having outside business interests in conflict with WSM's business; the board of WSM agreed with him.

The major problem was Jim Denny, who had grown too rich and powerful to be ignored, and who refused in previous meetings with DeWitt to divest himself of his outside interests. Roy Acuff began the final series of events when he complained to DeWitt about Denny giving him lesser bookings. The complaint was part of the power struggle between Acuff and Denny; both wanted to have the *Opry* as their own domain. Acuff eventually won that battle, but Denny may have won a bigger victory.

The ultimatum from DeWitt caused several history-making decisions. The WSM engineers closed down Castle Recording Studio because they did not want to lose their generous pensions from the parent company and because they wanted to be involved in the new medium of television. As a result, Owen Bradley's studio suddenly had a lot of new business. Bradley's business was the first to be located in the area that became known as Music Row. The reasons were financial. Property values were low there, and the area had been zoned commercial, so Bradley took advantage of the situation. Bradley would emerge with the major recording studio, which attracted business from record labels, whose business attracted publishers and songwriters. The old center for business had been downtown Nashville on Seventh Avenue at the headquarters for WSM and National Life as well as two streets over on Fifth where the Ryman was located. The new center for business would be in the area that became known as Music Row where Bradley had his studio.

In terms of the national media, country music was getting more coverage during the 1950s, receiving grudging respect for its economic success, but still saddled with an image of being backwoods and backward, and the victim of numerous stereotypical images conjured up by out-of-town writers.

In a 1951 article in the *New York Times Magazine* titled "Tin Pan Alley's Git-Tar Blues," writer Allen Churchill stated, "New York's writers of pop tunes look in envy and calculation at the 'Country' songsmiths now outsmarting the city slickers," and he continued, "Adding insult to misery is the fact that the bellwether song of the folk music trend seems destined eventually to unseat the Alley's favorite—Irving Berlin's 'White Christmas'—as the top popular tune of our time." The song he was discussing was "Tennessee Waltz," recorded by Patti Page and one of the biggest hits in 1951 but written by country songwriters Pee Wee King and Redd Stewart and published by the Nashville firm of Acuff-Rose.

Churchill went on,

> New Yorkers have long been blissfully unaware of the fact, but this country contains two great song-buying areas. One is the city field, which goes for "pop" songs from Tin Pan Alley, Broadway shows, and Hollywood musicals. The other is the country field, the territory outside cities, especially in the South, where music is taken more seriously than anywhere else. Music enjoyed in this vast area consisting of all types of hillbilly, mountain, Western and old-time folk tunes, jumbled together under the encompassing name of country music. . . . The financial success of top country singers has aroused the envy of city folk.

Don Eddy's article "Hillbilly Heaven," in *American Magazine* in 1952, began,

> If you don't mind, I will write this report lying down. I feel giddy. Before my eyes are funny little men chasing each other with pitchforks and banjos. In my ears ring mournful sounds such as never were before on land or sea. No, it's nothing I et. It's because I have been exposed, in person, to a national phenomenon called Grand Ole Opry, and I'm afraid it bit me.

The writer continued in the smarmy, cutesy vein: "This noteworthy nation has been taken down bad with an epidemic called hillbillyitis." He noted there was a lot of money in country music and added, "For guys who were skinning mules not too long ago, this is a lovely bale of hay."

A 1952 *Newsweek* article, "Country Music Is Big Business and Nashville Is Its Detroit," held that "country music has become more than a regional manifestation; it has become a national desire." It described country music as "this twang-wail-and-howl division of the electronics industry. . . . Whether heard on TV, radio, jukebox, phonograph, or by orchestra, this shouting or moaning from an old transatlantic past is doing a sturdy fifth of the dollar volume of the music for which the United States pays money to hear."

> ➤ *A 1952* Newsweek *article: "Country music has become more than a regional manifestation; it has become a national desire."*

Rufus Jarman wrote "Country Music Goes to Town" for *Nation's Business* in 1953. The country music industry grossed an estimated $25 million a year, and Jarman observed, "These country glamor boys are as big—sometimes bigger—in record sales and juke box popularity as Bing Crosby or Frank Sinatra. . . . They live in mansions with swimming pools attached in Nashville's fashionable suburbs, drive immense automobiles bearing their initials in gold, and wear expensive Western getups."

"Hillbilly Music Leaves the Hills," in *Good Housekeeping* in 1954, presented an overview:

> Who would have thought ten years ago that a group of country singers and a few musicians playing guitars, banjos, and fiddles could fill the auditoriums of big cities? What, no tricky pianist, no singer with sexy eyes, no smooth star belting the latest Broadway ballad? No, just simple songs and dances performed in homespun style—and all over the country people are "naïve" enough to pay money to hear it.
>
> As a matter of fact, country-music concerts have become astonishingly popular in the last three years. Most curiously, they've been particularly popular in the big towns—in Cleveland, St. Louis, Baltimore, Philadelphia, Cincinnati, San Francisco, and even conservative Boston. In fact, about the only big town hillbilly music has not invaded is New York City. Small groups performing such music are traveling to America's small towns, playing jamborees. Mountain music has left the mountains and gone down to the plains.

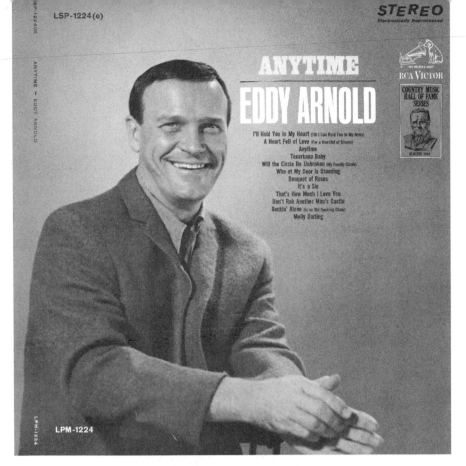

In *House & Garden*'s 1954 article "Folk Songs," Roy Harris commented,

> Hillbilly music emphasizes the lovelorn, the country fiddler, the camp meeting and occasionally the goings-on of country bumpkins (both sexes and all ages). The tunes and the harmonies are all about the same, rearranged to fit the words, some fast, some slow. The hillbilly racket begets some of the poorest music that ever entered human ears and yet it seems to give pleasure to many people.

In 1956, *Life* ran "Country Musicians Fiddle Up Roaring Business":

> Up until a few years ago one half of the popular music fans of America had no idea what the other half was up to. One half listened to slick songs from Hollywood and Broadway. The other—mostly from rural districts—was devoted to a brand of music loosely known as hillbilly. . . .
>
> This year some 50 million country music records will be sold, which is 40% of the total sales of all single popular music records. . . . Nashville has become the country's third biggest record-making center, just behind New York and Hollywood.

16

Eddy Arnold's Wilderness Years

The years 1957–63 may be considered the wilderness years for Eddy Arnold. But like Winston Churchill's wilderness years, they were deceptively busy and laid the groundwork for a successful future. Eddy Arnold has always been a man with an enormous amount of energy, working hard at his career. But during that period, he tended to devote most of his energies to his businesses and outside investments, away from the spotlight.

In the decade after his first record was released, Arnold had an amazing batting average with chart records: sixty-six out of sixty-eight of his releases had landed in the top ten on the country music charts at *Billboard*. The two that missed the top ten made it up to number twelve; one was a Christmas song, "Christmas Can't Be Far Away," in 1954, and the other was "Don't Forget" in 1955. During 1955, Arnold had ten songs on the country charts—nine of them in the top ten and two of them number ones. The year 1956 began with a top ten song, "Trouble in Mind," then the next, "Casey Jones (The Brave Engineer)" made it only to fifteen. The following number, one of Arnold's most memorable ballads, "You Don't Know Me," made it to number ten. The three were his only chart singles in 1956.

In 1957, Eddy Arnold had only one chart record, a remake of "Gonna Find Me a Bluebird," and he had *no* chart records in all of 1958. In 1959, there were two chart records, including "Tennessee Stud," which landed at number five, but in 1960, he once again failed to reach the charts for any of his releases. In 1961, he had three songs on the charts—but none of them came close to being in the top ten.

In 1962, Arnold bounced back with four songs on the charts—all top tens ("Tears Broke Out on Me," "A Little Heartache," "After Loving You," and "Does He Mean That Much to You?"), but in 1963, none of his three chart releases reached the top ten.

Requests for Arnold's personal appearances decreased significantly; he no longer went on tour. That was partly because the demand for country artists had dropped precipitously after rock 'n' roll hit. In 1956, Fort Worth reporter Bud Shrake wrote about the problem:

> The old whining hillbilly artist, who sang as if his boots were stuffed with ants and his nose with straw, is a dead item on the modern music market . . . a new style of music has taken over. It's hard to say what to call it, except that it's rock-and-roll by hillbilly musicians. . . . Popular music, hillbilly and rock-and-roll have gotten all mixed up.

▶ *The drop in demand for personal appearances coincided nicely with Arnold's desire to stay home and spend time with his children.*

The drop in demand for personal appearances coincided nicely with Arnold's desire to stay home and spend time with his children. For someone who grew up without a father, he knew the importance of having a dad around. On December 21, 1957, his daughter Joanne turned eleven, and on January 2, 1960, his son turned eleven—the same time in Arnold's life his own dad had died—and he wanted to be around to share those years with his children.

Eddy Arnold spent some of his time thinking about his life and career, and he wondered if he should hang it up as a country artist. He had made some good investments and was set for life, so there was no pressure to perform in order to buy the groceries. Sometimes he felt the music industry had passed him by; the pop style that he loved so much just didn't seem to appeal to teenagers, and the older audience was too busy making a living to buy many records or see many concerts. Radio and TV weren't very receptive to country music. Besides, he had ten years at the top, and few performers last that long; it was hard to imagine he could ever be as successful as he had been in the past after he passed his fortieth birthday in 1958.

As much as he knew he didn't have to sing, he couldn't shake the *desire* to sing. He loved singing and performing; they were as much a part of him as breathing. Something deep inside him wouldn't let it go, couldn't let it go, so he kept recording. No matter how successful artists become, the real reason they sing and perform is the drive to perform. Eddy Arnold never really lost that drive. No man ever forgets his first love, and singing was Eddy Arnold's first love.

So he stayed before the American public through radio and television appearances. In early 1955, as RCA mounted a special promotion to celebrate Arnold's tenth anniversary with the label, NBC did a special on Arnold. His half-hour show *Eddy Arnold Time* was syndicated in 1955–56, but the show lasted only thirteen episodes. In 1956, *The Eddy Arnold Show*, a half-hour television show on ABC, began on Thursday evenings during prime time; that same year *The Eddy Arnold Show* began on the CBS radio network and was broadcast over one thousand stations in the United States and Canada.

Arnold became much more involved in the Nashville community, both in business and in social events. In 1957, he starred in a play *School Daze* at the Ryman put on by the PTA. In 1959, he was master of ceremonies at a Boy Scout banquet (his son was in the Boy Scouts). He also appeared at a Fourth of July parade in Atlanta sponsored by WSB and was involved in the Day Care Center for Emotionally Disturbed Children and the Fannie Battle Day Care Center, which provided day care for indigent working women.

In many ways his life was that of a successful local businessman: going to his office every day, being home for dinner on most nights with his family, attending school and community events where his children were involved, and socializing with a small group of friends and business associates.

The 1950s were the Eisenhower years. Eddy Arnold felt comfortable in those years, and he admired President Eisenhower a great deal. In 1939, Eisenhower—at the age of forty-eight—defined happiness in a letter, stating "only a man that is happy in his work can be happy in his home and with his friends. Happiness in work means that its performer must know it to be worthwhile, suited to his temperament, and, finally, suited to his age, experience, and capacity for performance of a high order." This description could have been written for Eddy Arnold.

Biographer Stephen Ambrose described Eisenhower's effect on the nation as

> so comforting, so grandfatherly, so calm, so sure of himself, so skillful in managing the economy, so experienced

in insuring America's defenses, so expert in his control of the intelligence community, so knowledgeable about the world's affairs, so nonpartisan and objective in his above-the-battle posture, so insistent on holding to the middle of the road, that he inspired a trust that was as broad and deep as that of any President since George Washington.

Clearly, Eddy Arnold agreed with the biographer's assessment of President Eisenhower. Like Eisenhower, he liked business as usual, stuck close to a routine, and spoke and acted in moderation with a disdain for extremes. On most issues he held a moderate, middle-of-the-road stance and always sought to be flexible in his professional decisions.

Even Arnold's off-hours mirrored the president's tastes. For relaxation Arnold joined a country club, played golf, and spent time at Claude Cook's plantation in Hazelhurst, Georgia, hunting quail—all favorite activities of Eisenhower.

Always interested in politics and well informed on national and local events, Arnold had gotten more involved in politics through his personal friendship with Tennessee Governor Frank Clement. The two became close, and Clement often called Arnold to come over to the Governor's Mansion for a chat. Clement was a country music fan and liked Eddy Arnold; to a large extent, the country music community was treated well at the top levels of state government because of Clement.

Clement ran for governor of Tennessee in 1962. At that time, the governor was not allowed to succeed himself, so Clement became governor, then had to sit out four years before he could run again. During the 1962 campaign, Eddy Arnold (as well as a number of other country music acts) appeared with the governor around the state and sang a few tunes, then gave his endorsement. The man who was generally governor during the years that Clement wasn't, Buford Ellington, was also friends with Arnold, and during 1962, Arnold sang at his birthday party.

Tennessee was a Democratic state at that point; there was hardly any Republican opposition. But Eddy Arnold was a Republican; during the 1960 presidential campaign, he appeared with Richard Nixon to sing a few songs and give an endorsement. Arnold had been a Republican as long as he had voted, but since there was virtually no Republican party in the South during the 1950s and most of the 1960s, Arnold befriended Democratic officeholders. Besides, the conservative South was more Republican in spirit and policies than the liberal Democrats of the North. The strength of the Democratic party in the South up through the 1960s reflected history: the Republican party was the party of Abraham Lincoln, and since the Civil War, that was not a party that Southerners wanted to belong to.

On the national level, Arnold had met Senate Majority Leader Lyndon Johnson in 1958 at the dedication of a television station in Temple, Texas. Arnold had gone down for the event as a favor for Harry Stone, who was working for the station. In October 1959, Arnold went to the LBJ Ranch in Texas for a party for Mexican President Adolfo Lopez Mateos. Then in July 1961, Arnold was invited to the LBJ Ranch to entertain at a party Vice President Lyndon Johnson gave for Pakistan's President Ayub Khan. The performance didn't go as well as it should have; Arnold took out his guitar to play *after* President Khan was introduced—a victim of poor timing by Johnson—and had to sing while politicians swarmed around the Pakistani president. As soon as he finished his songs, Arnold packed his guitar and left the ranch.

Eddy Arnold also continued some promotional efforts for his career. In September 1961, he went to Chicago for the Music Operators of America convention, and on October 3, 1961, he went to RCA's record pressing plant in Indianapolis to honor the one billionth record pressed by the plant (it was one of Arnold's own records!).

Mostly, however, Arnold concentrated on his business ventures. He was part owner in the minor league Nashville Vols baseball team and served as vice president of the team. In that role he managed to go to the World Series and attend sports banquets, training camps, and baseball games.

In addition to the baseball team, Arnold was an investor in the Standard Record Pressing Co., Inc., was on the board of directors for an insurance company, and had real estate developments that included a car dealership (Frank Davis Buick), a Texaco filling station, and an ice-cream drive-in in Madison. Arnold's primary interest was in real estate; he purchased some land in Brentwood and began to develop it, building houses and selling them. He bought other parcels and held on to them, waiting for the value to increase before he sold them. Beginning in 1962, his income increased because President John Kennedy had lowered the top tax rate on annual income from 90 to 50 percent. More pictures showed him in a suit and tie rather than a sports coat and open-necked shirt.

Eddy Arnold appeared on NBC's thirtieth anniversary show in 1958, and during the heyday of *The Ozark Jubilee* TV show from

Springfield, Missouri, he was a guest host. Before ABC dropped the program in 1960, because host Red Foley's tax problems had landed him on the front pages, the producers asked Arnold if he wanted to take over the show; he declined. The Brown brothers had relocated to Springfield where they set up an advertising agency to work with the Springfield TV shows. But Charlie Brown dropped out of the agency to run for Congress (he was elected).

> ➤ *Country boy ... knows the ways of the city but never has turned his back on his heritage.*

After *The Ozark Jubilee* went off the air, finding country music on television was difficult. In 1962, at a TV appearance in Detroit for the United Foundation campaign, Eddy Arnold addressed the problem, stating, "It's because most of the producers of variety shows like Ed Sullivan have never been west of the Hudson River. They think country stuff is corn. Maybe some of it is, but people love it. . . . What those TV guys forget is that a lot of our so-called country artists are really versatile performers."

In the interview Arnold said, "I call myself a country-pop singer, and I think that's just what I am. There's some country music that I won't even sing. It has bad lyrics, bad melody. But some of it is beautiful."

He still performed occasionally, and following a performance at a nightclub in Houston in early 1963, a reviewer noted that

the crowd was with him all the way. . . . From the lone woman who kept calling out for "Molly Darlin'" to the majority who spontaneously started clapping rhythmically to "Up Above My Head," his final number. . . . He dipped in a folksong bag and came up with such numbers as "John Henry" and "Getalong Home, Cindy," passing them out with an easy, off-hand manner. And as the evening progressed with a lilting "After Loving You" and a lowdown "Lovebug Itch" and an almost sophisticated "You Don't Know Me," he emerged in the mood of a country boy who knows the ways of the city but never has turned his back on his heritage. He toyed around a bit with the yodeling in "Cattle Call," sang about why he's the "richest man in the world" with a humpbacked mule and a pond of trout, trotted out "Molly Darlin'" and some of the others he's identified with. Maybe it was the atmosphere of the receptive audience, but Arnold, backed by the Don Cannon band, worked in an amiable, intimate manner which was most appealing.

Another reviewer commented,

Well, it's just hard to beat Eddy Arnold, and he may easily have the most winning show in town at the Continental-Houston Hotel. Eddy is doing an early performance in a room open to the public and a late show for French Quarter members, who packed the place last night. Eddy has that old charm and grace, and he comes on singing "The Wreck of the Old 97" and goes off singing many of his lonesome and/or happy cowboy numbers. Eddy makes you feel goooood, whether he's singing the blues or peppy tunes. He's a happy man and his songs have a happy, pleasing lilt. . . . This is an evening nobody should miss.

17

The Beginning of the Nashville Sound

The years 1957–63 were also wilderness years for country music; frantic activity in Nashville was, in many ways, a fight for survival. *Opry* attendance declined and in 1957 dropped under 200,000 annually for the first time. It was also the subject of some bad press: Ernest Tubb walked into the National Life building's lobby and shot a .357 magnum, intending to shoot Jim Denny. Tubb shot at the wrong man; fortunately, nobody was hit, but Tubb was arrested and charged with public drunkenness.

In 1957, there were some shifts in the WSM executive lineup with Irving Waugh named general manager of the TV station while Robert Evans Cooper was named head of the radio station, in charge of the *Opry*; while Dee Kilpatrick remained as the *Opry's* manager. Also in 1957, the *Friday Night Frolics* was moved to the Ryman Auditorium from the WSM studios and renamed the *Friday Night Opry*.

But the *Opry* had lost its unchallenged hold on Nashville's country music industry. During the decade after World War II (1946–56), the *Opry* dominated the Nashville country music industry, but in the following decade, a number of independent publishing companies and booking agencies emerged. Although the *Opry* remained important, it could no longer make or break an artist by admitting or denying membership in the *Opry*. Increasingly, a recording contract with a major label determined an artist's viability. With the advent of television, people listened less to live radio programs on Saturday night. They continued to listen to radio, but they wanted to hear records of top artists on their local station.

> For the country music industry in Nashville, the most significant thing that happened was the formation of the Country Music Association in 1958.

For the country music industry in Nashville, the most significant thing that happened was the formation of the Country Music Association in 1958. The organization would become the Chamber of Commerce for country music, serving as a booster organization for the entire industry, although Nashville, home of the CMA, would benefit directly as well.

At the end of 1957, the Country and Western Disc Jockeys Association met in Miami, Florida. Some internal problems plagued the organization and its future was in doubt. At the same time, several country music executives wanted it to have a broader appeal—not just disc jockeys—and wanted more control and say-so. They envisioned a booster organization to help the industry, which was in horrible condition throughout 1957 because of the popularity of rock 'n' roll.

Several key executives took the lead: Connie B. Gay, a Washington, D.C.–based radio station owner and concert promoter, Wesley Rose of Acuff-Rose, *Opry* manager Dee Kilpatrick, booking agent Hubert Long, and Jack Stapp, owner of Tree Publishing. The Country Music Association set up a two-room office in downtown Nashville toward the end of 1958 with a desk and typewriter borrowed from Hubert Long. Long also let the address machine at his booking agency be used for CMA business. For mailings and memos, Wesley Rose donated Acuff-Rose's services.

In November 1958, the young organization held its first board meeting at the Noel Hotel and elected Connie B. Gay president and Wesley Rose chairman of the board. In December, the organization hired Jo Walker as office manager. Early in 1959, it hired Harry Stone to be executive director. After Stone was hired he was surprised to find that there was no money, only 233 members, and that his job would essentially consist of fund-raising. Stone didn't work out, and within a year he was gone. Walker continued to serve as office manager until 1961 when she was given the title executive director.

The CMA established the Country Music Hall of Fame and elected the first members—Jimmie Rodgers, Fred Rose, and Hank Williams—in 1961. Since there was no building to house the Hall of Fame, the plaques were displayed at the Tennessee State Museum. The organization continued to struggle because of lack of money, but those involved were determined and dedicated. Frances Williams (she became Frances Preston in 1962 when she married) also became heavily involved in the CMA. She had worked as a receptionist at WSM from 1948 until she was hired by BMI to recruit writers and publishers in 1955. Williams established the first BMI office in the L & C Tower in downtown Nashville.

> *Music Row, the first country music business in that area was Bradley's Studio on Sixteenth Avenue South.*

Since the roots for the CMA had been in the disc jockey organization—and a number of the CMA's founders came out of the broadcasting industry—they were aware that the essential problem facing them was getting country music exposed on radio. That had become increasingly difficult after Elvis Presley and rock 'n' roll hit in 1956. They also knew the way to get radio interested was to get advertisers committed to buying time because radio programmers would follow the money.

In 1963, the Country Music Association held its first major sales presentation for advertising executives in New York; the following year the group held one in Detroit. The intent was to get ad agencies convinced that country music on radio was a viable buy, a good advertising medium. The advertisers were often less than enthusiastic; at one presentation the CMA gave away a Tennessee walking horse in order to keep the executives there throughout the entire presentation.

The programs worked, and the essential role of the CMA—marketing country music to the broadcast industry—was established.

Major record labels helped the CMA in its efforts to promote country music and, ultimately, establish Nashville as the capital of country music. In 1957, Steve Sholes was named head of RCA's pop division and moved to Los Angeles. Chet Atkins, who had been running the Nashville office since 1955, assumed more duties and began producing RCA's top act, Eddy Arnold. In 1957, RCA Victor built a studio (now known as Studio B) on Seventeenth Avenue South and established the first permanent office by a major label. It was in the area that became known as Music Row.

The first country music business in that area was Bradley's Studio on Sixteenth Avenue South, which consisted of a Quonset hut purchased from army surplus. The Bradley brothers—Owen and Harold—established a TV studio and then set up the first recording studio in the basement of the adjoining house. Since TV was becoming increasingly important, the Bradleys decided to set up a studio whereby they filmed singers doing a song with the idea of providing the film clips for TV programming. The idea didn't fly at the time, although twenty-five years later the music video industry would thrive with the same basic concept.

In 1958, Paul Cohen left Decca Records, and Owen Bradley replaced him as head of the country music division. Unlike Cohen, who was based in New York, Bradley remained based in Nashville.

Columbia Records purchased Owen Bradley's studio on Sixteenth Avenue in 1962; it had become the major recording facility in Nashville, hosting Columbia and Decca recording artists, and that committed the CBS organization to Nashville with a spot on Music Row. Bill Denny, son of booking pioneer Jim Denny, was put in charge of the studio while Don Law, head of country music for the label, remained based in New York.

Thus, a number of major players were in place: Owen Bradley at Decca, Chet Atkins at RCA, and Frances Preston at BMI. All of them would play a vital role in country music and the CMA in the coming years.

Country music was helped along by a trend in the nation after World War II as people increasingly moved to the suburbs. The move came from two directions: people in the city moved out while those in rural areas moved in. The shift in housing was aided by the government, which built roads out of the city for the suburbs, financed car transportation through road building and low gas taxes at the expense of public transportation, and backed low interest loans for home buyers through the Federal Home Administration and Veterans Home Administration.

The federal government also helped the country music industry in another way. In 1956, President Eisenhower signed into law a bill creating the interstate highway system. The idea came out of Eisenhower's concern for the nation's defense. He saw the interstate system as a way to transport troops and weapons quickly and efficiently across the country. The money for the interstate system originally came from the Defense Department. But the interstate system did more than just help the armed forces, it changed America by linking long distances with dual-lane roads. The system helped the creation of the suburbs and boosted the tourism industry because people increasingly drove long distances on vacations since traveling on interstates was convenient. The interstate travelers needed places to sleep and eat, so motel and fast-food industries developed chains situated along interstates.

The country music industry benefited directly from the interstates because performers could travel longer distances faster, and thus personal appearances increased. They could travel on the wide interstates with large buses, custom fitted for sleeping and traveling, making it possible for country artists to stay out on the road for longer periods of time in relative comfort. Prior to the development of interstates country performers traveled two-lane roads in cars; they arrived at their appearances tired from having to sleep sitting up. There was a limited amount of space available for equipment—a trailer and trunk could hold only so much—but the large buses had more storage space available for stage costumes and bigger and better equipment.

In its November 14, 1960, issue *Time* magazine published "Hoedown on a Harpsichord" about country music: "Its demise has often seemed near, but it is now going stronger than ever, and Nashville has even nosed out Hollywood as the nation's second biggest (after New York) record-producing center." The article pointed out that "one out of every five popular hits of the past year was written and recorded in Nashville" and, discussing the Nashville Sound, observed, "As nearly as anybody can define it, the Sound is the byproduct of musical illiteracy."

The term *Nashville Sound* as a synonym for country music was popularized by the article. From that point forward the media regularly used the term *Nashville Sound* in discussing country music, and the term held a built-in promotion for Nashville as the center of the music. Nashville and country music increasingly became inseparable in the minds of the followers of country music.

18

The Sixties Begin

For many Americans, the era of the sixties began on November 22, 1963, in Dallas, Texas, when President John F. Kennedy was assassinated. On that Friday, Eddy Arnold was at the new home he had just built in south Nashville when he heard the news. Just six months earlier, in May, President Kennedy had visited Nashville, and crowds lined the streets, cheering him.

It had already been a difficult year for country music, an entire year marked by death. In March there were three separate major tragedies. On the fifth, country stars Patsy Cline, Hawkshaw Hawkins, and Cowboy Copas, along with Cline's manager Randy Hughes, were killed in a plane crash. On the eighth, Jack Anglin, of the group Johnnie and Jack, was killed in an automobile accident while on the way to the funeral of the plane crash victims. On the twenty-ninth, Texas Ruby (Ruby Fox), wife and duet partner of *Grand Ole Opry* fiddler Curly Fox, died when fire swept their mobile home. In August, pioneer country music executive Jim Denny died.

The early sixties also saw the deaths of country stars Johnny Horton (1960) and Jim Reeves, who was killed in a plane crash at the end of July 1964. The plane went down just outside Nashville in Brentwood, near Eddy Arnold's home, and a number of country stars, including Arnold, joined in the search. Finally, the wreckage was found, and Arnold identified the body.

On February 9, 1964, a new era in American music began when the Beatles appeared on *The Ed Sullivan Show*, launching Beatlemania throughout the nation. The oldest baby boomers (those born in 1946) were turning eighteen and had to register with the Selective Service for the draft. The draft had not reached a confrontational crisis by that point; indeed, the Cuban Missile Crisis in October 1962 and President Kennedy's speech at the Berlin Wall in June 1963 had made the Communist threat even more palpable and real. There wasn't much news about the tiny Southeast Asian country of Vietnam, but those who followed the news of that region knew trouble was brewing; on November 2, just three weeks before Kennedy's death, South Vietnamese Premier Ngo Dinh Diem and his brother Nhu were murdered by military leaders.

When the Beatles appeared in America, they brought a message of individualism and questioning authority that American baby boomers would embrace. During the next decade, the conflict between young people coming of age and the older World War II generation would escalate until there was a major chasm between generations. For the World War II generation, who fought in Europe and Japan for four years to make the world safe for democracy, it was beyond comprehension that young men would just say no to military service in Vietnam. But to the young men called, it was beyond comprehension that their country would ask them to fight in a war they considered lacking in clear and reasonable objectives. The conflicting views between generations would split the United States for years.

Two weeks before the Beatles appeared on *The Ed Sullivan Show*, Eddy Arnold appeared on that same show. And about the same week of Arnold's appearance, singer-songwriter Roger Miller went into a Nashville studio and recorded an album of wacky songs that included "Dang Me" and "Chug-a-Lug," which would turn country music on its head and be heard on the same radio stations that played the Beatles, Motown performers, and the Beach Boys in 1964.

Eddy Arnold had not exactly set the musical world on fire in 1963; none of his three charted singles, "Yesterday's Memories," "A Million Years or So," or "Jealous Hearted Me," made it into the top ten. Still, he had signed a new five-year contract with RCA Victor on September 21 that was announced by Ben Rosner, manager of A & R for the label.

Jerry Purcell, Arnold's new manager, negotiated the new contract after the label considered dropping Arnold from the roster. Arnold's career was stalled, he performed a limited number of engagements, and his record sales had dropped, although he was still a profitable artist, making money for the label. Purcell went to Steve Sholes and requested a second chance for Arnold. Sholes agreed to re-sign the singer.

Eddy Arnold appeared on the ABC TV show *Hootenanny* on October 12, 1963, broadcast from the U.S. Naval Academy, and on *The Ed Sullivan Show* on November 10. It was also announced at the end of 1963 that the all-time top three sellers of recorded music in the history of the music business were Bing Crosby, Perry Como, and Eddy Arnold.

There were, however, some changes in the wind, and the first hint of the changes occurred on February 1, 1964, when Arnold's single, "Molly," recorded with the Needmore Creek Singers, entered the charts; it would come to rest at number five. Then in November 1964, "I Thank My Lucky Stars" entered the charts, and it would reach number eight. The two releases signaled some important events taking place in Eddy Arnold's life, which would lead him to emerge with a "new" career.

Joe Csida, who had been Arnold's manager since 1954, took a job with a record label and had to give up his management company; he "handed" Arnold over to Gerald Purcell, manager of RCA Victor act Al Hirt. Purcell began working with Arnold in 1963, and on June 6, 1964, an announcement in the trade press revealed that Arnold had signed a management contract with Gerald Purcell and Associates. In truth, there was no contract, just a handshake agreement, but Eddy Arnold's handshake has always been a solid commitment.

Csida initially did not want to give up management of Arnold, and he told Purcell the singer would probably retire. Purcell had known Arnold from their mutual association with RCA and liked him. He was not interested in Csida's other acts—a singer and disc jockey—but decided to work with Arnold. It would mark a major change in the business side of Eddy Arnold's career.

One key to the success of any artist is good management, and that is certainly true of Eddy Arnold. Tom Parker did a remarkable job getting Arnold money and exposure from 1945 to 1953, but from 1954 to 1963, Arnold floundered in his career. That was partly the result of shifting musical trends and tastes and partly the result of Arnold's desire to stay home with his family while his children were young. But he did not have a Tom Parker or Jerry Purcell working on his career at that time, either.

Arnold has always gotten management "outside" Nashville. Even though Parker moved to Nashville in the late 1940s, he was always an outsider with connections in Los Angeles and New York. Csida was a New Yorker, and so was Purcell. All of the managers represented Eddy Arnold's desire to transcend the image of Nashville and country music as rural and Southern. Purcell grasped the idea quickly and wanted Arnold to change his look and pursue new avenues in his performances by moving him uptown.

> *During his first decade recording for RCA Victor, Arnold was marketed as a traditional country act with a smooth voice and manner.*

The sound of Eddy Arnold had been changing and developing since he recorded "I Really Don't Want to Know" in 1953. During his first decade recording for RCA Victor, Arnold was marketed as a traditional country act with a smooth voice and manner. In the late 1940s and early 1950s, the honky-tonk sound dominated country music; it was the heyday of Hank Williams, Lefty Frizzell, Webb Pierce, and Faron Young. Arnold's material wasn't much different from that of those singers (in fact, he recorded some of the same songs they did), but his delivery was different. Arnold was blessed with a smoother voice than the classic honky-tonkers. Since he did not have the harsh country vocals of a Hank Williams or Webb Pierce, he developed his vocal abilities by increasingly picking ballads and pop-oriented songs. Further, Arnold regularly appeared on network shows—on radio and television—and grew comfortable in the larger pop music world.

Arnold recorded with Hugo Winterhalter's orchestra in 1955, and he continued to record with string sections supplementing the basic country rhythm section of guitar, bass, piano, and drums. He dropped the fiddle and steel guitar sound and adopted the background vocal accompaniment of two male and two female voices (usually the Anita Kerr Singers) that were part of the emerging Nashville Sound.

The material Arnold recorded was often a grab bag; sometimes producer Chet Atkins would find some new songs, sometimes Arnold would record hits from other singers from the country and pop fields, or sometimes a publisher would send a song. In the fall of 1963, he recorded an album of folk songs, trying to capitalize on the folk boom by doing "Where Have All the Flowers Gone," "Green, Green," "Cotton Fields," and "Blowin' in the Wind." Arnold never liked the rock songs of the 1955–59 period; he thought there was a lot of beat but the lyrics were silly and meaningless. He always loved a good lyric, a song that carried a message, although the message of the folk movement in the early 1960s wasn't always in line with Arnold's conservative beliefs. Still, a lot of the songs had a good melody and the lyrics conveyed a feeling. Unfortunately, Arnold picked the wrong time to get on the folk bandwagon; by the time he recorded the album, called *The Folk Song Book of Eddy Arnold*, Bob Dylan had already gone electric at Newport, the Beatles had hit America, and folk rock was about to explode.

Arnold's folk album was not mere exploitation of a current craze in the music business. Back when he started recording, what became known as country music was called folk, and he recorded his first album of folk songs in 1955. In the ensuing years, he had recorded a number of other folk songs and had always performed some of the songs in his live appearances.

But the folk music of the early 1960s was a different breed from the folk tunes that Arnold grew up with. First, the songs could more accurately be labeled acoustic rather than folk because they were often written by contemporary performers and recorded with just acoustic instruments. Next, the songs were increasingly political, and the politics were often "protest" politics, which ran counter to Arnold's conservatism. So Arnold's album became a transitional album for him, lost in the shuffle of shifting musical tastes and trends from a number of directions in pop music, country music, and the music of Arnold himself.

In the meantime, Arnold continued to record with string sections, although that sound didn't quite fit with the Bakersfield sound of Buck Owens who, along with Roger Miller, had the hottest new sound on country radio throughout 1964.

Eddy Arnold had thought about quitting the business now and then, but he just couldn't. He kept recording, hoping for some more big hits and continued record sales, and he wondered how he could reach an audience that "fit" him, one he was comfortable with. The left-wing folk crowd certainly wasn't it, although he knew their old songs. And rock 'n' roll was just too far removed from him; he couldn't even relate to that young crowd. It was just as well—his voice didn't fit rock 'n' roll anyway, and the baby boom teenagers couldn't relate to him, either.

The country sound of Buck Owens, with its driving, honky-tonk beat, wasn't him, although Arnold's musical roots went back to that sound. But he couldn't see himself singing behind a walking bass, searing steel guitar, and nik nik news fiddle again. He knew there must be an audience of people like him—moving into middle age, with tastes for a softer, smoother music—but he just didn't know exactly how to reach them. He knew he liked the Nashville Sound and the new attitude of Nashville: taking country music into the cities and showing people that those in country music could be as intelligent and sophisticated as anyone else. Like many others in the Nashville country music industry, he intensely disliked the image of country singers as hicks, hillbillies, and hayseeds that many in big cities—especially New York and Los Angeles—associated with that field. He wanted that image tossed aside and replaced with a wholesome respect for the music as well as the people who made that music. And so he continued to record songs that could be played on country or pop radio, songs with strings and smooth background vocals that would prove to anyone listening that the guy singing wasn't some twang town, whiny, through-the-nose redneck singer.

> ➤ *The image of country music established after the war laid the groundwork for the image country music has had in the media capitals (particularly New York and Los Angeles) since that time.*

Still, Eddy Arnold's roots were in country music, and he felt an allegiance to it; he promoted country music as a genre whenever he could. More than any other Nashville artist, by 1964, Eddy Arnold had become a spokesman for country music and Nashville.

Arnold obtained a contract promoting Eastern Airlines in 1964 that made him more visible. The airlines sponsored a fifteen-minute nightly radio program *The World of Folk Music*, and Arnold attended the World's Fair in New York, talking with visitors for a radio show sponsored by the airlines. He also did a series of radio promotions for the Social Security Administration.

Arnold preferred the look of the businessman when he went out in public. During one of his personal appearances in Charlotte, North Carolina, a newspaper reporter observed, "The singer was wearing a conservative summer suit, a light blue shirt and a tie with diagonal stripes at a luncheon. No guitar in sight."

Eddy Arnold was clearly fitting in with the image that the Nashville country music community was trying to give to the world in the 1960s. It was an image designed to counteract what had been force-fed to the public by the national media in a steady diet during the twenty years since World War II had ended.

The image of country music established after the war laid the groundwork for the image country music has had in the media capitals (particularly New York and Los Angeles) since that time. And it explains, to a large extent, why country music never received the respect it should have during those years.

Still, most articles gave grudging respect to country music, usually acknowledging that it was the music of choice for many in middle America. Richard Marek's "Country Music: Nashville Style" appeared in *McCall's* in 1961. He wrote that country is "the most popular music in America today," although "the new sound at the *Opry* is less authentic country music, more akin to the popular styles of today (although not strictly pop songs)."

The observation that country music was absorbing the sounds of popular music was a common one that began in the early 1960s, as the Nashville Sound was developed and promoted, and right after the first rock 'n' roll revolution. The simple fact is that country music has always been influenced by popular music from its earliest recordings.

When Fiddlin' John Carson recorded "The Little Old Log Cabin in the Lane" in Atlanta, Georgia, in June 1923 and began what became the country recording industry, he recorded a song written by Will Shakespeare Hays for minstrel shows—the popular music of its day. And Jimmie Rodgers, the "father of country music" who first recorded in August 1927 and who recorded with the Carter Family, was most instrumental in creating the commercial country music industry; he was heavily influenced by popular music and never really considered his songs hillbilly, although he appealed primarily to rural audiences. Bob Wills was a country boy who grew up in the Jazz Age. He had a swing band with traditional country instruments and was always insulted when people confused his music with hillbilly music. The earliest *Opry* shows often began with a string band doing "There'll Be a Hot Time in the Old Town Tonight." The list can go on to performers who became popular after World War II or even into the 1990s, but the point is clear: country music has never been a rural, isolated folk music dominated by British ballads collected in the mountains and passed down by oral tradition. Still, the image persisted.

19

A New Beginning for Eddy Arnold

Eddy Arnold says, "I never really knew what good management was until Jerry Purcell came along." Indeed, the New York–based Purcell was a major factor in Arnold's rise as the primary exemplar and spokesman for the Nashville Sound in the mid-1960s.

There were some bumps in the road, however. Arnold put his career in Purcell's hands and followed his manager's direction. And when Joe Csida's job with the record company fell through and he decided to return to management, his announcement to the trade that he was resuming his relationship with Eddy Arnold caused a bit of a problem for Arnold. But Arnold decided to face it head-on, and he flew to New York where he met with Purcell and Csida together. "I love you both," he told them. "But I'm going to stay with Jerry." Arnold had seen some of the fruits of Purcell's efforts and caught his vision of Eddy Arnold as a pop singer.

In early 1965, Jerry Purcell wanted Eddy Arnold to try something new: he insisted Arnold buy two fitted tuxedos and booked him on a tour where the singer was presented as a smooth, uptown countrypolitan singer who did concerts instead of appearances at fairs and rodeos. At first Arnold was skeptical and complained about the costs of the new outfits ("I could buy several good suits for this money," he told Purcell) but agreed. Purcell had promised to underwrite the six-city tour in April 1965 of Cleveland, Cincinnati,

Philadelphia, Chicago, Toledo, and Dayton. On the tour, Arnold appeared with Roger Miller, who was the opening act and hotter than a firecracker in country as well as pop. He had swept the Grammy Awards in March that year.

The tour was a revelation to Eddy Arnold. It all came together—the look, the sound, the feel of what an evening of Eddy Arnold music should be. The crowds were large and enthusiastic; and the whole show was a class act. It was where Arnold knew he belonged.

After the tour he flew to New York and met with Jerry Purcell, and they talked; Arnold admitted Purcell had been right. Purcell was pleased with the result but there was still an accounts payable outstanding. Eddy Arnold had not been paid for the performances. Purcell told Arnold he owed the singer $30,000 and that he wouldn't take a manager's commission; Arnold pulled out his own checkbook and wrote a check for $15,000 to Purcell. Now it was time to launch the new career full speed ahead.

> *"I never really knew what good management was until Jerry Purcell came along."*

The first step was hit records on the charts. But not just any hit record; the sound had to be right. Although that ground had been laid beginning with "I Really Don't Want to Know" in 1954, the ball had really started rolling for the "new" career several months before the tour. On November 11, 1964, "I Thank My Lucky Stars" entered the charts; it was a smooth, pop-sounding song with the message of positive love. That became his second top ten song, reaching number eight. ("Molly" had reached number five.)

Then on January 13, 1965, Arnold recorded a song that would be his first number one in a decade: "What's He Doing in My World?" The session was recorded with a large string section—there were seven violins, a viola, and a cello, led by Bill Walker—and included two other songs, "What-Cha Gonna Do?" and "Laura Lee," from the Columbia picture *Major Dundee*, on the session. For "What's He Doing in My World?" a song that had not been the subject of a big arrangement, singer Anita Kerr wrote out a string arrangement during a break in the session. The song entered the charts on March 27, 1965, and lasted twenty-five weeks, ending up at number sixty on the pop charts. That would mark the beginning of a string of sixteen songs that not only reached the top ten in the country charts, but also landed on the pop charts.

After the success of "What's He Doing in My World?" the decision was made to do an album; Eddy Arnold decided on the title, *My World*, and he and his producer Chet Atkins set about finding songs. Arnold had heard the song "Make the World Go Away" on the radio by a female singer and liked it immediately. Purcell had also heard it performed in Las Vegas. It was written by Hank Cochran, a Nashville songwriter who had also written "I Fall to Pieces" performed by Patsy Cline, "A Little Bitty Tear Let Me Down" for Burl Ives, and numerous others. Arnold had, in fact, recorded songs by Cochran in the past. The song was published by Nashville's Tree Publishing, and Arnold checked to see how the song had done with sales. He discovered it had sold fifty thousand units as a single, and he felt he could do much better with it. He was unaware the song had previously been recorded by Ray Price and Jim Reeves.

On June 25, 1964, Eddy Arnold recorded "Make the World Go Away." It was the second song on a four-song session produced by Chet Atkins; the first song was "Mary Claire Melvina Rebecca Jane," and the other songs were "Here Comes My Baby" written by Dottie and Bill West and "You Still Got a Hold on Me" written by Merle Kilgore. At the beginning of the session "Make the World Go Away" was not viewed as a potential single, but as they listened to the playback, "it sounded mighty good," remembers Arnold. Both he and Chet Atkins began to consider the song as a single.

The session had a rhythm section of Floyd Cramer on piano and harpsichord, Grady Martin and Velma Smith on guitars, and a group of five violins, two violas, and a cello arranged by Bill Walker. The Anita Kerr Singers (Anita Kerr, Dottie Dillard, Louis Nunley, and William G. Wright) provided background vocals.

"Make the World Go Away" entered the country charts in *Billboard* on March 27, 1965, just before Arnold's six-city tour with a new look, and quickly went to number one, remaining on the charts for twenty-five weeks. On October 16, it entered the pop charts at *Billboard* and went to number six. From the end of March 1965 through the rest of the year, Eddy Arnold had a major hit on American radio.

In October, the *Miami Herald* reviewed Arnold's album *My World*: "This isn't country music, friends, this is a collection of ballads, love songs and mellow swingers by a topnotch singer who can put voice and style on the line with Martin, Bennett, Como, Goulet, etc., and come out the winner. There's not a yodel in the lot, and only a hint of the Nashville sound."

Another article discussing "What's He Doing in My World" stated that the record

> represents the Nashville sound at its best. The title tells
> the whole story of the song. . . . The Tennessee Plowboy
> is now wearing a tuxedo, doing guest-shots on network
> TV shows and night club dates. It's a far cry from appear-
> ing at country fairs and rodeos, and Eddy loves it. Some
> of his old died-in-the-wool fans resent his departure from
> straight country music, but for everyone who does, Eddy
> has gained a dozen new fans. After 20 years he has been
> "discovered" by thousands of youngsters.

The country music industry in Nashville attempted to solve the problem of the pop music world looking down its nose at country music with the creation of the Nashville Sound. The "sound" could never quite be explained because, in reality, it wasn't really a sound as much as it was an attempt to change class and rise above country music's blue-collar, working-class roots. In other words, the Nashville Sound was the antidote to the notion that country music was white trash music.

In 1964, *Time* published a major article, "Country Music: The Nashville Sound," that attempted to define the Nashville Sound: "More than the drawling, sow-belly accents and nasal intonations of the singers, it is the background music provided by the sidemen on twangy electric guitars." Despite the cynicism, there was a point to be made in *Time*'s observation.

In terms of the actual "sound," it was created by a relatively small group of musicians who performed together day after day in the Nashville studios, working on most of the recordings that came out of the city. Many of the musicians may have been musically illit-erate in the traditional sense, but they were certainly accomplished musicians. They had the ability to learn and play almost anything quickly and well.

The key instrument was the acoustic rhythm guitar, played with a pick and strum, full strum (from the lower register strings down), or an up-and-down strum (the strings strummed from the lower reg-ister downward, then the pick coming back upward across the high register strings in a steady rhythm) over open chords. There was also an electric "lead" or "take off" guitar that played an instrumental riff, a variation of the melody during a break in the song, some fills, and, occasionally, a rhythm. A piano, drums, a bass, and a six-string bass guitar were also essential elements of the sound. The electric steel guitar, fiddle, and harmonica were also involved on some sessions, but increasingly, the Nashville Sound kept the steel guitar in the background and replaced the fiddle with violins or background vocals (and sometimes both). Traditional acoustic instruments such as the mandolin, banjo, and Dobro were *not* part of the Nashville Sound. Those instruments were absorbed in bluegrass music, which had continued the string band tradition in country music as commercial country music moved toward a more pop-oriented sound.

Chet Atkins once jingled some coins in his pocket when asked to define the Nashville Sound. Atkins was making a point about the economics of country music. By using the same group of musicians on all the recordings and structuring the sessions as head sessions, or sessions where the musicians played by ear and not from sheet music, in three-hour blocks of time where three or four songs were recorded, country music was economically viable. The structure of the recording process meant country music could keep costs down by recording quickly and economically; since a record company makes money only when a recording is sold (it receives no money from radio airplay or artists' personal appearances), then country music did not have to sell many records to be profitable. So, from an economic standpoint, country music made good business sense to a record label's home office.

But the Nashville Sound was more than just a musical production factory and an economic system. In a very real sense, it was an attempt by the people within country music to transcend their working-class roots, to better themselves, if you will, and to get rid of the old stereotypes about country bumpkins and hicks and be accepted into the American middle class. The Nashville Sound embraced background vocals creating a smooth sound that softened the harsh edges of the traditional country vocals. The strings made the music more palatable to the pop audience, or at least to the audience who didn't care for the old, twangy sound of rural country musicians and their string bands. With the Nashville Sound country music discarded the fiddle in exchange for the violin; country musicians and executives hoped to cover up their blue-collar roots and escape the working class for the suburban middle class.

But it wasn't that easy. The audience for country music remained a working-class audience, the artists still came primarily from the working class, and the sound of country music still had working-class elements in the lyrics that expressed the sentiments of the everyday working American. The executives marketing country music often did not have working-class roots or, more likely, had escaped their blue-collar roots. Also, the newer executives often did not have the Great Depression and a rural background as their defining passage in life. But the blue-collar audience was still there. And it demanded a country music that related to the working class.

> *The Nashville Sound was the most visible example of the struggle for respect. Ironically, the Nashville Sound closely identified country music with Nashville.*

What emerged was a conflict between country music connected to the working class and a country music industry trying to escape (or deny) the blue-collar connection. So the story of country music became an effort to sign and produce artists who appealed to the traditional audience while, at the same time, signing and producing artists who were more pop and who, it was hoped, appealed to a more broad-based audience or an audience that was *not* blue-collar working class.

Again, the story of country music is essentially a struggle for respect. That struggle has been borne by artists, musicians, and executives, and often the visible results have been a type of country music intended to transcend the working class and be palatable to the broad cross section of middle-class tastes.

The Nashville Sound was the most visible example of the struggle for respect. Ironically, the Nashville Sound closely identified country music with Nashville. Even the Buck Owens sound from Bakersfield, California, became known as Nashville West as the image of country music increasingly centered on Nashville, Tennessee. This solidified Nashville as the capital of country music at the same time it tried to divorce country music from its rural audience.

The dichotomy was especially apparent in the 1960s when national attention focused on the Nashville Sound and country music. On the one hand was the smooth, pop-oriented music coming from Nashville; on the other hand, Buck Owens and the Bakersfield sound were having a major impact on country music. The dichotomy was also evident in the career of Eddy Arnold, who began as a traditional country artist but was soon accepted outside the field.

The story of Eddy Arnold is also a struggle for respect. He wanted to sing country music with dignity, wanted to achieve success and respect with middle America. That was part of the reason he pursued success in the business world, outside country music. And it was also the reason he was attracted to the Nashville Sound. It was a way he could attain the respect of the entire music world with his music. And so, in many ways, the joining together of Eddy Arnold and the Nashville Sound was a marriage made in heaven.

20

Back on Top Again

January 1965 marked Eddy Arnold's twentieth year as a recording artist for RCA Victor. To promote the year, he scheduled a series of major media appearances. The year began with a TV appearance on the *Bell Telephone Hour*. Then in February, he appeared on Danny Kaye's TV show. Back in Tennessee, his good friend Governor Frank Clement declared February "Eddy Arnold Month." In September, he appeared on the *Steve Lawrence Show* on CBS and taped an appearance on the *Jimmy Dean Show*. Although Eddy Arnold had spent the bulk of 1955–63 off the road, he remained visible with the American public through TV appearances. Thus at this key point in his career, he was in demand as a guest on TV shows; in 1965, his TVQ, which measures how recognizable a person is with TV audiences, was thirty—a very high, respectable figure.

In addition to appearances on other performers' TV shows, Eddy Arnold had his own TV show, *Today—On the Farm*. He spent a week in Chicago on WIND as a guest disc jockey, and in June, he was in Indianapolis to host the Miss Indianapolis Pageant. He also had two radio shows, *Eddy Arnold Sings* and *Eddy Arnold Time*.

Arnold's hits and tour led to more exposure in the media. In September, an article by Wayne Trevathan in the *Sunday Courier and Press* in Evansville, Indiana, was headlined "People Don't Forget Eddy." Trevathan highlighted the singer's "niceness," stating,

> The genial entertainer has delighted the nation's country and western music audiences for more than 25 years with his mild manners, mellow baritone voice and back-on-

the-farm aura surrounding him. Arnold makes himself
comfortable wherever he goes and whatever happens.
Although a millionaire, he can gracefully
adjust to a bowl of soup at a truck stop
or a plush restaurant.

> ➤ *Arnold makes*
> *himself*
> *comfortable*
> *wherever he*
> *goes and*
> *whatever*
> *happens.*

   Arnold talked about the obligations of
fame: "They all recognize me. I autograph for
everybody. I walk in and they start asking for
autographs. I said, 'Well fine, just let me order
some food first.' They see me, they recognize
my face. And then some will think they've met
me somewhere. They think I'm an old friend
or an acquaintance."
   Arnold then talked about his career:

> Doing an act, if a performer is any kind of a performer,
> and has ever given any thought to being a performer, he'll
> have a system. Cause being a performer is a business just
> like any other; you strive for perfection, and if you don't
> you are not going to stay in the business. It takes you a
> long time to become a good entertainer. You don't become
> a good entertainer overnight. There is nothing easy about
> it; nothing easy. . . . The hardest part is conditioning
> yourself, learning your songs, disciplining yourself, being
> a gentleman, keeping your life straight.

That was certainly part of the "Eddy Arnold Philosophy" of
show business.
   On fans coming around he observed,

> Without it, you'd be out of business. Now, I'd be less than
> honest with you if I didn't tell you I get tired of it. I only
> have a normal body system like anybody else and my
> energy runs out after awhile. Like anybody else, I get
> tired, sure. . . . I like to work. . . . I'm still young enough
> that I have enough energy that I still want to work and be
> productive.

   Some of the old magic was back. On June 29, fans in Anderson,
South Carolina, mobbed him. In an interview there he said,

> Country and western music is current. It's modern, it's
> being written right now. . . . Live audiences always seem
> to be after something more than just country music.
> There are a few still playing and singing in the old tradi-
> tion, but the moderns are the ones with the big appeal
> now. Many radio stations which played only "top 40"
> tunes and rock and roll during the last decade are now
> operating on a modern country format. . . . This is giving
> the music a wider exposure than it has ever had before.

Perhaps the biggest surprise—and the harbinger of things to come—for Eddy Arnold occurred on December 11, 1965, when he performed with the Dallas Symphony. When the symphony called Arnold's manager with the request for a booking, Jerry Purcell relayed the request to Arnold, who said over the phone, "What the hell am I going to do with a symphony?" It was one thing to put on a tux and change your image—but a ninety-two-member symphony seemed like a world away. Still, Arnold was flattered and intrigued and decided to do it, even though he felt a vague uneasiness. Somehow he felt he might be stepping a little too far out of bounds, out of his league with the symphony booking because it would be a new audience. Arnold got with his arranger, Bill Walker, who had been traveling with him and conducting a small string section, and they decided to take the existing arrangements and "extend them out" to include a larger symphonic section. Then he structured his symphony show like his regular show.

On March 29, 1965, RCA Victor held the grand opening for its new offices and studio. The 95,000-cubic-foot studio represented a $1 million investment in Nashville. Arnold, Chet Atkins, Owen Bradley, and Al Hirt were there. Elvis was *not* there, but his gold Cadillac was parked outside. However, the future wasn't all bright and rosy, and RCA must have wondered if it had made a mistake with its $1 million.

In April the announcement was made that 16 percent of the staff in Nashville was let go. The problem, it seems, was that many in Nashville thought that the folk music craze would benefit Nashville, so a number of artists (including Eddy Arnold) recorded folk albums. But they were two entirely different audiences; for country music, folk represented a return to the older, simpler times while for most young people, folk meant a way to protest what they

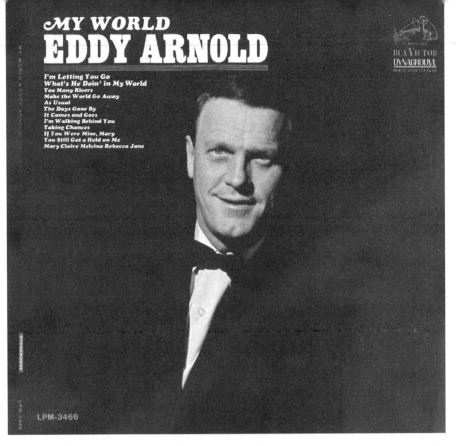

perceived was wrong with America. The country music crowd, in general, thought there was more *right* with America, so the protest songs fell on deaf ears.

Eddy Arnold addressed the issue in an interview and talked about the changes in country music: "The folk thing, as we knew it a couple of years ago, is going by the wayside. I think the next thing will be modern country western music." He was making a major tran sition himself during the year; as "Make the World Go Away" was hitting, Arnold's current album was *Folk Song Book*.

A number of people were writing about Nashville and the boom in country music. In "Sing a Song of 60 Million: Sound of Music Pays Cold Cash in Nashville" Arthur Whitman wrote in the *Commercial Appeal Mid-South Magazine*,

> The noise used to be called mountain music, and it was a twangy, nasal thing that went with corn liquor, family feuding, and barefoot courting. A few years back, though, Nashville image builders rechristened their musical lingo, added new sounds and lyrics, and came up with the style that's called Country and Western, known simply as C&W in the trade. Since then, the Nashville sound has come

rolling down the mountains, spread to the far corners of the continent, and now is beating on distant shores.

There are some 200 stations throughout the country programming it. Despite all this burgeoning acceptance, no one has yet defined just what country music is. It has roots in the songs and laments the earliest colonists brought over from 17th-century England, but it has since had infusions of new vitality from almost every mode of popular music from high society jazz to lowdown blues to gospel songs. Today, it is as cosmopolitan as Rome.

Whitman discovered that in Nashville there were a dozen talent agencies, twenty-six record companies, four record pressing plants, and 265 music publishers. Ten major record companies had recording studios, Decca and RCA Victor had both recently expanded their facilities, and more than five thousand people were estimated to be connected to the country music industry.

> ➤ *"Arnold is pretty unique, as his 40 million records testify."*

By the end of 1965, it was obvious that the Nashville Sound was changing country music.

In an interview for the *Gary Post Tribune*, Arnold remarked, "The wholesome, melodic appeal of country-western songs is unchanging. But the By-Cracky-My-Aunt-Millie-Wanted-Me-to-Play-This-Here-Song bit went out with bib overalls."

Arnold was certainly leading by example. Another interview with him concluded, "That's how Arnold is, easy-going, impeccably honest, and thoroughly appreciative of other people. They are unique qualities to find in a show business personality. But then, Arnold is pretty unique, as his 40 million records testify."

21

The Era of the Nashville Sound

In 1966, the city of Nashville cranked up to firmly establish itself as the capital of country music. Mayor Beverly Briley donated some city land at the corner of Division and Sixteenth Avenue that had formerly been a park as the site for the Country Music Hall of Fame. A fund-raising committee comprised of Andrew Benedict (chair), Ed Shea of the Chamber of Commerce, businessmen Harry Sadler, C. A. Craig II, Fred Harvey Jr., Owen Bradley, and Bill Denny set about to raise $350,000 for construction costs. The governor at the time was Frank Clement, an avid country music fan, and the business community in Nashville had clearly seen the advantages of trumpeting their connection with country music.

However, many of the social elite preferred to think of Nashville as the Athens of the South and wished country music would just go away. But that street ran both ways; if the Nashville social establishment looked down their noses at the country music industry, it was often because the country music crowd kept their distance from the establishment types. Neither felt totally comfortable with the other, although city leaders knew the importance of country music—and cultivated the country music business—while some key country music executives made it a point to join mainstream business leaders. (Owen Bradley was elected to the board of directors for the Nashville Chamber of Commerce.) In an interview, Chet Atkins declared, "People down here now are accepting us because of profits and national image. Those of us who belong to the country club or the boat club have a social life that includes people from other walks of life. But in the main, the music people stick to their own."

The term *Nashville Sound* was used regularly to describe Nashville, and the image presented had two prongs. On the one hand, the city and the country music industry were viewed as vibrant and thriving with a lot of excitement and energy in the air. On the other hand, country music was viewed as the province of hicks, hillbillies, and hayseeds, albeit those who had seen the light learned how to thrive with the music. And the emphasis was on the idea that the once backward people weren't so backward anymore.

> ➤ *However, many of the social elite preferred to think of Nashville as the Athens of the South and wished country music would just go away.*

Newspaper articles were full of backhanded compliments. For example, "Country music has changed. No longer does a geetar, a natural (or acquired) twang, and a talent for shucking corn suffice. What really sends folk today are the tuxedos, the 15-piece orchestra, the sophisticated tones—in fact, call it country and urban music and you're nearer the truth." And in the *Boston Record American*, Bruce McCabe wrote,

> Take everything you've heard about Nashville, Tennessee—about the jug-eared hillbillies who subsist on corn "likker"; about the barefoot mountaineers who play squalky fiddles—take all that, and throw it into a cocked hat. Because Nashville is "Music City, U.S.A." . . . home of the hottest sound on the national airwaves today. It's the home of the "Nashville Sound."

The *New York Post* carried an article in July 1966 by G. Bruce Porter:

> Several years ago, New Yorkers viewed country and Western music in much the same way they look upon water diving, whittling, skinny dipping, butter beans, old time religion and voting Republican—a faintly interesting idiom of rubes and other culturally disadvantaged unfortunates but one which retained nothing but its offensiveness when shaken free of straw, lifted from the river bottoms, hay lofts and juke joints and transported from the hinterland to the big city. Somehow, songs like "Pickle Squirts," "Who Licked the Red Off Your Candy?" and "Gettin' Any Feed for Your Chick?" just didn't seem to enunciate the real concerns of people trapped in concrete boxes

and hot city streets. And until recently, anyone who wanted to listen to such stuff had either to tune his crystal into WWVA in Wheeling, W.Va. where the fiddlin' and twangin' is interspersed among advertisements for genuine bronze statues of Jesus Keeeriste, or wait for the occasional indulgence by the local pop or rock station.

Eddy Arnold was the focus of some articles on the Nashville Sound and country music, and he had to endure the slurs and indignities of the country hayseed stereotype. Commenting on Nashville and country music, a New York writer had this to say:

> Riding its crest, like a surfer heading for the sand, is a 48-year-old reconstructed Tennessee farm boy named Eddy Arnold who is becoming as familiar a figure on network television as he once was on the corn circuit of barn dances, plowing contests and country fairs. But as Northerners have reconsidered their distaste for country music, Arnold has moved a little away from the farm in recent years. Pure country music is all right for the home folk, he says, but what he needs to capture what he calls "the masses" is the "modern country sound," and even at that he still inserts among his upbeat songs of the sod a few that Northerners can recognize such as show tunes and popular ballads.

The writer then quoted Arnold: " 'Ih'm getttin' what Ih wont,' he said recently in a soft Tennessee voice. " 'Ih'm sellin' to the masses, and that's what Ih wont. Some of myh kuntreh boih friends put me down for that. But Ih'm not tryin' t'be a slick pop singer, but neither 'm Ih uh tywangy kuntre boih.' " Anyone who has known Eddy Arnold—or heard him speak—knows he doesn't talk like that. Yes, he has a southern accent, but he speaks well and clearly and enunciates his words. Still, the New York writer wanted to make him sound like some sort of Southern redneck to fit his own perception of country music performers. Arnold did not complain publicly about the articles, believing that in the long run, the exposure helped country music. But privately, he fumed. That was *not* the image he wanted to create, and he worked hard to educate himself beyond his country boy background. It was an insult to be profiled that way, but Arnold, as always, remained a gentleman in public.

Eddy Arnold fared much better when writers came to his concerts and reviewed them. Concert reviewers often noted his "smooth-

ness" and uptown sound. Consider this review of a concert in Hartford, Connecticut: "Showing real versatility—and a range from a
whisper to a clear call that kept the sound man busy—Arnold went
from 'Dear Heart' to 'Lonesome Me' then
slipped into 'Hello Dolly' with all the brass
anyone could want." A reviewer of his show
in Providence, Rhode Island, where Arnold
closed the show after performances by Jim Ed
Brown, Dottie West, and Don Bowman, stated,

> ➤ *I'm a man that likes to be honest in whatever I'm involved in.*

Arnold is one of the few, if not the only
performer in his field who has the ability
to relax an audience and make it concentrate on two things—the music and Eddy
Arnold. In a way, it's amazing, for he sings simple songs
simply and to simple people. What is not so amazing is
the fact that he has the knack to turn a sentimental program into a crying good time.

Still, Arnold never denied his country roots, as is evident in an
interview with Stephen E. Rubin of UPI:

> You know, you can't deny your background. I'm a man that
> likes to be honest in whatever I'm involved in. And that is
> my background, that is where I came from. No, I don't live
> in the country now. I live in the suburbs of a city and I
> enjoy the life and comforts that anybody else manages to
> have—read books and see shows and wear shoes and all
> those things. So, now I'm not a country boy, but that was
> my background and that was where I came from.

In that same interview, he talked about the changes in his music:
"I've changed the background, added a string orchestra, which I
wanted to do. I wanted to broaden my appeal. I never wanted to desert
the country field, and I will not. But I wanted to broaden my base. I
wanted my style and my image to be enjoyed and accepted by a
broader segment of the people."

When the reporter asked if success had "gone to his head,"
Arnold answered, "I'm sure some of it has. I'm a proud man. I came
from parents that were very poor, but very proud. . . . I have a fear of
winding up broke, and that's what's made me somewhat of a conservative. I like to conserve and invest what I earn. . . . I guess you're proud
of what you've accomplished."

Not all country fans liked the Nashville Sound and the trend toward making country music more pop-oriented. Some fans liked the hard core honky-tonk sound of country, believing country music should stick with those roots and that sound. So there was a backlash among country fans over the Nashville Sound and particularly Eddy Arnold. But from Arnold's vantage point, it was something he had to do; after all, his smoother sound had proven its appeal with huge record sales and large concert audiences.

Arnold told *New York Sunday News* writer John Patrick, "This may make the purists mad but I figure for every purist I lose, I gain five other fans who like country music the modern way. Actually, I don't think I have lost too many people because even though I've modernized to reach the pop market, I still keep my songs simple."

Despite the criticism, Eddy Arnold's moves into the pop world were working, and more and more people were seeing the fruits of the efforts. In *Record World*, Doug McClelland summed up Arnold's status:

> Arnold [has] proved himself without peer in country or
> pop fields. He is not only an artistic marvel with a voice
> that actually has improved with the years, but a music
> phenomenon who has managed to retain the loyalty of his
> initial following while firmly establishing himself in areas
> of the globe where moonshine means something to hold
> hands in while listening to Eddy Arnold recordings.

22

Carnegie Hall and the
Hall of Fame

For Eddy Arnold, 1966 was a landmark year for three reasons:
(1) he made his first appearance in England and had his first
international hit when "Make the World Go Away" became a
hit there; (2) he performed at Carnegie Hall in New York; and
(3) he was elected to the Country Music Hall of Fame.

Arnold made his first trip to England in January 1966 with his
manager, Jerry Purcell, when the two went over for some personal
appearances and to promote the single, "Make the World Go Away."
Because of his appearances and exposure in the media the sales took
off and the record sold 300,000 copies.

Arnold was surprised that several select appearances in the
media could blanket the entire country:

> I came to England . . . without knowing what the scene
> was. For instance in the States every city has at least five
> or six radio stations and at some places I have to do at least
> fifteen radio interviews. I did a couple of BBC shows, and
> an interview with Radio London over here—I thought that
> was because nobody wanted to know about me. When I
> arrived in Manchester for "Scene at 6:30" I assumed I
> would be interviewed by at least six radio stations, because
> of Manchester's population. When I was told that the BBC
> covered all of Britain and all you had to do was one inter-
> view for the whole country I was delighted.

He stayed at the Mayfair Hotel in London and charmed everyone around. By March 9, "Make the World Go Away" was number nine in Great Britain, behind "19th Nervous Breakdown" by the Rolling Stones, "These Boots Are Made for Walkin'" by Nancy Sinatra, "A Groovy Kind of Love" by the Mindbenders, "My Love" by Petula Clark," and "Barbara Ann" by the Beach Boys.

Country music was getting a good amount of international exposure: Jim Ed Brown, Marion Worth, Leroy Van Dyke, George Hamilton IV, Bill Carlisle, Ernie Ashworth, Billy Walker, Roy Acuff, and Roy Drusky all had international tours, mostly arranged through the USO for military bases. Most of the tours were in Europe to German military bases, although Roy Acuff visited Vietnam and Korea.

In England Arnold mimed his records on Radio Caroline's Saturday night dance at Wimbledon Palace, appeared at London's Marquee Club, and on the BBC's Light Programme and several other TV programs. He also did a number of interviews, including one with the *Daily Sketch* where the writer noted he "refused to disclose his age, but did admit to being a millionaire." Arnold had just turned forty-eight in a time when young record buyers were advised not to trust anyone over thirty. That was probably why one of his bios during that time had his birth date listed as 1928, ten years after he was actually born.

As a follow-up to "Make the World Go Away," Arnold recorded "I Want to Go with You," written by the same writer, Hank Cochran. The session, on October 25, 1965, was produced by Chet Atkins in Nashville. It featured the rhythm section of Floyd Cramer on piano, Ray Edenton, Jerry Kennedy, and Wayne Moss on guitars, Henry Strzelecki on bass, and Buddy Harman on drums, along with five violins, two violas, and one cello led by Bill Walker. There were also four background singers—William Wright, Louis Nunley, Dottie Dillard, and Millie Kirkham. Arnold recorded it on the first of three straight days of recordings to put together a single and an album to follow up "Make the World Go Away" and *My World*, both of which had achieved Gold status.

"I Want to Go with You" entered the American country charts on February 12, 1966, and rose to number one, going up to thirty-six on the pop charts in *Billboard*. It was also released in England. The song has the same big ballad feel as "Make the World Go Away" and sounds remarkably similar, a fact noticed by one British reviewer who compared "I Want to Go with You" to "Make the World Go Away" and said the former "possesses the same kind of basic simplicity of melody and charm that characterised his first big British hit."

> ➤ *A highlight of Eddy Arnold's life came on February 14, 1966, when he and Sally were invited to the White House by President Lyndon Johnson for a state dinner.*

The scruffy, long-haired look was in vogue, a sharp contrast to Eddy Arnold's clean-cut, conservative image. In an interview later that year Arnold admitted he was "slightly puzzled by his ability to get through to young people in an era which features 'kooky' types," although he had come to the conclusion that "the present set of teen-agers is probably not as different from youngsters of yesteryear as we're inclined to fear." Arnold declared, "There's a vast majority of fine young people in our country. Maybe they're a little more sophisticated than they used to be but that seems perfectly normal in view of a world of astronauts and rockets."

The writer noted that "the only lament Eddy makes about the young male singers today is that many of the long-haired variety too often look like their locks could do with a good shampooing. 'I'm almost resigned to fellows wearing long hair,' said Arnold, 'but just a little soap and water would add a lot to their appeal, to my way of thinking.'"

A highlight of Eddy Arnold's life came on February 14, 1966, when he and Sally were invited to the White House by President Lyndon Johnson for a state dinner. It was especially meaningful to Arnold because "I didn't have to sing for my supper."

The dinner was given for Haile Selassie, emperor of Ethiopia, and scheduled for eight o'clock that evening. A little snafu caused considerable consternation for the Arnolds as they were heading to the dinner. Outside their hotel room, the Arnolds pushed the elevator button and waited. And waited and waited and waited. A phone call confirmed that the elevators were out of order—and the Arnolds were on the ninth floor. There was nothing to do but race down nine flights of steps in formal evening wear.

Eddy Arnold—who hates to be late or for others to be late—was in a turmoil. By the time they reached the east entrance of the White House, President and Mrs. Johnson had already received the emperor in the Oval Room, colors had been presented at the foot of the stairs, and guests were being received in the East Room as the United States Marine Band played. As they waited to be received, Eddy Arnold looked at his wife and said, "It's a long way from Chester County!" That line would provide the title for his autobiography, which would be published several years later.

> *He was performing country music in the Big Apple, packing a crowd of urban sophisticates with a kind of music that many in the New York media looked down their noses at. And he even charmed the critics.*

Eddy and Sally Arnold were not seated together at the White House dinner. There were only 140 guests, and they were seated ten to a table where they dined on roast filet of beef, duchess potatoes, asparagus, and a salad. After-dinner entertainment was provided by Metropolitan Opera singers Richard Tucker, tenor, and Nedda Casei, mezzo-soprano. Arnold sat with Benny Goodman, and Hubert Humphrey barely acknowledged Arnold; instead the vice president spent the evening talking with Benny Goodman. It was another reason Arnold didn't particularly care for Hubert Humphrey.

Eddy Arnold began 1966 by doing a concert with the Phoenix Symphony, and he clearly enjoyed his new audience, new image, and big hits. In February and March, he was the spokesman for RCA's sales campaign, "Welcome to the Wild World of Country Music," that sought to capitalize on the renewed interest in country music and the success of the Nashville Sound. Then on May 19, 1966, he achieved a pinnacle in his career when he did a concert at Carnegie Hall in New York. He was performing country music in the Big Apple, packing a crowd of urban sophisticates with a kind of music that many in the New York media looked down their noses at. And he even charmed the critics.

Writing for the *New York Times*, noted critic Robert Shelton praised the performance: "Whether done in an intimate, personal fashion, or with a sweeping theatrical projection, Mr. Arnold was a sure-footed, expressive interpreter. He showed much of the unpressured crooning and relaxed phrasing that have made him such a long-standing favorite with listeners."

And a long review in *Time* magazine asked, "What was a li'l ole country boy doing in a big fancy place like that?" It quoted Arnold saying, "This is the fulfillment of a lifetime dream," and stated that he was "all fancied up in a tuxedo and string tie" with "a mellifluous baritone that poured out just as warm and creamy as milk fresh out of the barn cow." According to the review, Arnold possessed "a broad, half-moon smile and an ultra-relaxed manner that could charm the warts off a hog's back," and it pointed out that the appearance "marked a new era for country music. A few years ago, any country crooner billing himself as 'The Tennessee Plowboy' would have been run out of most Northern cities. But now, in an age of shifting population, country music has penetrated the metropolis in a big way."

The review continued, "Arnold has never gone in for the spangled Western getups, nasal mewings and twangy guitars that have made country music so tiresome. . . . He is more the Country Como, a slightly citified slicker in sports shirt and slacks, singing to arrangements laced with violins and a generally humming chorus." It then quoted Arnold on the "new" country music, "Once we cut out all the by-cracky nonsense and give respect to our music, then people will respect us."

The following night Arnold performed at the Brooklyn Academy of Music and won over those fans as well, performing a song set that included "Wreck of the Old 97," "Make the World Go Away," "Lovebug Itch," "Cotton Fields," "Dear Heart," "The Richest Man (in the World)," "Tennessee Stud," and "Cattle Call."

In March, Roger Miller swept the Grammy Awards for country music, winning six with his hit "King of the Road" leading the way. In fact, the only country Grammy that Miller did *not* win was for Female Vocalist, and that was won by Jody Miller (no relation) whose hit, "Queen of the House," was an answer song to Roger's "King of the Road."

Eddy Arnold was there, hosting the event as president of the Nashville office of NARAS. His album *My World* had been nominated for a Grammy but lost out in the Roger Miller sweep. The previous fall he had recorded one of Miller's songs, the ballad "The Last Word in Lonesome Is Me," which had been the B side of Miller's hit "England Swings." That became his follow-up to "I Want to Go with You" and entered the charts on May 14; it rose to number two on the country charts and number forty on the pop charts. In July, he released "The Tip of My Fingers," which reached number one on the country charts, and then in October, he released "Somebody Like Me," a more peppy, up-tempo number after five straight ballads, which reached the number one position on the country charts.

The greatest honor of Eddy Arnold's life came on Friday evening, October 21, 1966, when he was inducted into the Country Music Hall of Fame.

The induction came during the weeklong Disc Jockey Convention held in Nashville. On October 19, the *Billboard* Country Awards were presented, and Arnold received Favorite Male Vocalist. But Arnold picked up the flu that week and wasn't planning on attending the CMA banquet and dance that Friday evening. In fact, he canceled plans earlier that day to attend a football game at Battle Ground Academy where his son attended and played on the football team. Instead he stayed home in bed and would have remained there except his manager, Jerry Purcell, called and insisted he get out and come down to accept an award from *Cashbox* magazine. It was a ruse designed to make sure Eddy Arnold was there to get his Hall of Fame honor.

When Eddy Arnold's name was announced by Hal Cook, the CMA board chairman, the singer, wearing a gray suit and striped tie, came forward and said, "It's a long road. I'm delighted to be here." He cried openly and held hands with Sally in front of the audience of 1,150 as the applause engulfed them. When the applause died down, Arnold said, "Could we go now?" Even the great honor couldn't totally overcome the flu bug, so Arnold skipped the dance afterward and headed back home to bed.

Eddy Arnold was one of four inducted that evening in the Country Music Hall of Fame. The others were Judge George D. Hay, who could not attend, and two who were deceased: Uncle Dave Macon and Jim Denny.

Eddy and Sally Arnold at his induction into the Country Music Hall of Fame.

Arnold marked a lot of milestones in 1966. In addition to his trips to England, his appearance at Carnegie Hall, and his induction into the Country Music Hall of Fame, he appeared several times on network television shows, performed a number of personal appearances, played in the Music City Pro-Celebrity Golf Invitational tournament with partner Dizzy Dean, and served as the Middle Tennessee Chairman for the Red Cross Fund. ·

He had emerged as a country and pop superstar, but his image went beyond music. A number of articles stressed his role as a successful and wealthy businessman. In one article Arnold explained, "I swore to myself . . . that if I ever managed to make any money, I'd hang on to it."

In another interview he talked about his British trip: "It's funny you know during my near 30 years in show business, I haven't travelled all that much. That last English trip was my first and I have mainly been restricted to America and Canada. I would dearly love

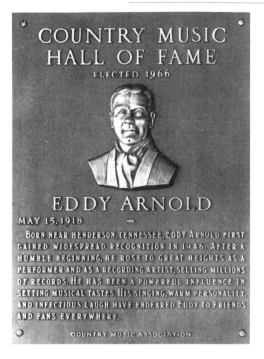

Eddy Arnold's plaque at the Country Music Hall of Fame.

to travel more, see all the things I've always wanted to, meet many new people and show my son the world." He talked about his family, saying of his son, "Dickie plays electric guitar & sings Beatles songs," adding that "I think I get on better with my boy Dickie than anyone else. He really is the greatest! I want him to come to Britain with me next time I'm over for there's so much for young people over here. All the clubs and the organisations."

He still had his television show on NBC, *Today— On the Farm*, and his radio show, *Eddy Arnold Time*. He remarked,

> I answer all my fan mail personally because I decided a long time ago that it helps sell records. If a fan writes in and asks me where he can buy a certain record I may have to tell him I never recorded that song, but in the letter I include a list of every side I ever cut and I may even tell him which one I think he might like. Now if that fan shows my letter to a few people, I've bought myself a lot of good will and happy customers just for a few minutes of my time and a stamp.

Eddy Arnold defended his desire to make money selling records, telling a British interviewer, "Heck, too many people in this line think that money and business are dirty words." Several articles included the information that he was on the board of directors of insurance and air-conditioning companies, was a partner in a land development company, and had been appointed by the governor to the Tennessee Industrial Commission.

He performed one week out of each month, had an annual income of more than $200,000 from his performances, was on the board of three companies, and owned a four-hundred-unit apartment house, a realty company, a water utility, a record pressing firm, a farm and a music publishing company.

He was increasingly mentioned as a candidate for political office, primarily because Tennessee Governor Frank Clement kept encouraging him to run. At that time, the end of 1966, Clement's term as governor was up, and Tennessee law stated a governor could not serve two succeeding terms. Buford Ellington, a Clement rival, wanted to run, and Clement wanted to head him off. Clement reasoned that if he could get someone he knew and trusted—like Eddy Arnold—into the office, he could head off Ellington, and Clement could easily reclaim the governor's seat in 1970.

Arnold thought about it but decided against it. First, he disliked the rough-and-tumble of politics, especially the fact that "everybody wants something from you." There would be a line of job seekers a mile long, and he would have to turn most of them down—something he was loath to do. Also, Clement was a Democrat, and Arnold would have to switch parties and run with Clement's Democratic machine. Arnold liked Clement's politics—it was Southern conservatism even though he was a Democrat. In July, he had accompanied Governor Clement to a Lions Club convention where Clement "blasted draft card burners" to thunderous applause while Arnold served as master of ceremonies on Tennessee Night and performed some songs. But Eddy Arnold was a dyed-in-the-wool Republican, and he would not abandon his party even though, in 1966, the Republicans were at a low point after Barry Goldwater's defeat in the 1964 presidential election.

Arnold also reasoned that he would have to give up a lot of income and that he couldn't perform after he left office because the dignity of the office wouldn't allow it. And his wife, Sally, hated the idea of her husband being in politics. So he decided to stay out of the scramble for political office, but kept his interest in politics as a contributor and observer.

He was also enjoying home life, and he told Margaret McManus for the *Milwaukee Journal*,

I enjoy a few comforts and I'm going to enjoy a few more. I'm about to get me a new boat. I'm not what you call frugal, but I'm conservative about money. I'll spend a lot of money on my home but I've also invested a lot of money. I belong to a little syndicate back home and I told those people, right before I came up here, "Now, that's the last I'm putting in those apartment houses. Now we're going to spend some."

23

Entertainer of the Year

Eddy Arnold capped a banner year in 1967 by winning the Country Music Association's Entertainer of the Year award. He also earned more money from appearing at fairs than any other entertainer, appeared at the prestigious Coconut Grove nightclub in Los Angeles, starred in several *Kraft Music Hall* shows, and had three more major hits: "Lonely Again" and "Turn the World Around" each reached number one on the country charts while "Misty Blue" reached number three. A fourth single, "Here Comes Heaven," entered the charts in December 1967 but did not reach its top position—number two—until the following year. All of those records also reached the pop charts in *Billboard*, although none rose past the fifties.

It was the "summer of love" for the rock world. In 1967, *Sergeant Pepper's Lonely Hearts Club Band* by the Beatles was released, and the Monterey Pop Festival was held in California. In San Francisco, young people wore flowers in their hair, played music in the parks, and took Timothy Leary's advice to turn on, tune in, and drop out. A cosmic cloud of smoke was hanging in the air in the Haight-Ashbury district, known as "Hippie Haven." Musically, it was a time for the Jefferson Airplane and Grateful Dead playing psychedelic musical jams that went on forever.

Despite the attention that rock music received—and it was indeed the music of the young generation—country music achieved substantial success. The liberal crowd never noticed; psychedelic sounds drowned out the Nashville Sound. But outside psychedelic circles, the combination of Eddy Arnold and the Nashville Sound was winning converts across the country. In Atlanta, columnist Dick Gray, reviewing an appearance of Eddy Arnold with the Atlanta Symphony, wrote, "I never was much of an Eddy Arnold fan until I experienced his Atlanta performance. But he sold me—just as he's been selling millions of people around the world for many years."

A number of other critics agreed. Al Freeders, in an article headlined "Country Music Makes It Out of the Backwoods," stated, "Eddy has converted a host of new listeners to uptown country music. To those who claim he has deserted country music, I say he's merely brought it out of the backwoods to show the rest of the world that it's here to stay." After a concert in Mobile, Alabama, the reviewer summed up Arnold in this way: "Far more than a wailer of hillbilly lamentations or a crooner of pop songs, he is first, last and always, a showman. Born to entertain, he has the heart of a Jolson or a George Burns and, happily, a heckuva lot more voice."

> ➤ *Outside psychedelic circles, the combination of Eddy Arnold and the Nashville Sound was winning converts across the country.*

In several interviews, Eddy Arnold defended the Nashville Sound and his move away from hard core country music. He told *Los Angeles Times* reporter John L. Scott, "I gave the traditional style a lot of thought, and decided to urbanize it into the mainstream of pop music. Pop-country has become a tremendous force in the recording medium. It always was big in rural and small town areas, but in the past few years we've been able to get it going in the big cities, too."

In another interview, Arnold pointed out that it wasn't just the music that was changing; country fans were changing as well. He told writer Rex Polier, "I got news for you, the country people are pretty well educated today. They like all kinds of music, too."

A key difference between country music and rock was the relationship between the performer and the audience. Rock artists sang at their audience, expressing themselves and daring the audience to agree. Country performers sang *to* their audience and wanted to make a connection. In one review, critic Dick Gray highlighted the point: "Mr. Arnold . . . is as down-to-earth and amiable as if he were one of us poor folks. . . . 'I'm not a singer,' he said. 'I'm a performer. . . . And I know how to sell.'" The notion that country singers were salesmen who "sold" a song was not a new one; Roy Acuff used the same analogy. But it brought home an important part of country music: the connection with an audience. And Eddy Arnold, who was comfortable in the business world, saw himself as someone who combined the world of business with the world of country music. In fact, in February 1967, Arnold received the award of Salesman of the Year from the Sales and Marketing Executives of Nashville. The award was given for Arnold's "selling Tennessee" to the world through traveling to England, performing at Carnegie Hall, and making numerous network TV appearances.

> ➤ *Rock artists sang at their audience, expressing themselves and daring the audience to agree. Country performers sang to their audience and wanted to make a connection.*

If the height of the rock world was the large, outdoor concert, the top of the pop world was the nightclub, while the top of the country music world was the state or county fair. Eddy Arnold hadn't performed much at either nightclubs or fairs until 1967, but that year he found both rewarding and lucrative.

Arnold had avoided fairs until the year before, when he began to perform for them. He explained, "I never played country fairs because the producers never put the stage close to the grandstand. But now they're getting smart and they're putting the stage where you can be close to the audience. I'll go in now, yes sir. If you're not close, you don't have the communication. I want to feel the presence of the audience." There was big money in fairs: in San Antonio, Eddy Arnold took home $40,000, and at the Houston Livestock Show at the Houston Astrodome he drew a crowd of 62,000 for two shows.

On TV Eddy Arnold was seen on the *Kraft Music Hall* with Perry Como, on the *Danny Kaye Show*, as a guest host on *Mike Douglas*, and as a replacement host for Johnny Carson on the *Tonight Show*. He also continued performing with symphonies, performing with those in Atlanta, Phoenix, and Beaumont, Texas.

In October, Arnold performed at the Coconut Grove club in the Ambassador Hotel in Los Angeles. In the audience were Pat and Shirley Boone, Judy Carne, Anjanette Comer, Omar Sharif, and Peter Duel. According to the reviewer, "He proved a hit with the celebrity-crowded audience—most of whom were surprised to see Eddy dressed as one of them. Instead of wearing western attire à la Roy Rogers, the singer donned a tuxedo with appropriate appurtenances. Didn't even wear cowboy boots."

Before performing at the Los Angeles club, he told John L. Scott of the *Los Angeles Times*, "For several years I played in small, smoke-filled joints and got to hate 'em. That's probably why I shy away from club dates now, although there are a few areas I'd like to work—Lake Tahoe for example. My personal appearances these days are mostly in the concert and state fair mediums."

He was careful with his bookings: "My managers and I have always agreed that either a booking would be something I'd be proud of or forget it. No matter what the money, you can't buy back your reputation." The Coconut Grove booking proved to be something he was *very* proud of.

Here is the review of the concert by Bill Libby in *Cornet* magazine:

> Opening night at the exclusive Coconut Grove in Los Angeles: From mansions in Beverly Hills and Bel-Air, the customers came, by invitation only, in long, shiny cars . . . celebrities . . . a mink-coat-and-tuxedo crowd—plus a number of stunning starlets wearing mini-skirted evening dresses with deep, plunging necklines, frantic fans waving autograph books, and the movie-magazine photographers popping flash bulbs. The elite swept through the ornate old Ambassador Hotel lobby to the great, dark, potted-palm-fringed room crowded with more than a thousand persons, including the short fat men and their wives whom no one recognized but who own the movie and TV and record interests, banks and insurance companies. As they ate their seafood cocktails and steaks, drank their Scotch, and waited for the show to begin, they marveled that they were here to hear a hick, a hillbilly, a country crooner. Eddy Arnold has given class to country music. He has backed it with violins and even full symphony orchestras; he has helped to bring it from the sticks to the big cities, and he has made many millions of dollars which, it is well known, he conserves carefully. . . . If he does not always wear a tux, as he did at the Grove, he wears sports shirts and slacks, never star-spangled cowboy suits. If he cuts up country style, he doesn't overdo it. "I know better," he says, grinning. "I don't dig this by-cracky nonsense myself and if I hear it on a

country-and-western radio station, I turn it off. I love the
music and I've always believed that if you present it with
respect, the people will respect it." . . . He had rehearsed
four hours just before the precedent-shattering show and
he worked for more than an hour, singing more than two
dozen songs. He was sweating, weary, and wilted when
he took his last bow. Backstage, he shrugged. "I don't
mind working hard. I have found that you have to work
hard for anything worthwhile."

At the end of the evening, he was exhausted and told the
reporter, "I enjoyed the performance—I always enjoyed performing—
and I enjoyed meeting the prominent people, but the party pooped
me out. Oh my, but it was an ordeal." In response to what he thought
while he was performing and at the star-studded party later Arnold
replied, "I thought the same thing I thought when I performed for the
President at the White House last year. I turned to my wife and I said,
'Well, baby, it's a long way from Chester County.'"

Eddy Arnold was enjoying the life of a major star, although he
had learned to avoid one temptation. Admitting there were a number
of letters at the Ambassador Hotel for him, he declared,

> Most of these are from women who want to meet me or
> spend some time with me. They're wherever I go, as I
> suppose they are for most entertainers. Here, in Holly-
> wood, they're more persistent. They come up to you in
> the lobby or knock on your hotel room or come back to
> the dressing room, rubbing their minks on you, and prac-
> tically ordering you to come have a drink with them.
> Oooweee, I'm no prude, but I been there before, when I
> was younger and more open to temptation, and I ain't
> about to start going back there.

In 1967, country music began giving awards to bring recognition
to its performers. It was the first year of the Country Music Association Awards, held at the Municipal Auditorium but not televised.
Eddy Arnold was performing at the Coconut Grove when he received
a phone call informing him he had just been awarded the top honor,
Entertainer of the Year.

In the public eye, Eddy Arnold was always smooth and polite,
and he made people feel at ease. In Camden, New Jersey, at a
Korvett's store, a reporter described the scene: "Arnold acted like a

politician, posing for pictures, hugging record clerks, bussing customers and autographing records." And he made no bones about why
he was there: "I'm not here to plant a cornerstone. I'm selling albums.
We've got 26 of them here." One of those albums was *The Best of
Eddy Arnold*. RCA had put the package together and named May
"Eddy Arnold Month." Arnold went out to promote his catalog. The
album joined the *My World* album by reaching Gold sales (more than
half a million copies sold).

Finally, he had some advice for other country singers who
wanted to enter the world where he lived: "If you don't overdo the
cornball humor and the cornball clothes, if you present your music
simple, straight, with dignity, and give it quality backing and setting,
it will sell. There is a great audience for our music and we have
tapped only a part of it so far."

24

A Calm in the Storm: Country
Music in the Mid Sixties

The sixties came to a head in America in 1968. During that
year, the Viet Cong launched their massive Tet offensive, and
the United States responded with stepped-up fighting and
more troops. On March 31, President Lyndon Johnson
announced on television that he would not seek reelection after Senator Eugene McCarthy won a surprise victory in the New Hampshire
primary. Robert Kennedy would soon join the race while, in the
South, George Wallace attracted the attention and support of a number of voters, especially in the country music community. On the
Republican side, Richard Nixon, whom many had written off after
his defeat for governor of California in 1962, was gathering strength
and support.

A week after Johnson's surprise announcement about not seek-
ing reelection, Martin Luther King was assassinated in Memphis,
Tennessee, which led to race riots in several cities. Then in June,
Robert Kennedy was assassinated in Los Angeles just after winning
the California primary. That led to Hubert Humphrey's nomination as
the Democratic standard bearer, but riots in Chicago during the
Democratic Convention seemed to seal his fate as a failed presidential candidate. For many Americans in the middle class, the country
was simply out of control. Antiwar demonstrations increased
throughout the country, radical students took over universities, lock-
ing themselves in administration buildings, and black athletes at the

Olympics accepted their medals with a Black Power salute. In November, Richard Nixon was elected president.

> ➤ *The middle class was comprised mostly of those who wanted a safe, secure America, who had worked hard for their success.*

It was painfully obvious that there were two different Americas in 1968, and the gap between them was increasingly wide. On the one hand were the young students who objected to the Vietnam War, wanting to smoke pot and do their thing. On the other hand were the hardworking parents who had sacrificed during World War II to make the world a better place for the young people.

The middle class was comprised mostly of those who wanted a safe, secure America, who had worked hard for their success, and believed in the values of fighting for the flag, obeying laws, and observing common, personal decency. They could not understand a world where young men snubbed their noses at American patriotism and the value of hard work to embrace drugs or a culture that valued dropping out more than it did pitching in. Neither side could see the other's point of view, and neither side could really understand the other. If the American Civil War was brother against brother, then the Vietnam War was father against son.

The world of middle-class values was the world of Eddy Arnold. He had become a spokesman for country music and the Nashville Sound; now he became a spokesman for the hardworking middle class—the "silent majority"—and he sang for them. In a world dressed in jeans and tie-dyed T-shirts, Eddy Arnold wore a tux; in a world of shaggy hair and beards, Eddy Arnold was clean-cut and neat; in a world of drugs, Eddy Arnold was straight. And in a world of liberalism and radical activism, Eddy Arnold, like so many in his generation, was a conservative.

Still, he remained friends and allies with a number of Democratic politicians in Tennessee. Tennessee (and Southern) politicians and voters have generally always been conservative, but they were almost always in the Democratic party. As the years rolled by—from the 1960s to the 1990s—the bedrock beliefs of Southern voters and politicians remained fairly constant, but they shifted party affiliation from Democrat to Republican. Eddy Arnold was way ahead of the curve.

The 1968 elections confirmed Arnold's conservative beliefs and his connection to the Republican party.

The news of the day was filled with riots on campuses against the Vietnam War, footage from Vietnam that brought the war into American homes, civil rights discord, and angry young men and women. Years later, the sixties, especially 1968, would be viewed through a haze of tumultuous change and confusing forces pulling in all directions. Those who remember those years often remember a time of confusion, yet it was also a time of simplicity. It was a time when the liberal agenda held sway, but it was also a time when a conservative backlash was making itself felt.

To look back to 1968 and to see country music become so popular in America, or an artist like Eddy Arnold become a major star in both the pop and the country fields seems almost to be an anomaly. Then again, Eddy Arnold spoke for the great majority of Americans who did not deny problems, but wanted them solved civilly; did not deny injustice, but wanted it corrected in an orderly and peaceful way; and did not deny there were things wrong with America, but thought there were more things right with the country and wanted to see wounds healed rather than opened wider.

Nineteen sixty-eight was a watershed year for country music as well as the country. The country-pop sound that Eddy Arnold had pioneered and the uptown image for country music that he had cultivated became the sound and the look of the day. Two of the top country artists that year were Eddy Arnold and Glen Campbell, both of whom had a clean-cut image that was a marked contrast to the shaggy look of unkempt youth.

In terms of the popularity of country music, Arnold told the *Louisville Courier-Journal*,

> Television has had a lot to do with it, but radio is the real
> factor. In almost every major city now, there is a station
> that uses nothing but country music, modern country
> music. I was in Philly the other day, and one of the big
> stations—I mean a 50,000 watter—is doing it and their
> revenues and listenership are way up.

In that same article, Eddy Arnold attempted to promote a more cosmopolitan view of country music:

As of this moment, in every major city in this country—
New York, Chicago, Minneapolis, Los Angeles—you have a
country music station. I sell more records in New York than
I do in Nashville. Maybe it was true ten or 15 years ago that
country music had appeal only in the South, but we've
taken the hayseed out of it; it's gotten exposed on major TV
shows. It's a lot more acceptable than it ever was before.

But there is another side of country music—the hard-driving,
traditional sound of honky-tonk that represents the working class.
That group was represented by Merle Haggard, who finished the year
as one of the top three artists in country music, and by Buck Owens,
who finished in the top ten for radio airplay and country sales. Haggard
and Owens were from Bakersfield, which was challenging
Nashville as a creative force in country music. Still, of the top
twenty-five artists in country music during 1965, the great majority
(twenty-one out of twenty-five) were "Nashville" artists.

Despite the tremendous growth of country music and the
Nashville Sound, there were still, of course, the snide comments
about country music coupled with some backhanded compliments
from the media, especially the New York–based media. An article in
the *New York Daily News* in early 1968 began, "There's golden music
in them thar hills, folks. And if you don't believe us, just take a look
at the record—the record business. Country music, once fluffed off as
corny 'hillbilly' noise, is now a multi-million dollar enterprise."

Here is an article from *TV Guide* in January 1968:

Let's see: there's corn pone, corn fritters, corn meal, corn-
starch and corn sirup [sic]. Among the uses of corn there
is another that emanates from 16th Avenue South—so-
called Record Row—in Nashville, Tennessee, and sup-
ports a $100,000,000 a year industry with tentacles into
every state and to some 400 radio stations broadcasting
an unvarying and largely uninterrupted quota of Country
and Western Music. . . . Funny thing about Nashville! It
stands at the crossroads of several great music traditions
that have roots deep in America's memory: Negro blues,
Southern mountain balladry, "Bluegrass" string bands,
and work songs. And yet the city has become to many
music fanciers the international symbol for a musicality
of such numbing mindlessness and banality that some
either won't or can't listen to it. . . . The automatic

assumption about Country and Western music is that it is the private domain of rural white Southerners and that the better educated and more affluent Northern urbanites are much too sophisticated for it. . . . Time was when the banjo, mandolin and dobro guitar were the staple instruments of Country and Western music. Now violins and pianos and harps provide a more elegant background for the same soppy sentiments that always have characterized the more commercial aspects of Country and Western music.

If "clothes make the man," as the old saying goes, perhaps they make the music as well. Writers and critics had been surprised for years that Eddy Arnold dressed in conservative outfits. It was a never-ending source of amazement for writers and reporters from the mid-1940s onward (more than twenty years!) to discover Arnold dressed fashionably instead of decking himself out in rhinestones or duding up like a cowboy. In "Clothes Show He's No 'Plowboy' Now," Lou Ganim wrote that during their interview, Arnold "was wearing a herringbone jacket and sporting a bright orange turtleneck underneath it—a far cry from the 'frizzles and pintos' of other country singers."

Eddy Arnold knew that sounding more poppish was not enough; he had to look the part as well. Never one for cowboy garb (except for his appearances with Pee Wee King's Golden West Cowboys or at the Houston Fat Stock Show) or loud, flashy rhinestone outfits, Eddy Arnold had worn semidressy slacks and a shirt, often with a sports coat, during his entire solo career. Still, the image of country artists for many in the media was someone either dressed as a cowboy or covered with rhinestones. Arnold always made it a point to let writers know that image of country music didn't fit him. One interviewer stated, "In terms of stage apparel, Arnold disavowed the rhinestone look. 'I never did dress like that,' he said. 'I usually wore a plain sports shirt and a nice pair of slacks, and I still do at fairs and things.'" At a press conference in Beaver Falls, Pennsylvania, a reporter observed that he had on a "brown sports jacket, flashy green turtle neck." Still, many newspaper writers continued to find it difficult to believe that Eddy Arnold didn't dress to fit in with the old stereotype. At a show at the Academy of Music in Philadelphia, the reviewer began, "One may have expected him to appear in cowboy garb, but Eddy Arnold, king of the country and Western singers, looked handsome in a tuxedo."

For a number of years, Arnold had not considered himself just a "country singer," and he made that plain to interviewers in 1968. He preferred "singer," but if there was a category or label, he told Ronnie Joyce of the *Pensacola (Florida) Journal*,

> ➤ *Arnold described himself as "a Heinz 57 singer. A little bit of western, a little bit of pop, a little bit of folk."*

I'm a country pop singer. . . . I want you to know though, that I'm not taking anything away from the country and western or any other kind of music. They're all important to the entertainment field. Country music has been good to me, and it still is. But, like I say, I don't really consider myself a country singer anymore. . . . I want people to think of me as a more versatile singer. I hate the thought that I've worked so hard these many years and not achieved broad recognition.

He attempted to define himself beyond the limits of country music. He told a writer in Monroe, Louisiana, "I sing a combination of country, folk, and popular music, and to me it all goes together." He commented to one reporter, "I've been gradually moving towards being a performer rather than a country and western singer." In several interviews Arnold described himself as "a Heinz 57 singer. A little bit of western, a little bit of pop, a little bit of folk." The combination of singing poppish love ballads and dressing conservatively worked for Eddy Arnold.

Arnold told Monte Zepeda of the *Charlotte Observer*, in an article headlined "I'm Really a Pop Music Artist," that "since I started in this business I've never thought of myself as a country and western singer. With the type material I do, I'm really a pop music artist. But I don't play to any particular type of audience. I want my songs to be accepted by everyone." He was described in an Orlando newspaper headline as "The Frank Sinatra of the Pop Country Field."

He admitted the "new" look and sound of country music weren't really all that new for him. "I was flirting with a more sophisticated urban style in the late Fifties but it just didn't come off for me," he said, referring to his recording of "I Really Don't Want to Know." "It was sometime in late '65, I think, that I found the song 'What's He Doin' in My World' and it was right for this treatment. Right after that I got 'Make the World Go Away' and made my transition."

When Arnold performed with the Hartford Symphony, the reviewer was favorably impressed:

> From conversations overheard in the lobby during inter-
> mission, it would seem that country music buffs from far
> and near had gathered to acclaim their idol. Arnold's ver-
> satility sets him apart from the "run of the mill" country-
> western balladeers, and popular ballads, novelty songs and
> cowboy tunes were included in his repertoire. . . . Blessed
> with a pleasing, not particularly unusual voice, the singer
> uses it in a way which makes his audience cry for more.

Eddy Arnold always saw his music in simple terms—a good lyric, a memorable melody, presented in an easygoing, straightfor-ward, relaxed style. The "other" kind of music in 1968 seemed too confused, so complicated, without melodies, and with convoluted lyrics. Arnold told a reporter for the *Watertown Daily Times*, "There always will be a place for simple music, you can't forget the feeling in a song. It is not my intention to be strictly a 'country boy' per-former and it is proving out. I stick to commercial songs and giving them a pop treatment."

An article from the *Napoleon, Ohio, Northwest Signal* summed up Eddy Arnold and his importance to country music in 1968:

> Above all of them, Eddy Arnold has brought sophistica-
> tion to the Country and Western field. He's helped to
> build Nashville into a recording mecca where, like New
> York and Hollywood, the kids go with their dreams and
> talent. You listen to Eddy Arnold sing something like
> Roger Miller's "If That's Not Lovin' Me" and you can sit
> back and relax. It's a good voice, an untrained voice, but
> the voice of someone you'd like to know well enough to
> call friend. There is a youthfulness to the Eddy Arnold
> sound, something comfortable, something grand. The
> sound comes at you like the village minister helping you
> through a time of grief, the family doctor cooling your
> fever. Eddy's like the Pied Piper. If you hear him and like
> him, you stick to him. You can't shake him.

25

In Concert

E
ddy Arnold spent much of 1968 on the road performing, and it paid off handsomely for him. A concert at the Corn Palace in South Dakota in the fall grossed $169,244, and Arnold took home $77,222. During an eighteen-city tour late that year, the shows grossed $550,000, and Arnold carried home $300,000. His concerts became smooth, relaxed affairs, and both audiences and reviewers responded enthusiastically.

A reviewer of his Milwaukee show praised Arnold:

> He's a talent, a pro. Wearing a blue sports jacket, blue shirt and blue tie, he prowled the stage to be sure all the spectators had a good view and shuffled his feet in "aw, shucks" style whenever applause greeted his efforts. Arnold has the relaxed execution that makes his work appear effortless. The effect is like entertaining a guest in your parlor. There is a lot of the old Nashville sound left in his delivery of ballads, pop and country western, but all the corn is shucked.

In Monroe, Louisiana, a reviewer commented on his song selections: "Many of the tunes were songs that possibly appealed more to the older folks. Not to say the young ones didn't enjoy him, but songs like 'September,' 'Tips of My Fingers,' 'Bouquet of Roses' and others he made famous, are usually more appealing to the 'older set.'"

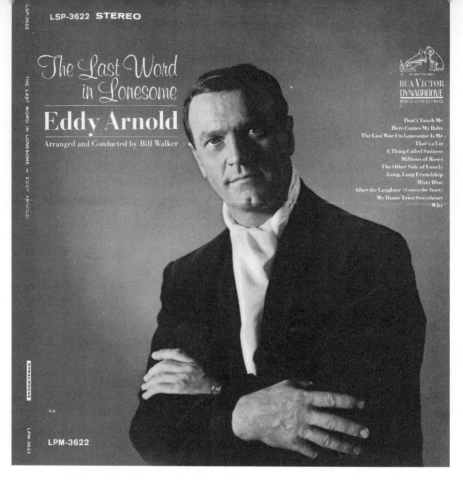

On the album cover:

LSP-3622 STEREO

The Last Word in Lonesome

Eddy Arnold

Arranged and Conducted by Bill Walker

RCA VICTOR
DYNAGROOVE
RECORDING

Don't Touch Me
Here Comes My Baby
The Last Word in Lonesome Is Me
That's a Lie
A Thing Called Sadness
Millions of Roses
The Other Side of Lonely
Long, Long Friendship
Misty Blue
After the Laughter (Comes the Tears)
My Home Town Sweetheart
Why

LPM-3622

Another concert reviewer stated, "Don't let the shiny suit and the Ivy League tie fool you. That was a country boy who brought down a sold-out house at the Eastman Theater last night, and he did it with plain old ordinary country charm, easy and relaxed as a Southern summer evening."

He was adjusting to performing in a concert setting. During a concert in Monroe, Louisiana,

> spectators seemed to annoy Arnold by snapping cameras in his face, and he asked seriously, that anyone who had a camera and wanted to take pictures, to come forward and take them while he could pose for them. This held the show up for a few minutes, but as Arnold put it, "Taking pictures during a sentimental love song just don't go good, and besides, other people have to look at your backsides."

Having attended Arnold's show in Portland, Oregon, Charlie Hanna liked what he heard:

Easy Ed kept up an almost constant flow of past and current record hits while moving easily about the stage as he sang. Arnold's baritone holds a ton of magic, and his imperturbable pace shows that he's in complete control. Still, though a ton of mellow is always mighty nice, a body gets thinking along about the 1,999th pound how just a little ginger might come in nice. Still again, Arnold takes on just about every type and tempo of song any kind of singer has a right to take on. Along the way he does justice to a broad range, the likes of "Hello, Dolly," "The Last Word in Lonesome is Me," "Up Above My Head," and new "super-country" or "super folk" such as "By The Time I Get to Phoenix" and Jimmy Rogers' composition, "It's Over." Arnold's ease and grace are delightful, and he would be the first to admit that 30 years experience has helped a little in putting on the polish.

Samuel Singer reviewed the Academy of Music Show in Philadelphia:

Arnold himself chatted with the audience, but not at great length; the songs were the thing. His wisecracks earned chuckles, not belly laughs. They usually had a bizarre twist that made the audience do a mental double take. "I wasn't born here," Arnold informed the audience. "but if it should happen again. . . ." Arnold . . . sings in a serviceable baritone that can do tricks. He slips into falsetto with ease, or dips into the bass register for an effect. But it is his straight-forward style that holds the greater part of his manifest appeal to both sexes. . . . Yes, the girls—of all ages—would squeal when they recognized a tune in a medley. . . . Arnold is a homespun fellow and many of his songs are homespun.

Even a reviewer who didn't particularly care for country music or Eddy Arnold gave grudging respect. This review by Bob MacKenzie for the Oakland, California, newspaper, which caused both ire and humor with Eddy Arnold, was found by his manager, Jerry Purcell, and sent along with a few choice comments:

Arnold, for those who don't dig country scene, is a nice-looking soft-talking gentleman with a plain straight face, friendly gray eyes and a comfortable midriff who sings

rural songs in a trickless straight-forward way, owns some
20 million dollars and doesn't bother to get his teeth
capped. He is a plum likeable cuss, and his music is easy
to take, even for a non-addict of C & W music. Arnold's
tunes are not the hard-core twang-and-moan hillbilly stuff,
they are softer and mellower, somewhere between country-
western and popular songs. His delivery is sincere and
easygoing; his songs are sweet ballads with sentimental
lyrics, corny but nice. When he tries a swing tune or a pop
ballad with no country flavor, he sounds a little better
than the average shower baritone, but not much. But when
he gets into a country tune he puts his heart in it and
sings it as only a genuine country boy could.

In March, Eddy Arnold made his second Carnegie Hall appearance and once again wowed the New York crowd, including the
media. Robert Shelton wrote in the *New York Times*,

His singing is smooth, earnest, buoyant and uncomplicated. He is sentimental and direct. For women he seems
to be a sort of no-challenging romantic figure, and for
their husbands is non-threatening. . . . Mr. Arnold has
sophisticated many elements of country music to the
point where identification with straight country songs
comes only after he dismissed a large orchestra and
perches on a stool with his guitar. In ballads or country
song, he is one of the pinions of our pop music, and it
looks as if he'll be around a while.

A reviewer in another New York paper said that "Arnold takes
the twang out of the music, substituting soft strings and orchestral
effects."

During the concert, RCA executives Norman Racusin and Harry
Jenkins presented him with a Gold Record to commemorate 50 million records sold. He was only the fourth artist in the music business
to accomplish that feat; the other three were Bing Crosby, Elvis Presley, and the Beatles. He was also given an award from the National
Association of Record Merchandisers (NARM), which represents
retailers, for Best Selling Male Country Artist in 1967.

In addition to his active schedule of personal appearances, Eddy
Arnold appeared on a number of TV shows. The most prestigious

was an NBC special on country music, *American Profile: Music From the Land*, which Arnold narrated. He appeared on six *Kraft Music Hall* shows on NBC during the summer, the *Jackie Gleason Show* on CBS, and a *Kraft Music Hall* Christmas special; he was the host for *The Hollywood Palace*, a guest on *The Red Skelton Show*, and a guest host for Johnny Carson on the *Tonight Show*.

In May, Arnold filmed a pilot for a proposed TV show, *Mr. Deeds Goes to Town*, based on an old Gary Cooper movie. When asked about the taping, Arnold said, "Nothing has been finalized on the series and it may or may not be," then added, "I'll level—I'm not overjoyed at the prospect. I suppose I could do it but, gee, it's a lot of work. They promised me a schedule I could live with—a four-day week and one week off a month. If I get it, OK, if not, I'm just as happy on my boat." He got his wish: the pilot wasn't picked up by the networks.

It was a big year for country music on television in 1968 because the Country Music Association's Awards Show was first telecast. One of the great untold stories is the importance of advertising agencies in the history of country music. In 1939, the William Esty Agency bought advertising time on the *Grand Ole Opry* for their client, R. J. Reynolds, and thus launched the *Opry* as a major player in country music. From 1945 to 1956, the Brown Brothers Agency bought advertising time for their client, Ralston Purina, that played a key role in the national exposure of Eddy Arnold. And in 1968, the J. Walter Thompson Agency's client, Kraft Foods, would become the sponsor for the Country Music Association Awards Show, giving that show network exposure in prime time.

The first awards show—in October 1967—was held at the Municipal Auditorium in Nashville; the following July a group of CMA board members—Hubert Long, Jack Stapp, Frances Preston, and Bill Denny—had lunch with Irving Waugh, head of WSM television in Nashville, and sought his help in getting a network slot for the next CMA Awards scheduled in October. That lunch was on a Friday; on Sunday night Waugh and Jack Stapp caught a plane to New York where, on Monday morning, they called on an old friend of Stapp's, Dan Seymour of the Thompson Agency.

Kraft Foods had long been a sponsor of music shows—Kraft's *Music Hall* series—and that show had featured Eddy Arnold a number of times. A *Kraft Music Hall* show scheduled for October was entitled "Texas State Fair," to be hosted by Roy Rogers and Dale Evans. Seymour made some phone calls, and the show was changed to the

Country Music Association Awards Show with Roy Rogers and Dale Evans as the hosts. The New York agency was reluctant to let country music performers appear, and since the sponsor retained creative control, some noncountry acts appeared on the show to appease the New York advertising executives. However, the show was so successful that the Country Music Association obtained creative control by the eighth broadcast and eliminated most of the noncountry elements.

The televised awards show did more than just put the Country Music Association's Awards program in prime time; it also put the organization on firm financial footing. In the first year the network paid the CMA $25,000 for the show, but as the show became more popular, and the CMA obtained more clout, power, and control, the show brought millions of dollars into the CMA's coffers, allowing that organization to go full steam ahead in its efforts to promote country music. No longer would the CMA have to worry about funds or try to come up with ideas for fund-raisers in order to do its job—the awards telecast took care of those problems.

In Nashville there was a building boom to capitalize on the success of country music. The previous year the Country Music Hall of Fame, located at the head of Music Row on the corner of Sixteenth Avenue South and Division, opened. New buildings were under construction to house the performing rights organization ASCAP; publishers Tree, Cedarwood, Hill and Range, and Pamper; and talent agencies Moeller and Show Biz. And there was an announcement about a fourteen-story building on Music City Boulevard. The boulevard was planned to be a four-lane road that would follow Sixteenth Avenue South from Demonbreun to a point north of Belmont College—where it would veer west and join Hillsboro Road in the vicinity of Fairfax Avenue. The multistory office building was scheduled to be constructed on the east side of Sixteenth Avenue between South Street and Grand Avenue. The investors in the office building included Eddy Arnold; however, the boulevard was never built, and neither was the office building.

RCA planned a fifty-foot extension to its building on Seventeenth Avenue South while WSM announced it had hired Economic Research Associates of Los Angeles to study the feasibility of an entertainment complex called Opryland USA. That same firm aided in the development of Disneyland and Sea World.

On the personal side, Arnold was enjoying family life, especially when he had a chance to get out on the lake in his boat. In July, he spent three weeks off the road, enjoying his boat. He talked about his thirty-foot boat with Frank Langley of the *Boston Herald*:

> Every man should have one great love other than his family or his work. Mine is that boat. Every time I can put more than two days back-to-back, no matter if I'm in New Orleans or New York, I zip back home and make a beeline for the lake. Out there on that boat it is just me and whoever I bring along. Sometimes I look on it as almost unnatural, the calm, the peace and most of all just being alone.

In answer to a question about "slowing down" he said, "Maybe someday I'll have to, but I'm sort of like Bob Hope and Bing Crosby, I guess. I can't quit. I'd be bored stiff. I have to have the sense of creating something or else my ego is not satisfied." There was a little bit of tragedy, though, because his dog, Nuggles, died in 1968. He had originally bought the dog for his daughter, JoAnn, but she left it with her parents when she got married.

As for the demands of fame, he summed up his feelings: "I love it all and if I didn't I wouldn't still be in the business." And he told a reporter for the Fort Smith, Arkansas, newspaper, "Show business requires a dedicated pride. If you don't love it, you will not be successful."

➤ "My tastes are simple. Ever since I started singing, I've had the fear of making a lot of money and then ending up without any. I've seen it happen to too many others."

In terms of record sales, country music was booming—and moving into the middle class. The Armed Forces Radio Network announced that 65 percent of all records sold at military post exchanges were country music records. The number of radio stations playing country music was steadily increasing, and country music was visible in the national media. When the country records of 1968 were tallied up, Glen Campbell emerged as the top-selling artist, with Merle Haggard second and Eddy Arnold third. Clearly, there were two directions for country music: the smooth pop-type sound of Campbell and Arnold, and the traditional honky-tonk sound of Merle Haggard.

At the end of May, the presidential race heated up, two months after President Johnson announced he would not seek reelection. A number of Nashville country artists endorsed third party candidate

George Wallace, although Arnold preferred Richard Nixon in the November elections. Arnold never really considered endorsing Robert Kennedy, but he felt the tragedy of Kennedy's assassination in a personal way; on the day Kennedy died, Arnold gave a concert in Portland, Oregon, and the air was heavy with grief.

As a businessman, Arnold was spokesman and representative for Mary Carter Paints during the year. Also, he was chairman of the board for the newly formed Tennessee Fried Chicken, Inc. Fried chicken franchises had been popular in Nashville; entrepreneurs Jack Massey and John Jay Hooker had made fortunes with fried chicken enterprises from their Nashville base.

At the end of the year, Arnold told a reporter with the *Charlotte Observer*, "My tastes are simple. Ever since I started singing, I've had the fear of making a lot of money and then ending up without any. I've seen it happen to too many others. So I live in a simple house, nothing elaborate. My car is several years old. I've gotten used to it like an old pair of shoes."

Finally, just before Christmas, a reporter from *Music City News* asked Eddy Arnold what he wanted most for Christmas. He replied, "I wish someone would turn up my first guitar, the one I started strumming with 20-odd years ago in Tennessee. My mother bought it for me, and it's how it all began."

26

A Conservative in a Liberal Era

T he last year of the sixties was the year of country music on television. *The Johnny Cash Show* and *Hee Haw* debuted while *The Glen Campbell Show* continued its successful run. Eddy Arnold served as host on the *Kraft Music Hall*, and by the end of the year, Eddy Arnold had appeared on a total of eleven *Kraft Music Hall* shows, a summer *Kraft Music Hall* series titled "County Fair," and a *Kraft Christmas* Special.

The popularity of country music on TV inspired Mary Ann Lee of the *Memphis Press-Scimitar* to note,

> Once regarded as somewhere beyond the range of the TV screen, the popularity of music with a country twang has been slowly building over the years—a song here, a special there, Eddy Arnold as host of some "Kraft Music Hall Specials" plus the success of "The Glen Campbell Show"—and this summer the trend is in full swing.

Financially, it was a good time for Eddy Arnold; a column by Walter Winchell announced that he earned about $300 a minute on stage or about $22,500 for a seventy-five-minute concert. During a thirty-city tour that year, he grossed approximately $750,000, and a subsequent nineteen-date tour grossed $574,655 with attendance of 171,253 for a personal take of $342,670.

The year before he had turned fifty and found himself at the top of both the country and the pop worlds as a superstar. He enjoyed his success more the second time around and continued to receive rave reviews. Fred Cicetti of the *Newark Sunday News* found Arnold to be an exception in the entertainment world:

> The man is candid in a trade that thrives on sham. His attitude toward his fortune is especially refreshing. He's not ashamed to reveal his pride in his ability to accumulate comforts and security for himself, his wife, and two children. . . . Eddy Arnold's decades in show business and years in corporate board rooms have made him cautious. Routine questions are pondered. His responses are delivered carefully. Inquiries he would rather not answer are simply not answered; he smiles warmly and stares interminably. The wordless message is clear: "I don't want to have any embarrassment here. I don't want to refuse you, but the truth is a private thing and I'm not going to give you the baloney. Go on to another question, please."

> ➤ *The man is candid in a trade that thrives on sham.*

He loved performing and told Harold Stern of the Inter-Press Feature Syndicate, "Personal appearances and concerts allow me to come into contact with the people and that stimulates me. Knowing there are live bodies out there inspires me. I like to see the whites in their eyes, to feel their reactions."

For the *Memphis Statesman*, Bruce Ebert wrote,

> Mr. Arnold said his personal pride caused him to change his style of singing. "I felt that my kind of thing should appeal to the general public, not just to a specific minority. I realized that if my singing was to earn the respect I wanted it to, I had to smoothen it. I wanted to present a more polished sound. So, I added the violins and the orchestral accompaniment." He continued that "I'm happy that I'm now regarded as Eddy Arnold the performer, not just Eddy Arnold the country singer. I once performed strictly in the West and the South. Today, I can perform all over the country, including the colleges. This change in style has afforded me the opportunity to do many things I could not have otherwise done, such as appear on national TV and in cities outside the South."

In terms of losing the traditional country fans, Arnold remarked, "I'm sorry about this, however, for every fan I lose because of that, I find I have gained three. Those down home people are the most avid of all music fans. They stay with you and love you."

As for future ambitions, he admitted that "I wouldn't mind doing a good movie with a good part that I could fit into comfortably. That would offer me a challenge. But that's about the only thing I haven't had a chance to do."

Country music had come a long way in the twenty-five years since the ending of World War II, and some explanations were offered. "I think the writers deserve a great deal of credit for this," said Arnold, discussing the appeal of country music.

> Country songs are now more tasteful than they once
> were. Time was when every country song was about some
> catastrophe—mother dying, poverty or something like
> that. Today, they're written about love. . . . Because peo-
> ple like the simplicity of the country song combined with
> the smoothness of the ballad, I believe country music will
> continue to be the accepted thing.

As for the popularity of the Nashville Sound, he observed,

> It seemed like the right time for this kind of thing to hap-
> pen. Country music got a little more dignified. It got more
> exposure on TV and radio. I think the whole movement is
> responsible for it. I know I started to change my back-
> ground, adding softer guitars, violins, more of a pop
> music feel to give me wider appeal. . . . Many of the other
> boys started getting national exposure, national accep-
> tance. Now in every major metropolitan city is a radio
> station devoting itself entirely to the modern concept of
> country music. The radio stations got rid of the "hay-
> seed" disc jockeys, the ones that said, "Hello, by cracky,
> my grandma sent me a cake." They have given country
> music some dignity, started to respect it. The only way
> for the public to respect it is for it to respect itself.

In 1969, Eddy Arnold returned to Las Vegas, where he had not appeared since 1954. The terms were appealing: a $1 million long-term contract by the soon-to-be-finished International Hotel. The deal meant that Arnold would headline at the International four weeks a year for the next five years. It would mark the beginning of an era when he became a top nightclub performer in Las Vegas in addition to being a top concert draw throughout the nation.

In July and August, Arnold was at the Las Vegas International; at the end of August, at the Sahara in Lake Tahoe; and at the end of September, at the Nugget in Reno. He conquered the world of Nevada clubs in short order; still, a reviewer couldn't resist making a few digs at Eddy Arnold and country music in the high-rolling world of the clubs. Rick Pavlik reviewed one of his shows at the Circus Room of the Nugget Casino in Sparks:

> Arnold is as American as Mom, apple pie, the flag and the Washington Monument. He's the prototype of Mr. Straight and the people love him—at least the country-western, middle America, silent majority hardhat, cow country types do. The audience . . . was made up primarily of these types, and they loved every minute of the Tennessee Plow Boy's hour on stage. He sings 24 songs, spins some cracker barrel stories about the folks back home, and drawls a few risque jokes that add spice to the evening's dialogue—not much, but just enough to let you know he's kind of earthy and just a "real folks" type. . . . Arnold is good. He's a charmer with a good personality and all this folksy charisma certainly helps. But, best of all he's a singer and as good a country-western type as I've ever heard.

Along the way Arnold had developed a tried-and-true method that prepared him for his shows, which involved an intense rehearsal before each show. He told Joan Smith,

> I always go to rehearsal. If I go, I can get along with the stage hands and sound people. I can get more out of them than anybody else just by looking them in the eye, shaking hands, and saying "thank you." I always go meet them; I don't want them to come to me. I go up and say, "I'm Eddy Arnold, how are you." . . . I'm a live kind of a person and I like to communicate with an audience. I work a lot with a hand mike . . . it makes me feel closer to people. I work the whole stage. I perform for every audience as though it were a challenge, and I'm trying to sell 'em something—trying to sell 'em me. I want them to leave liking me. . . . I need it; I love bein' loved.

Eddy Arnold and Louis Armstrong with Mike Douglas.

By 1969, he had developed his method of performing. He would come to town and spend the afternoon rehearsing his show with local musicians hired for that evening. He always brought along a guitar player, Jim Lance. In Ellsworth, Maine, a reporter watched the rehearsal and reported that at 3:00 P.M., "wearing a trimly cut suit and a bright yellow turtleneck," he appeared for the rehearsal:

> On stage he was all amiability and ease. He raced through the layout of his show with the light heart and confidence of a professional who knows his work. The skips and double-timed spins, which might have passed for extemporaneous clowning, were actually a fast run-through of every well-practiced movement that accompanies his performance. He seemed to take himself, the band, and the program very casually, like a businessman who is perfectly familiar with his stock in trade. He

smiled when he gave the band instructions, and he
joked when he told a man at the amplifier where to
pitch the volume, but he made his points very clear and
he didn't waste a word. Whatever he said and did, it
was always with the same good-humored ease. On stage
he offers a smooth parody of the classic country boy, but
in person he is quiet, sincere and unpretentious. He is
perhaps the most courteous individual in the entertainment business.

When the reporter asked him what he thought about while
singing, Arnold replied,

Mostly the thought running through my mind is whether
the people out there like what I'm doing. Am I getting to
them is evermost in my mind. I always wonder if they
like me, if they like what I'm singing, if they're pleased.
I'm always concerned with their reaction to me. As far as
my own feelings go, it's been years since I had stage
fright. I did once, but I'm relaxed now.

He admitted that "when I'm not rehearsing or giving a show, I'm
usually in my hotel room. I'm very seldom any place where there's
anything I really want to see," although he did admit that the previous summer, while appearing at the Illinois State Fair, "I made a visit
to Lincoln's house and his tomb. I enjoyed seeing them. The state
police gave me an escort there." He added,

It's not easy for me to sight-see. People recognize me. No,
there aren't mob scenes, but I always end up signing
autographs. I don't get to see much. If I stop to read a
sign, all of a sudden a little lady is tugging at my arm saying "My daughter will kill me if I don't get your autograph!" Then I turn a corner and someone is pulling on
my other arm and asking for another autograph and then I
spend the whole afternoon saying "Yes ma'm. Thank you,
ma'm. You're welcome, ma'm. All right, ma'm." And I
don't see anything.

When Arnold made his New York nightclub debut at the
Waldorf, he received $10,000 a week to perform. Of Arnold's perfor-
mance, Ray Knight wrote,

Even for a staunch country music non-fan like me, Eddy
is a pleasure to hear. He can and does sing "Hello Dolly"
and other citified ditties without the use of his nose. And
he has such a good voice that his country songs, also
non-nasal, are easy for anybody to take—especially
backed by a 22-piece orchestra.

A review of the New York show in the Hackensack, New Jersey,
paper by Dan Lewis began:

Call me a silo sophisticate or a hoe-down snob if you
choose, but the truth of the matter is that I enjoy listening
to Eddy Arnold immensely. That's why I could even condition myself to sit through the ya hoos who frequently
and incongruously pierced the elegant Empire Room at
the prestigious Waldorf-Astoria Hotel Monday night
when the old Tennessee plowboy created some sort of
history by ascending its stage and singing country-western, hoe-down and clippity-clop music before a black-tie
audience. . . . In the main, the simplicity of his performance added to the beauty of the songs and made for a
worthwhile evening. Most of it was also warmly—in fact
enthusiastically—received at the Empire Room, although
I'm sure curiosity created as much of the interest as anything else. People wanted to know just how well a country-western singer could do.

Reviewer Jerry Parker offered this opinion: "Arnold was not
awed by the big city surroundings. He may be country, but he's no
bumpkin. 'I played the Coconut Grove in Los Angeles and I sang at
Carnegie Hall twice,' he said, 'and that ain't exactly Flatbush, you
know.' Parker observed that he "bristled when someone commented
on his urbane appearance. 'I'm from the modern school of country
boys,' he said. 'Don't you go trying to put boots on me! I'm not a cowboy. The only time you'll see me in a fancy shirt or boots is at a rodeo,
when everybody is wearing them.' "

As the sixties came to a close, many viewed the country in a complicated, complex maze. Antiwar protests were rampant on college
campuses while President Nixon announced a Vietnamization plan
for the withdrawal of American troops from that country. Former
President Dwight Eisenhower had died that March, and in July, Neil

Eddy Arnold the businessman in his office.

Armstrong walked on the moon. It was the summer of Woodstock and
the autumn of the largest antiwar rally in Washington, D.C., when
250,000 protest marchers descended on the capital.

It was the heyday of the counterculture, which had books such
as *The Making of a Counter Culture* by Theodore Roszak and *Do It*
by yippies founder Jerry Rubin. The voices of the counterculture
were answered by Vice President Spiro Agnew who called war pro-
testers "anarchists and ideological eunuchs" and the national press
"an effete corps of impudent snobs who characterize themselves as
intellectuals." He called journalists "nattering nabobs of negativism"
and then called for "a cry of alarm to penetrate the cacophony of
seditious drivel."

But though the world seemed a complex maze for young people in search of themselves while wearing illegal smiles, for Eddy Arnold it was a simple time, a time to stick to the basics of hard work, honesty, respecting others, patriotism, and self-responsibility. Love songs are timeless, so he sang them. And he believed strongly and deeply that people should be polite, decent, and loyal. Yes, there might be problems, but the problems are solved best within the system—not by trying to tear the system down.

> ➤ *Many of those Americans liked Eddy Arnold's old-fashioned values, enjoyed his relaxed performances in the midst of the cultural upheaval, and agreed that romance and love songs were timeless.*

Eddy Arnold stood opposite the sixties counterculture, but he stood right in the middle of American values. In an era often characterized as anti-business and anti-establishment, Arnold was a marked contrast.

Arnold's ideas and views might have been out of step with the counterculture during its heyday, but they were firmly in step with many Americans who found the whole counterculture to be an example of how *not* to fix America's problems. Many of those Americans liked Eddy Arnold's old-fashioned values, enjoyed his relaxed performances in the midst of the cultural upheaval, and agreed that romance and love songs were timeless. In many ways, Eddy Arnold was an anchor for a culture adrift, a rock in a sea of change, and his audience responded by clinging to him.

Nineteen seventy began as just another year in the sixties. Nothing much changed really, except the year started with a seven instead of a six. In 1970, Richard Nixon gave a speech where he first used the term *the silent majority* to describe most Americans. That seemed to sum up those not in the news who comprised the bulk of the population.

Some newspaper writers realized country music was the musical voice of the silent majority. In her column, "Prime Time" in *Cocoa (Florida) Today* in January 1970, Margot Reis-El Bara wrote,

One of the reasons for the nationwide growing popularity
of country music may be the songs themselves. In an age
that is so fraught with problems and complicated technology, country music simply tells a story. The music is
down to earth, putting in the simplest words imaginable
the problems of domestic life or the nostalgia for the freedom of a less hectic era. The tunes and verses, with a simple guitar beat, are neither complicated nor unfamiliar.

Country music was certainly getting respect. The column "On
the Scene" by Mike Jahn summed it up:

Right now country and western ranks second only to rock
as the most-widely-heard form of American music. Its
geographic boundaries encompass virtually the whole
country. Country stations are heard in most big cities—
including New York. In Los Angeles it is almost impossi-
ble to watch evening television without turning on a
country show. The Apollo 12 astronauts had country
music piped up to them on the moon. Network television
carries a respectable amount of it. . . . Country music is
unpretentious, uncomplicated, easily sung and it makes
you feel good.

Times had certainly changed for country music. Arnold told
Roger Doughty of the *Miami News*,

When I first started in the business, you couldn't get a
country record played on a big city radio station outside
the South no matter what you did. If you were lucky you
might find a station where the morning man would play a
couple around 6 A.M., but that was it. Now you can't turn
a radio on without hearing Johnny Cash or Bob Dylan or
even groups like Crosby, Stills, Nash and Young doing the
same kind of music we couldn't get on the air. I always
felt our kind of music would be in the mainstream someday, but I was considered to be something of a radical by
my contemporaries. They thought I was too pop and not
enough country.

At the end of the year, in an interview with LaVelle Alexander,
Arnold stated,

You almost have to be reborn once in a while in this business. The best years of my career have come since then. . . . I had to be able to reach more people. I wanted my songs to appeal to middle-America. I knew I would lose some of the country fans. I was willing to take that chance and I've been well rewarded for it.

27

Tragedy Strikes

On August 1, 1971, Eddy and Sally Arnold were on their boat on Old Hickory Lake with their friends, Frances and E. J. Preston. It had been a nice, relaxed day, far away from crowds and telephones. But when they arrived back at the club where they docked their yacht, there was an emergency phone call: there had been a horrible accident.

Dick Arnold had just graduated from the University of Alabama with a degree in broadcasting and journalism. He had come home for the weekend and then, with a Sigma Alpha Epsilon fraternity brother, headed back to school to pick up some belongings at his apartment. Dick was tired and let the friend drive his little red sports car. In Bessemer, Alabama, a car pulled out and hit them, smashing the sports car. An ambulance rushed Dick to the Lloyd Nolan Hospital in Fairfield, just outside Birmingham, where he lay unconscious.

A plane was chartered for Eddy, Sally, and their daughter to take them to Birmingham; they arrived at midnight. Arnold wanted to cancel his personal appearances but was persuaded to fulfill his obligations, and he did so. But from October to the following February, Eddy Arnold did not perform, spending that time at home with Dick.

Dick stayed in a coma for nine and a half weeks. During that time, his parents were with him at the hospital; they played some of Eddy Arnold's records, and the TV in the room showed some Eddy Arnold performances. Finally, he regained consciousness and said his first word, "Sally." The Arnolds took him home to Nashville where he began his long road to recovery.

The accident devastated Eddy Arnold, but he was determined to help his son any and every way possible. For months he lifted Dick out of bed and bathed him. He purchased a metal walkway with rails and helped Dick stand there and try to make his way to the other end. At first it was just a shuffle; gradually, Dick's steps returned. The accident had bruised Dick's brain, and he had to relearn a number of things. Throughout the whole ordeal, Eddy Arnold stood with his son, helping him, encouraging him. It was the greatest test of fatherhood a man could ever face, and Eddy Arnold met the challenge.

➤ *When your son has been hurt badly, things like a recording career, hit records, and personal appearances fade in importance.*

When your son has been hurt badly, things like a recording career, hit records, and personal appearances fade in importance. Although Arnold continued to make selective personal appearances, TV appearances, and recordings, he did not have a single record reach the top ten in country music during the entire decade of the 1970s.

He had been slowing down for a while, tired of the one-nighters and a schedule that had him flying into a city, rehearsing all afternoon, then performing a concert at night. Having to meet the obligations of a performer on the road—doing the "meet and greets" backstage, talking with the media, staying up and friendly for everybody, giving everyone a little piece of himself, giving up his privacy to sign autographs, posing for pictures, and shaking hands and chatting with whoever showed up—took much of his energy.

He had always preferred a quiet lifestyle off the road. He told one reporter that he lived "a very frugal life, just like anyone in the middle income bracket." In answer to a question about whether he played music in his home, he said, "I don't perform at home. We have a piano and we all enjoy music. We put on records or tapes and if we have friends in and someone wants to play the piano and sing a song, that's great; but it's never something we plan, always something that happens spontaneously. I guess that's how I live my whole life." Sally admitted she liked to listen to Andy Williams, Perry Como, and Bing Crosby.

Arnold liked entertaining at home. "I love to have my friends in," he told a reporter. "We tell a few corny stories and have a couple of laughs." Arnold especially enjoyed grilling steaks for his guests.

He had a good marriage. He said, "I think a marriage, to be successful, must have its bad times and good times. There just have to be differences, but above all a couple has to really know each other well, all of the time." He enjoyed his family and commented to a reporter, "We've kept our kids out of the show-business limelight. They don't even listen to my music, and they don't know many of our show-business friends. I did not take them with me when I traveled."

"On holidays," he stated, "we have a big turkey. My wife, Sally, loves to cook the dinner. It's really our family day." Sally noted, "Our children planned our holiday dinner years ago and we always have the same menu for both Christmas and Thanksgiving. We have roast turkey, dressing, giblet gravy, ham, string beans, creamed potatoes, candied sweet potatoes, congealed salad, hot rolls and about four kinds of dessert." She added that "coconut cream pie is Eddy's favorite dessert."

Arnold added, "Our holidays are spent with just the immediate family and a few close friends. I'm a very private person. When I'm home, I'm a husband and a father. I don't like going out to night clubs or big parties. If you invite me to a party where you're going to have 200 or 300 people, I will say, 'Thank you very much but I won't be there.' People pull or drag on me if I'm at something like that, especially when everybody's in the music business. Many of my closest friends are not in the music business, and do you know something, I never hear them talk about business when we go out socially."

He still played golf occasionally but admitted, "I really don't play enough golf to consistently break 100. . . . I like golf. . . . But I kinda let my game go a couple of years back when I discovered boating. Now I'm really hooked on boating." At that time he owned a thirty-four-foot Hatteras that could sleep six with a pair of 290-horsepower Chrysler marine engines.

With one reporter he enthusiastically discussed life on the lake:

> Those Tennessee Valley Authority lakes are the greatest
> in the world. They provide the most pleasant boating
> you'd ever want to find. I can't tell you how great it is to
> stay out for days. Why, once three of us took our boats
> from Old Hickory Lake in Tennessee right on through
> four other lakes all the way into Barkley Lake in Kentucky. That was about 150 miles. It's really something
> tricky to maneuver those boats through dams and locks.
> We were out 12 days.

Eddy Arnold performing.

Earlier in 1971, Arnold had closed his fried chicken operation; he attributed the failure to the high overhead cost the company incurred: they "were competing with the Kentucky Colonel, but we went about it wrong. First off, we built very elaborate buildings. I figure we spent 60 percent more on each building than the Colonel does. We went bust pretty quick." But, he noted, "I want you to know we paid all our creditors and abolished the corporation. Nobody except the four original investors ever lost any money, and we lost that in stock. I lost about $150,000. I know I shouldn't complain because I can afford it, and I'm gettin' it back in dribs and drabs as a tax write-off. But, oh, my how I hate to lose money. I was a Depression child. I never will forget bein' hungry and I'm very frugal."

Early in 1971, he returned to Las Vegas at the Sahara; in the seventies, he concentrated on appearances in Nevada, generally two-week stands three times a year at Harrah's in Lake Tahoe and Reno.

Even though he worked less, he still had the same work ethic he always carried, as reported by John F. Steadman in the *Baltimore News American*:

> The formula is still hard work. If he's at a party with
> friends, it's not that he's anti-social, but Eddy excuses
> himself before the hour grows late and makes sure he's
> going to get a full night of rest. This afternoon, he'll
> rehearse four hours. . . . Later in the day, he'll order a cup
> of soup from room service and take a nap before the
> show. [He has] impeccable attention to detail, to his
> appearance and, of course, the material he sings. The last
> thing he puts on are his trousers in the dressing room
> because when it's time to go out and sing for the people
> he doesn't want his pants to be a maze of wrinkles.

In March 1972, Arnold appeared at the Circle Star Theater in San Carlos, California, with the Mike Curb Congregation. Curb was a music business wunderkind. He was the twenty-seven-year-old leader of his vocal group, which had a pop hit with "Burning Bridges" from the movie *Kelly's Heroes* in 1970, and he had been president of MGM Records since 1969. He and Arnold hit it off, and at the end of the year, Arnold left RCA after more than twenty-five years with the label and signed with MGM.

The decision to leave RCA was difficult; Eddy Arnold is a loyal man who sticks by old friends and associations. But things had

changed a great deal at RCA Victor since he had first signed in 1944.
Chet Atkins, who had produced Arnold's 1960s hits, was tired of the
corporate routine and wanted to just be a guitar player; in December
1973, he would step down as head of the label, and Jerry Bradley, son
of Owen, would take over as label chief. Atkins had been producing
a large number of acts and could not give Eddy Arnold as much attention as the singer needed, so Arnold sought some fresh input and
began to work with new producers.

Both Arnold and Atkins owed a lot of their success to Steve
Sholes. In the summer of 1957, Sholes was named head of RCA's pop
division and moved to Los Angeles. Sholes would no longer be Eddy
Arnold's producer, and Chet Atkins would have additional power in
RCA's country division and would take over production chores for
Arnold's recordings. Arnold had enjoyed working with Sholes and was
reluctant to take on a new producer, but gradually, Arnold and Atkins
developed a good working relationship, culminating in the series of
hits in the sixties. But that was changing in 1972, so the idea of going
to MGM to work with Mike Curb seemed appealing to Arnold.

While at MGM he rerecorded some of his old hits and released
nine singles that charted. At the end of 1975 his contract was up, and
Curb was no longer head of the label, so Arnold returned to RCA.

Some major changes were afoot in Nashville in the early 1970s.
In 1971, the first Country Music Fan Fair was held, attracting ten
thousand fans, and the National Life and Accident Insurance Company broke ground on a theme park to be called Opryland.

At the end of May 1972, Arnold did a one-week stand at the
Shady Grove Music Fair in Rockville, Maryland. By that time Dick
was recovering well and told his dad he wanted a dog—and he
wanted it to be a bulldog. Arnold found a bullmastiff advertised in
the newspaper and went out to the owner's home to see it; he
arranged to buy it and have it sent to his home. Dick named the dog
Hoss, after the character on *Bonanza*, and the two became great
friends. Unfortunately, after about seven months, the dog wandered
out on the highway and was hit by a car. Both Dick and his father
were devastated; Arnold wanted to buy another dog, but Dick wasn't
interested. Finally, Eddy bought another bullmastiff from the same
parents, and Dick named it Big Ed. Arnold then fenced in about an
acre for the dog to run in. It was a good dog—but it wasn't Hoss. Still,
it helped Dick in his recovery.

He continued to play in Nevada. In an appearance in Las Vegas
in 1977, he proved he had not lost his touch with an audience.

According to the reviewer, "Arnold epitomizes the country boy who can reach the most sophisticated cabaret audience by his simple, honest delivery. No gimmicks or stage tricks for this man—he sings 'em straight and there's something about his open-faced look that just makes you a believer."

Toward the end of 1972, he talked openly about retiring. "I've talked to my wife, my son and my daughter," he told a reporter.

> ➤ *I can't say that I have ever been disappointed in this business. Tired maybe, sometimes disillusioned, a lot of things, but disappointed. I don't think so.*

And I've told them, in a general way, that I'm thinking about it. I don't know when, but I'm not gonna keep singing all my life. A man needs to start thinking about what he'll do when he retires, how he'll keep involved in life. I'm involved in a little real estate, and I have a boat that I just love, and I think I could be happy retired. It's just that the thought keeps coming up in my mind more than it used to . . . but I don't know yet.

In a reflective mood he commented to writer Peggy Russell,

I suppose that I'm the type of guy who appeals to the average person, country or non-country. Sort of middle-America, bread-and-butter kind of guy. I would like to think that I was wise enough to see several years ago that there was an added market there for me if I wanted to reach for it. At that point my records were selling to a minority of people, what we call hard-country buyers who like that type of music and that alone. I like that kind of music but I also knew I liked a little more modern song and a little more modern arrangement, and I wanted to do that. . . . That's the way I feel about music, all fields of it, whether it's rock, country, pop or what. I just know what I like. I can listen to the Carpenters for hours and I like Kenny Rogers.

When asked if he had any disappointments during his career, he answered, "Disappointments. I really don't know . . . disappointments come in personal lives. I can't say that I have ever been disappointed in this business. Tired maybe, sometimes disillusioned, a lot of things, but disappointed. I don't think so. It's a great life. I've been very fortunate."

Also at the end of 1972, he talked about his son to a reporter, stating that Dick "should be back in shape in about another year." He said that he called his son every night he was away and that "people have asked me about 100 times in the past few years what my goal is. Well, I tell 'em my goal is to get my son well and back in the main-stream!"

28

The Outlaws Arrive

During the early 1970s, some of country music's pioneers passed from the scene. In 1972, Elton Britt, whose hit "There's a Star Spangled Banner Waving Somewhere" defined country music in World War II, died. In 1973, *Opry* comedian Stringbean and his wife were murdered. In 1974, Tex Ritter and Nelson King (a disk jockey from 1946 to 1970) died. King was one of the founders of the Country and Western Disc Jockeys Association back in 1953. In 1975, promoter Oscar Davis, comedian Clell Sumney (Cousin Jody), artists George Morgan and Lefty Frizzell, and Audrey Williams, wife of Hank Williams, passed away.

In 1975, Ernest Tubb handed over his *Midnight Jamboree* to his son Justin, and the Music Row area got new names for streets. Formerly known as Sixteenth and Seventeenth Avenues, they became known as Music Square West and East.

Out in Branson, Missouri, a small group known as the Baldknobbers Band opened the Hillbilly Jamboree Theater in 1973. Nobody in Nashville noticed, but that would mark the beginning of Branson as a major tourist attraction for live country music shows.

In the spring of 1974, President Richard Nixon came to Nashville to inaugurate the opening of the new Opry House at the Opryland Theme Park while the last *Opry* performance at the Ryman was held, marking the end of an era.

By the early 1970s, it was difficult to find the traditional, hard core country music sound. The countrypolitan sound pioneered by Eddy Arnold seemed to have won the day; in 1973, Roy Clark won CMA's Entertainer of the Year, and in 1974, Charlie Rich won the honor.

By 1975, country music had reached the limits of the country-politan sound. That was the year John Denver won the CMA's Entertainer of the Year award, and "Back Home Again" by Denver won Song of the Year honors. Charlie Rich, the previous year's Entertainer of the Year winner, showed his displeasure by opening the card that announced Denver's selection, then setting the card on fire in front of the television audience. The previous year Olivia Newton-John had won CMA's Female Vocalist of the Year award.

> *The outlaw movement effectively ended the era of the Nashville Sound.*

A major national recession occurred in 1975 from the oil embargo, which resulted in a vinyl shortage and a cutting back in the number of records pressed. It also led to the decrease in the older, or catalog, recordings. For an artist like Eddy Arnold, whose catalog of recordings continued to sell, that hurt.

In 1976, the outlaw movement brought a whole new group of young fans to country music. Along the way, the outlaw movement effectively ended the era of the Nashville Sound. The outlaw movement represented a rebellion of artists against the Nashville system of producers and session musicians being in control of the music. Leading the outlaw movement were Waylon Jennings and Willie Nelson, two longtime Nashville recording artists who achieved a degree of success in Nashville, but also felt thwarted in the efforts to expand their artistic visions.

In the early 1970s, the producers held the power over the music; they generally picked the songs—or approved them—and they chose the studios and musicians. The system was developed in part because artists had to spend so much time on the road performing. Since artists had to incur such a large overhead—transportation, equipment, an office, travel expenses—to maintain a career and keep a cash flow, they were not in town much to look for songs. Their bands were chosen to accompany them on tour; they had to play the same songs over and over again. Often the road musicians joined in hopes of becoming studio musicians, but were then thwarted in their attempts because they weren't in town enough to do sessions and couldn't expand their musical talents through challenges in the studio to play a wide variety of music and sounds, and because the A team of studio musicians jealously guarded their privileged positions. Also, producers generally had to work with a number of artists, and they liked the idea of forming a team of musicians who worked well together and understood each producer's needs and could meet those needs quickly and effectively. The idea of bringing in a group of untried and untested studio musicians they didn't know—and whose allegiance was to the artist—was not something they wanted to do.

The producer's actions were justified to an extent. Some road musicians could not perform well in the studio. Playing in a studio is much different from playing live; musicians must learn a song quickly—often a song they've never heard before—develop a new and exciting instrumental lick to fit the song, often on the spot, remain in a relaxed, friendly mood, and get it all done under intense pressure within three hours.

On the other hand, some artists—especially those who wrote their own songs—could work out their songs while on the road with their musicians. And artists who had been with their group for a long period often felt more comfortable with those musicians than with a group of virtual strangers they saw only for recording sessions.

In many ways it was a power struggle; on one side were the producers and executives, and on the other were the artists. By the mid-1970s, many of the artists were merely singers. The actual artists were the producers, who found songs, developed musical styles, and had a vision for where the music should go.

Waylon Jennings and Willie Nelson were different. First, both wrote a number of their own songs; next, they had bands that had been with them for a long time; and finally, the Nashville system just wasn't working that well for them. They had spent years on the road in front of crowds and they knew what the crowds wanted—and it wasn't the Nashville Sound anymore.

It is significant that Waylon and Willie came from Texas and both performed a lot of shows in that state. There is a significant difference in the audience for country music in the two states because Texans danced while people in Tennessee, particularly Nashville, didn't. Nashville has long been known as the buckle of the Bible Belt, or the Protestant Vatican. It is the home of the Southern Baptist headquarters and numerous churches and religious schools. For most of the people in the southern religious community, dancing was sinful. So the music that came out of Nashville tended to be music you sat and listened to; the music for Texas was music you could dance to.

There were other factors as well. The dream of joining the establishment and being respected in the middle class—which was once part of the dream of the country music community—was thrown out

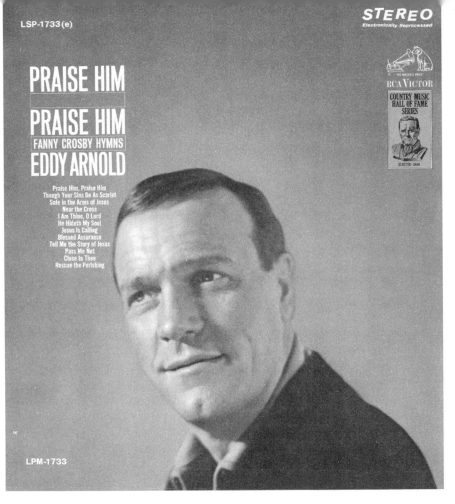

the window in the early seventies. The sixties counterculture turned a lot of that on its head. Although the South was slower than the East and West Coasts to have the movement hit home, it did by the 1970s. The long-haired look came to town, and laissez-faire individualism came into full bloom.

Ironically, Waylon and Willie had been part of the Nashville establishment for years. They knew the system, and they knew the rules when they began their revolution of producing their own recordings. The other part of the revolution was drugs. No longer were the artists content to sip martinis for relaxation; no longer was liquor the drug of choice. Liquor is a depressant and renders you incapable of making decisions; marijuana and speed are stimulants and put you in action. The change in the method of escape would have a profound effect on the way Nashville did business.

Of course, along with the drugs and changes in the cultural landscape came an antiauthoritarian attitude. Ever since Vietnam, people who were given orders demanded to know why and, if the answer wasn't satisfactory, chose not to follow the order. All of that bled over into other parts of society. People in charge had to "earn" respect; there was no more following orders "because I said so." Rank still had privileges, but it also had obligations. And those in charge could no longer expect their decisions to be carried out by those below; those below had ideas of their own.

> *If Eddy Arnold has ever been the subject of criticism, and you've got to look awfully hard to find any, it has usually centered on the fact that he doesn't look like a country singer.*

And so the outlaw movement ushered in the next phase of the country music business, a phase that returned the musical decisions to the artists. The Nashville Sound was not dead; studio musicians still worked on the bulk of the albums from Nashville, as well as advertising commercials, gospel product (Nashville became the center for contemporary Christian music and southern gospel), and other projects. The idea that country music had to be smooth and pop-oriented to achieve respect and success in the middle class went out the window as well. The outlaw movement featured a sound with rough edges, more raw with a heavy beat, and no aspirations toward middle-class respectability. The very term *outlaw* made that plain.

The outlaw movement changed country music because it brought in young people and baby boomers who had previously shunned country music. No longer was the country music audience representative of the World War II generation; now the Vietnam generation was in the audience as well. Instead of driving cars with bumper stickers saying "America: Love it or leave it," country fans could be found driving pickup trucks with bumper stickers saying "Question authority."

With the rise of the outlaws, country music let its hair grow long, and it got a new attitude. It was essentially the rock 'n' roll attitude of rebellion and doing your own thing, and it attracted the Vietnam generation like no other movement in country music had done before.

Eddy Arnold returned to RCA in 1976, and his first release there, "Cowboy," rose to number thirteen—his best showing since 1969. He continued to have chart singles throughout the 1970s for RCA, but none hit really big.

Although Arnold was not an outlaw in country music by any stretch of the imagination, he applauded their success:

> Those guys aren't doing anything except making records with a little heavier beat and singing some pretty good songs. . . . Guys like Willie and Waylon are doing a fine job. Heck, I've known Waylon for years, and those guys aren't doing anything but helping this business. Maybe their lifestyle is something else—letting their hair grow long, skipping a couple of baths and puffing that stuff—but their music is fine.

Arnold continued to appear in Nevada. In 1976, he appeared at the Sahara Hotel in Las Vegas, and at Harrah's in Lake Tahoe and Reno. After one of his Las Vegas appearances in 1977, the reviewer stated, "Arnold epitomizes the country boy who can reach the most sophisticated cabaret audience by his simple, honest delivery. No gimmicks or stage tricks for this man—he sings 'em straight and there's something about his open-faced look that just makes you a believer."

Then in 1979, he announced he was going to resume his recording career. The effort paid off; in 1980, he had two top ten records, "Let's Get It While the Gettin's Good" and "That's What I Get for Loving You." With those two songs, Eddy Arnold achieved the distinction of having a chart record in five decades: forties, fifties, sixties, seventies, and eighties. And he continued to have chart records throughout the 1980s, although he failed to have a big single.

In an interview Arnold said he wanted to resume his recording career "because I'm an ambitious person and an egotist, too. There's nothing wrong with ego. I think we all want to feel productive. Actually, I guess I've just decided to outlive the tax man."

The decision to resume his career came about for several reasons. First, his son Dick had made a remarkable recovery from his automobile accident, although he still walked with a limp. In 1978, Dick got a job in Nashville and moved out of the Arnold home into an apartment. Next, Arnold wanted to have a chart record in the eighties, which would mean he had been on the country charts for several decades. It was a long time to be an active force in the country music business, and Arnold was both proud of and amazed by his continued success.

In terms of his longevity and business acumen, he stated, "It's no lark. I advise young people to get a good accountant, a good lawyer, a good manager and listen to them. Then, if you have a show to do, show up on time. I've never missed a show in my life and I've never been late. And I've never shown up any other way but sober."

Since he was going to concentrate on recording again, he knew he needed to look for material:

> I'm only as good as my songs, and I pick the best I can find from professional writers. I don't fool with amateur songs because they are never good. Lots of people think writing a song is a lark. They think all they have to do is make a few rhymes and they have a song, write to Eddy Arnold or somebody and he's going to make them a millionaire. All of them need to go to a music publisher. They need tutoring as a writer. They have to pay their dues. A writer of songs must have experience . . . he must have someone say, "This is lousy. Go back and write the third line." That is what the music publisher does. My producer and I listen to as many as 150 songs for an LP. Sometimes we have to rest and wait awhile because they all begin to sound alike. In some instances, we take as long as three weeks to find a song. We're not in a hurry.

In terms of finding songs, Arnold stated, "It boils down to my tastes. My producer also listens for me, and he listens very well for me. Then we both get together and listen together. It's a long process and sometimes it gets very boring just sitting and listening. Sometimes . . . you have to get up and walk away from it and give your ear a rest."

The commitment Arnold made to his recording career led him to concentrate on his recordings, some personal appearances, and generating publicity. The image of Eddy Arnold was pretty well set: he was known as a class act in country music.

Eddy Arnold may have been a country crooner wearing tuxedos, but he still got asked about cowboys. It was a logical question in 1980 when *Urban Cowboy*, a movie about a contemporary cowboy riding mechanical bulls in Houston appeared starring John Travolta, and cowboy mania swept America. Plus, Eddy Arnold's most famous song was "Cattle Call."

Still, Arnold set the record straight whenever the subject was broached:

I never tried to be a cowboy because I wasn't a cowboy. I
came from a rural area, and I knew country life. When you
dress like a cowboy, people ask all kinds of questions and
make all kinds of remarks. If you don't have on cowboy
clothes, you don't have to answer all those questions—
"Do you have a horse? Do you ride a horse?"

He admitted he grew up loving Gene Autry but didn't want to follow in those bootsteps:

I just really wasn't interested in being a cowboy. I liked
and admired the cowboys who sang, but I knew I wasn't
a cowboy and I knew cowboy songs per se normally
didn't become too popular. I always felt like if you were
going to be a cowboy, you had to sing cowboy songs
rather than love songs and even though we all love
"Tumbling Tumbleweeds"—it's great nostalgia—if you're
going to be an artist who sells records, you gotta sing
love songs.

29

The Performer

By the 1980s, Eddy Arnold had defined himself: he was a *performer*. It was a part of his life that he approached seriously in a businesslike manner. In 1983, Arnold told Dave Bittan with the *Philadelphia Daily News*, "My first love is still performing. I work because, like anybody else, I want to feel a sense of accomplishment. I want to create something. I don't want to sit on my laurels. I'm not going to retire. They may ask me to, and say 'Hey man, you've had enough.' "

Talking with reporter Jim Ruth in Hershey, Pennsylvania, Arnold said,

> Frankly, I wanted to become a performer. I was going along making records, singing and that kind of thing. What I really wanted to develop was the art of performing. I think that's what moved me. There are some people—and I was one of them—who made records but didn't spend a lot of time learnin' to communicate with the audience. There's a great difference between record artists and performers. I just got out there and started to put a lot of thought into it, building an act. I even took some dance lessons although I don't dance, just to loosen me up. I went into training. I don't stay quite as active as probably I should. I used to do a lot of TV but not anymore. The variety shows are gone. That's the biggest reason. I may be square but I always hesitated singin' about triangle love. I always preferred singin' about love between two people. I've noticed you can take any audience, let an old couple come up who've been married a

long time, and it'll always put a warm feelin' in the
hearts of people.

He told one reporter,

> *People write
> and ask me all
> kinds of
> questions. And I
> answer them. I
> acknowledge all
> the mail I get.*

I don't want to sound boastful, but I've
given an awful lot of thought to performing. Not just singing now, but performing.
I've always thought of it as a business. I
know that sounds very straight-laced and
square, but I do. And every day when I'm
not on the road I go to my office and I
answer all my mail. People write and ask
me all kinds of questions. And I answer
them. I acknowledge all the mail I get.
And another thing. I have never walked on stage drinking. Never given a drunken performance. Never missed a
show. I don't want to sound like I'm bragging about
myself, it's just the way I am about all my little businesses.

He told another reporter,

I'm still basically a country boy and always will be but
I became a performer instead of just a singer. . . .
I entertain. That's my style. That's my way of thinking. I just picked the route of pleasing people. If you
don't please them, you'll be out of the business. If I'm
going to sing for art's sake, I couldn't make a living. You
can't put art in the bank. I'm not ashamed of what I do
and make no apologies for it.

In the age-old debate of "art" versus "business" in the music business, Arnold was emphatic. Nancy Bigler Kersey of the *Cleveland
Plain Dealer* reported Arnold's position: "I'm not stupid. It's all profit
and loss. If you want to be an *artist* get a brush and start painting. I
want to make records that please the most people." And he told S.
Lovejoy of the *Phoenix Gazette*, "Whenever I have to listen to people
talk about strings in the background damaging the authenticity of my
music, I just say you can't put art in the bank. I had to make saleable
records or get out of the business."
Then he gave an example from 1955:

There was a disc jockey from Knoxville. . . . I mean this
was a country jock and I remember him saying, "I don't
like that there record; they got all of them bugles in
there." Well, I guess I was a little concerned at the time. It
was 1955 and what we did was do a remake of "Cattle
Call" using a big orchestra. Well, sir, that record went on
to sell a half-million copies, and I mean to tell you, that
was a lot of records back then. Well, when I saw what
was happening with the record, I stopped worrying. I just
cried all the way to the bank.

His attention to his performances paid off handsomely for him.
A concert review by Mel Shields began,

In a world of live entertainment where it is becoming
the norm to act as if an audience is assumed, where ego
seems the key word, where superstars consider it a priv-
ilege granted to showgoers even to appear, where audiences are insulted for not reacting vociferously, or for
being small, or for just being an audience (translate "little people")—in such a world it's nice to have Eddy
Arnold still with us. Arnold gives his audience an hour
of good, old-fashioned manners. His respect for those
paying to see him is almost tangible. He's a millionaire
many times over, but the ones who feel rich when he's
on stage are those listening. . . . Young entertainers
should be required to see him just to learn style. Parents
should take their children ("Awww, Mom—-who's he?")
just to learn that quiet grace is often as effective as
sound and sight attack.

The review by Gerald Nachmann of his Reno show appeared in
the *San Francisco Chronicle*:

Around here they eat up Eddy Arnold like 99-cent break-
fasts. . . . He quietly leads you into a land that's less bitter,
mean and mawkish than the one inhabited by the Tammy
Wynettes and Merle Haggards. Hearts break more gently,
and are more repairable, in Eddy Arnold country. . . . He
seems at first suspiciously pleasant, even pat, as set in his
unthreatening, law-abiding ways as the nasty outlaw
singers are in theirs. . . . He's as basic, direct and middle-
of-the-road as Gerald Ford. He ropes you in with his

warm, understated, understanding style, and darned if
you don't find you like it in there. . . . Country songs now
fill the sentiment void. They deal with complex emotions
bluntly stated (the lyrics aren't sophisticated, but the feelings are), with love, romance and lost and found hearts.
Eddy Arnold is all gently plucked heartstrings, with a
honey-coated twang.

Howard Rosenbert wrote in the *Hollywood Reporter*,

Eddy Arnold is a classy example of one of today's
handful of performers who dare risk a showroom
appearance sans the protection of the standard over-
charted, overamplified, prepackaged production.
Arnold is a singer, recognizes that's what he does best
and what the folks have come to hear and places his
major emphasis accordingly. His voice improves with
age, has become even smoother and more mellow,
washing over the room like cool spring water, not a
sharp edge anywhere, even when he finds it necessary
to gently rebuke a couple of talkers intent on horning in
from the audience. He paces a turn well, shrewdly
breaking the musical segments with some of the oldest,
corniest, most appallingly tacky, yet bitingly funny
jokes ever. With his altar boy twinkle, slow, measured
Southern Drawl and wickedly disarming delivery, both
he and his stories are just about irresistible.

> ➤ *"I lead a very quiet life. I'm even a little surprised when anybody wants to interview me. Because I don't really think I'm news."*

It was true that Eddy Arnold's voice
wasn't as strong as it used to be and he
couldn't hit the high notes like he used to
do. But as he noted to an interviewer, "I've
been around long enough I feel like I can do
whatever I want to do. There is an audience
there for it."

And, of course, he had to answer the
question about groupies who cast their aspirations upon him. The question made him feel
awkward, and he squirmed, then said,
"Awww gee. I'm not in such great demand.
Oh, I appreciate the thought, but honestly I
lead a very quiet life. I'm even a little sur-

prised when anybody wants to interview me. Because I don't really think I'm news." He admitted there had been some women who "try to take me off stage and take me home. But obviously I've tried to discourage it because I just want to perform. Besides, I know my body is no different from any other man's body."

30

The Personal Side

Eddy Arnold is proud of the fact that "I never beat my wife and I never went on stage drunk." While Eddy Arnold's personality and lifestyle might be considered more like the "ordinary" middle-class American than some others in the fast-paced world of show biz, this left him susceptible to the charge of being "boring" to those who like entertainers to have lifestyles of the wild and reckless. This may lead some to call him "boring," but that is an accusation he has always been willing to defend.

He noted, "Entertainers are nothing special. Maybe we have a talent for singing a song, but other people have talents. I wish fans would just come up and say 'hello,' before asking for an autograph. I wish they would just say, 'Hello, I'm so and so, and I just want to shake your hand.' I'm impressed when I find people like that. Most people just say, 'Sign here,' and treat you like a statue."

An article in the *Boston Globe* by Steve Morse quoted Arnold saying, "I'm a cornball, I don't know any better. That's why I stay so happy." The writer commented about

> the ageless, fit-looking crooner, who paved the way for Nashville pop by introducing violins and orchestral arrangement to country music during the 50s. . . . His inimitable soothing voice has lost a touch of its strength, but he continues to entrance his diehard listeners with a blend of unabashed sentimentality and boyish naivete.

Arnold told reporter John Fisher,

I'm not an exciting person. Sometimes I'm a little surprised that people even want to interview me, but anyway my strength has been all through the years the fact that I can make an album and it will keep selling for years. In other words my catalogue will keep selling and that's where I have gained an awful lot of, what you might say, continued record sales.

The *Nevada State Journal/Reno Evening Gazette* reported this Arnold comment: "I'm just an ordinary guy, so I can get very close to my audiences—country people or sophisticates—from overalls to fur coats."

Although he was a wealthy man, he declared, "I decided a long time ago I didn't want to make all the money in the world. I want to sing a few songs and pat my wife on her backside and lead somewhat of a normal life. I hoped it would become popular, but I never dreamed it would have this kind of acceptance.

"I do live a very conservative lifestyle," he said. "My 53-foot Hatteras is the only thing I have ever been extravagant on." Arnold loved talking about his yacht: "I'm a pretty good captain. I polish the chrome and I hose it off. If you came to visit, I'd even pour you a lemonade." On the boat, "I don't have to talk about my latest recording. Most people never say hello. They talk to you as though you were an automatic soft drink machine, push and pick on you and are gone. I love to sit down and talk to somebody and be a human being. I want to know the people I do business with. That's what I like about where I live. There's nothing like living in a place where you know the man who runs the hardware store or the people who work in the supermarket. It's my kind of living."

> *"I want to know the people I do business with. That's what I like about where I live. There's nothing like living in a place where you know the man who runs the hardware store or the people who work in the supermarket. It's my kind of living."*

On his daily life he said, "I stay on the telephone most of the day—talking to either my manager or somebody connected with radio, publishing, or my own little businesses. I have little businesses myself—and I try to stay on top of them. Or I try to help somebody find a job." He also indicated that he regularly read the *Wall Street Journal* and *U.S. News & World Report.*

As for his off-hours, Arnold remarked, "I like to run my boat. I have a 53-foot Hatteras that I operate myself on the lakes around here and down the Mississippi to New Orleans and over to Florida—where I use it as a condominium."

Arnold said of life with his wife, "Our best times are on the boat or in the car. No phones. No interruptions. These are the happy times." His wife "never misses Las Vegas, likes to play cards." In discussing his marriage he confessed, "I don't know the secret. We have fought less than most couples. It's not normal not to fight."

In regard to his wife's attitude toward his sex appeal to other women he said, "Well, I'm sure it must have bothered her a little bit and that she had some problems with it. But she certainly lived with it. And I'll tell you what I learned right away, early on. When she was with me in public I had to MAKE them respect her . . . many, many times. They would walk on her, step on her, trample on her and ignore her. And I wouldn't let them do that to her. I would take her by the arm and say, 'My good people this is my wife.'

"When I'm home I go to lunch with a fellow nearby who owns a local hardware store," he said. "We sit there in one of the booths and tell each other stories. That's the way I live, and that's pretty much the way I perform. I haven't been an altar boy all my life [but] suggestive lyrics bother me. When it comes to sex, well, I think a real pretty love song is the answer."

Commenting on his autobiography, *It's a Long Way from Chester County*, published in 1969, he said, "The book wasn't exciting enough and I'm not an exciting person. A book about me is not good because I'm still living with the same wife, I never beat her up, I've never smoked pot and I've never walked on stage drunk. I'm just an average human being that can sing. People want to be able to say 'Gee, did he get drunk or did he beat his wife?' and then go back to the show. They don't want to read about ordinary people. It must be sensational and spicy."

At the end of the year he had fond memories about a boyhood Christmas. He received a toy butterfly that was mounted on wheels so that when he pulled it, the wings moved. "It was fantastic," said Arnold. In the RCA newsletter he was asked what he wanted for Christmas and replied, "A case of clam chowder."

In some interviews, Arnold reminisced about his childhood: "I was too young [to leave the farm], I guess, but my situation had reached the point where I was just existing, not living. There was nothin' on the farm to look forward to and not much in Henderson, so one day I just lit out."

On the music he listened to while growing up he said,

> It was just music. The only kind I heard, the only kind I knew. It was happy music, sad music, foot-stomping music for a dosey-do, and spirituals that could, I thought, stop the birds from flying south, as they heard it drift across the valley. My family used to sing around the house but we didn't call what we sang "country music" because the term wasn't around back then. The term came along later when the music industry wanted to dignify what a lot of people thought of as "hillbilly music." So when I was growing up I never heard of "country music," even though that was what I was singing.

He noted that growing up out in the country

> you manufacture your own entertainment. We really had no electricity and no plumbing. We used to sing a lot—at school, in chapel, at family gatherings. My mother's side of the family was very musical. All of them played instruments. My dad had a slight interest in music but as far as my immediate family, musically I was it.

He particularly remembered the song "If You'll Let Me Be Your Little Sweetheart." He told an interviewer, "I had the record when I was growing up on the farm there and that's the first song I did on the radio. Strummed the guitar too.

"I was a country boy all my life," said Arnold. "And so I guess that's why I became a country singer—I understand that kind of life. But I've always liked all kinds of music. All I had was a record player when I was growing up, and I listened to everything—everything from Bing Crosby to Gene Autry." Then he added, "Sure, I'm a country boy and I'm proud of it, but that doesn't mean I can't like other things."

He also had some ideas about raising children, which came from an experience with his father. He related a story to reporter Mel Shields:

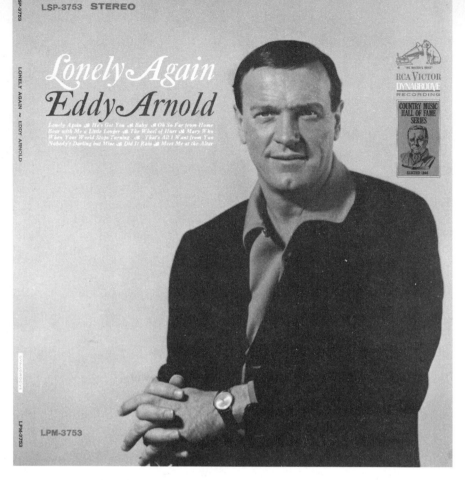

"Son, hand me that stick," my father said. "Uh-uh," I said. "Son, hand me that stick,' he said again; he had a very strong voice. "Uh-uh." My daddy got up, walked over, picked up the stick, turned me across his knee and whipped me. Then he put the stick back and said, "Hand me that stick, Son." He whipped me again; and then again after I still refused. But the next time he asked me for the stick, I handed it to him. I was only six or seven then but he never had to whip me again. I have a sort of philosophy about that, despite all the current philosophy about not punishing children: I believe that children lean on authority. I know I did. You can try to reason with a child, but you'll find out quick enough that he doesn't think like an adult. If he's to live in this world, he's got to learn to mind young, just as I did; and he's got to learn to respect his mama's and daddy's authority.

In 1980, Eddy Arnold found a presidential candidate he was excited about. "Reagan is my man," he declared. The excitement generated by Reagan caused Arnold to become more involved in Republican politics. He liked the way Tennessee and the country were headed; in 1980, the two senators from Tennessee, Howard Baker and William Brock, were both Republicans, and the future governor's race had a promising Republican candidate, Lamar Alexander, who would win in 1982. In September, Eddy and Sally attended a $1,000-a-couple Republican fund-raiser at the Hyatt Regency in Nashville. At the event were Senator John Warner and his wife, Elizabeth Taylor. On October 16, Arnold was pictured with Ronald Reagan.

> ► *By the 1980s, Eddy Arnold had emerged as one of the most articulate spokesmen for country music since World War II.*

After the election Arnold told Allan Horton of the *Sarasota Herald Tribune* that he was "right of center" in his political ideology and he lauded the election of Ronald Reagan for "a healthy return of conservative influence." He liked the fact the new president was "willing to bite the bullet on inflation" and had "the gift of appealing to the same audience which gives country music its strength—the common man." He said Reagan, whom he knew as an actor, "has the same gift of communication which gave Franklin D. Roosevelt's popular 'fireside chats' their common appeal."

Arnold said of President Reagan that "he is the first president in a good while who speaks the common language to the American people where the average man can understand what he's talking about. If we're going to do things in this country, we've got to talk to the common man."

At the beginning of May 1983, Arnold went to Washington for the Seventy-first Annual Meeting of Chamber of Commerce of USA and entertained. President Reagan delivered the major address to the group. A month earlier he had appeared on the Country Music Association's twenty-fifth anniversary show on network television. Also in 1983, Arnold went to Fort McHenry in Baltimore to lead the pledge of allegiance to the flag along with Maryland Governor William D. Schaefer and Lieutenant Governor Joseph Curran.

Arnold had been one of the major developers of Brentwood, a subdivision south of Nashville. In early 1981, he sold the utility, the Brentwood Water Company, to the city for $3.2 million. He said of the water company, "It needed money to survive. We took the stock approach, raised the necessary funds and put the company on its feet. Then we were able to meet the water needs of both homes and businesses."

At that time he owned about 300 acres in three major parcels, located in prime developmental areas. He was the landlord for a Buick agency and had just sold off 17 acres for a housing development.

At the end of 1982, Eddy Arnold appeared on the Country Music Association Awards show to announce Marty Robbins had been inducted into the Country Music Hall of Fame.

By the 1980s, Eddy Arnold had emerged as one of the most articulate spokesmen for country music since World War II. He told one interviewer, "In the old days, the better musicians looked down on Country music. They didn't think it was respectable. Today, of course, it's a homogenized part of our popular culture, and I think it's good that Country is finally getting the respect it should have gotten a long time ago."

In 1980, Barbara Johnson reported Arnold's comments about country music:

> I've been there when it wasn't considered popular to like it. And that used to bother me because the music as an art form wasn't respected. I think all music should be respected—even though there's good and bad in all of it. Country music is THE popular music now and all the singers are country oriented. If you stop and think for a moment, you don't have the Perry Comos, Andy Williamses and Eddie Fishers coming along anymore. All are coming out of the country field—like your John Denvers, Kenny Rogers, so forth and so on. Many have come over to the country field because it fills a void. They're looking for a pretty song and that's where they're finding it. Not the nasal kind of country, you understand, but the pretty ballads. If Irving Berlin were writing today, he'd be mighty close to a country boy.

In 1983, he told Stewart Ettinger,

> Everybody doesn't like country music you know, but everybody doesn't like chocolate pie either. The more exposure country music gets, the more it moves into the mainstream of music and the entertainment business.

Television and movies are part of it and the other part is
that radio stations are programming it. I'm talking about
stations across the United States. It used to be you didn't
even have a small station in the East and North playing
it. Now you have plenty of stations playing it 18 to 24
hours a day.

Regarding the state of country music in the early eighties, he
said,

I think it is very healthy, you have some people out there
that are very strong at the moment and it's getting pretty
much in the mainstream of what you call popular music.
Popular music is whatever is popular. Rock still has the
edge in overall sales, but the rock artists, bless their
hearts, there's no longevity for the most part. You have a
group now that is real popular, but in six months they are
gone and you have another group. They don't treat their
profession as a business. Once you fail to do that you just
will not stay around for a long time. You must treat it as a
business and I mean that as a compliment.

Then he gave some advice: "There is so much more to the music
business than just memorizing a song and walking on stage and
singing it. There is much more that goes with it." Some of those
things included keeping up with "trends and handling your business.
Directing yourself, being managed properly, showing up on time,
keeping your nose clean."

Finally, he appeared to resign himself to the day when he wasn't
a superstar any longer: "I won't always do this. There'll come a time
when the people won't want me, and I'm talking about in numbers.
There'll come a time when I'll have to hang it up and I realize that,
but everything has to come to an end, there is nothing permanent in
this life."

31

Country Music's Odyssey

T he significance of the Nashville Sound era, led by Eddy Arnold, Chet Atkins, Owen Bradley, Floyd Cramer, and others, is that country music, like the post–World War II population of the United States in general, moved into the middle class. In 1956, for the first time, the United States had more white-collar workers than blue-collar, in terms defined by job description (that is, management and clerical workers rather than agricultural or assembly line workers). In economic terms, there was a huge shift in the population from lower class to middle class, primarily due to the downward shift in wealth because of government spending and the tax codes. Essentially, what happened was that the group of people who used to be defined *working class* is now defined as *middle class*. This shift in terms comes through an economic definition (an increase in income) although according to social and cultural definitions of class, these middle class white-collar workers often remained working class, albeit with higher expectations, more material possessions, and more access to upward social and cultural mobility. In short, during the fifty years after World War II, country music changed collars—from blue to white.

But by the mid 1980s, sales of the country-pop type sound pioneered by Eddy Arnold declined while country music executives found it increasingly difficult to relate to the core country audiences. The *New York Times* published an article by Robert Palmer stating that country music was, effectively, dead. The article noted that sales of country records had suffered a sharp decline and that it was "the end of an era." Palmer noted that:

It's not just the Nashville Sound that seems to be dying; it's the Nashville *dream*. For more than four decades, young people with musical talent growing up in the South and the Middle West have dreamed of making it in the big time by singing, playing and making records in Nashville. They're still coming to Nashville, but most of them would like to be rock rather than country stars."

Arnold's manager, Jerry Purcell, sent a letter to the writer arguing against these conclusions. Ironically, the country music industry was "saved" by the new traditionalists, led by George Strait, Ricky Skaggs, and beginning in 1985, Randy Travis. When Travis hit, it was a shock to many in the Nashville music industry who were convinced there was no market for this sort of old-style country sound. The *New York Times* article noted that "the pop-oriented arrangements helped the music attract a mass audience," but that particular mass audience was getting older and not buying records. The Nashville community was concerned about its future, but few thought the "new" country music would be a return to the older sound of country music that Eddy Arnold recorded during the 1940s and early 1950s.

> ➤ *Few thought the "new" country music would be a return to the older sound of country music that Eddy Arnold recorded during the 1940s and early 1950s.*

While many viewed this "new" musical trend as a necessary course correction—country music's way of finding its soul—it could also be viewed in another light because the American middle class was slipping backwards to its working-class roots instead of continuing on its path of being upwardly mobile. Indeed, the term *middle class*, which used to mean home ownership, vacations in Orlando, and college for the kids, had shrunk to a group struggling to get by. During the 1980s, as the price of housing and college tuition went shooting through the roof, the median household income remained stuck where it had been ever since the late 1970s, at about $30,000 a year.

There were income gains from working-class families during the 1980s, but these came from working wives whose extra income was increasingly needed to keep their families afloat or by family members either working overtime or an extra job. In May 1989 there were 52.8 million women working, an increase from 28.9 million in 1970.

The struggles of the middle class to make ends meet played a large part in the success of mass discounters like Wal-Mart and K-Mart, which are really contemporary versions of the old style country store that had a little something for everybody, built on a grand scale. And the success of these discounters played a direct role in the success of Country Music.

Consider these facts: in 1980 there were 276 Wal-Marts and they sold $1.2 billion worth of merchandise; in 1990 there were 1,528 Wal-Marts and they sold $26 billion worth of merchandise. These facts, in essence, explain the incredible explosion in the sales of country music during the 1980s because mass merchandisers like Wal-Mart sold about 75 percent of all country recordings. Or, to put it another way, Sam Walton had as much to do with country music's explosion in sales during the 1980s as Randy Travis, George Strait, Reba McEntire, Garth Brooks, or any other country star.

Sam Walton wasn't the only person who thought discounting was the wave of the future. The same year he opened the first Wal-Mart three other companies began discount chains: S.S. Kresge opened KMart, F. W. Woolworth started Woolco, and Dayton-Hudson opened Target. KMart was the most successful from the start; by 1967 it had 250 stores with sales of over $800 million while Wal-Mart had only 19 stores and annual sales of about $9 million.

The mid-1980s and 1990s was the period of the large discounter. In 1981 Sears was the country's largest retailer; by the end of the decade KMart had claimed the number one spot. And during the 1990s, Wal-Mart surged past KMart. It was also the end of the reign of the shopping centers, brought on by shifting consumer buying as well as overdevelopment. Thus as the dominant retailers for Americans shifted from shopping centers to the mass merchandising discounters, the sales of rock music—whose strength was in the mall stores—leveled off while the sales of country music—whose sales came from stores like Wal-Mart—zoomed upward. If there had been Wal-Marts and K-Marts stocking Eddy Arnold records in the 1945–1955 period, there's no telling how many records he would have sold!

But there was another factor involved in the growth in sales from country music linked to retailing. And it came from the bar codes and computerized scanners that have become an integral part of retailing. These electronic scanners at checkout counters scan bar codes and automatically record the item purchased, subtracts it from the store inventory, tallies up the price, and shows the consumer how much to pay. In addition to having an impact on the retailers, who can keep up with what's selling and what is not, and consumers who spend less time in the checkout lane, these scanners have also had a tremendous impact on the country music charts located in trade magazines.

The information on the sale of recordings is collected by a company called SoundScan. This computerized information is collected each week by *Billboard*, a music industry trade magazine which compiles charts of the top songs and albums in the nation in all music fields. Retailers and wholesalers use these charts as a barometer for consumer demand and to determine what to stock. This SoundScan technology has been in place since 1991 and gives a quick, accurate reading of what sells and what doesn't. This differs greatly in the way charts used to be compiled.

Before SoundScan, *Billboard* and other trades regularly called a pre-selected group of record stores and distributors (called "reporters") around the country and asked a manager or assistant manager (or whoever was in charge of giving the report) to tell them the top sellers in the various categories (country, rock, rhythm and blues, etc.). Sales figures were *not* collected; the stores only gave a relative ranking. In other words, the top seller was such and such, the second was such and such, on down the line. Country music suffered from an inherent prejudice; stores regularly underestimated country sales and, since it was stocked in a section outside "pop" or "rock" music, the sales weren't really considered comparable. This affected Eddy Arnold, particularly during the 1960s, when he had to be considered a "pop" act in order for his records to achieve big sales. Just being a "country" artist limited record sales and mass market appeal.

With the advent of SoundScan, all those prejudices were eliminated; instead, the raw data of unbiased sales figures were reported. And it was discovered that country music competed with pop sellers; indeed, it even outsold a number of pop music sellers. This had been an open secret within the music industry for a number of years, at least among those in the accounting departments at the major labels. But the pop music world in general refused to believe that country music could sell in such huge numbers. Again, Eddy Arnold's career reflects this. A number of collections of "pop" music from the 1940s and early 1950s have been compiled—but none include Eddy Arnold, although Arnold outsold the entire pop division of some major labels during those years. A song like "Bouquet of Roses" is not included on any "pop" music collections of the greatest hits from 1948, yet that record outsold almost every recording included on such collections. Such was the plight of being a "country" artist during the years before SoundScan.

Buyers for stores generally use the trade charts as a gauge on which to measure what they should buy, and stores like Wal-Mart, which depend on a quick turnover, routinely buy the top 15 sellers in country, rock, and R&B based on the *Billboard* charts. So if an album is selling well, it will be ordered so it can sell even more. Thus the big sellers can generate even more sales; whereas country music once was happy to have gold records signifying 500,000 units sold, now it sells triple and quadruple platinum (platinum is one million units sold). Stores in malls or free-standing locations also began to order more country music because the figures showed it was selling well. Since music is often an impulse item, having country albums on hand when consumers are browsing leads to more sales. And so country music spiraled upward.

The final factor integral to understanding the jump in country sales during the 1980s and 1990s is to understand working women. By 1994 almost half the work force (45.6 percent) consisted of women; they made their own money and they bought what they wanted. And many bought recordings.

Music industry studies in the 1980s showed that about half the country recorded product is sold to men and the other half to women, although that varied from artist to artist with some artists appealing more strongly to women while men are dominant buyers of other artists. By 1996 studies showed that women accounted for approximately 65 percent of all country music sales. But country music marketers have sometimes jokingly referred to the "nag factor" in explaining country music sales to show that up to 80 percent of sales can be traced back to a woman. In other words, a woman will buy albums herself, but she will also persuade her husband or boyfriend to buy others.

The struggles of the middle class to make ends meet, a product of a combination of stagnant incomes and increased demands for material goods, led many to keep up a middle-class lifestyle through the use of credit cards.

Borrowing has always been part of American economic life. Before World War II people usually had "accounts" at local stores, such as the grocery or general store, which allowed them to go into short-term debt. Then, after World War II, installment loans exploded as people bought homes, cars, or appliances such as refrigerators on a monthly or weekly payment plan. In fact, between 1945 and 1960, consumer credit went from $2.6 billion to $45 billion; a decade later it was $105 billion. In many ways, this reflected the optimism that people held that tomorrow would be better than today. And, for the most part, it was a safe bet. Income improved for most Americans between 1947 and 1959, when

the percentage of families earning less than $3,000 annually dropped from 46 percent to 20 percent. Meanwhile, the percentage of families earning an annual income between $7,000 and $10,000 (high middle-class income) rose from 5 percent to 20 percent within this same period.

The cards and their usage grew: in 1960 there were 233,585 BankAmericards in use; by 1968, there were over a million while credit cards overall accounted for $59 million worth of sales in 1960 and $400 million by 1968. In 1967 there were a total of 32 million credit cards issued and in 1974 there were over 200 million credit card transactions; by 1992 that figure had risen to six billion. There were over 300 million credit cards in circulation by 1993 and 220 million active accounts, or an average of three active credit card accounts for each of the nation's 70 million households.

Just as important as the actual change in the economic well-being and improvement of Americans was the change in attitude towards debt. For those raised during the Great Depression, like Eddy Arnold, a fear of debt haunted them and they studiously avoided financial risk; however, for those who came of age after World War II, debt became the way to a better life. And, since income kept growing, debt became a way to quickly acquire the possessions that defined and improved middle-class life, as what was once unaffordable became affordable. Still, for the most part debt after World War II was controlled by others, who had to approve a loan or payment. With credit cards there was no one but the customer himself to decide whether or not to borrow to spend. And, with computers, this decision became easier to make because computer technology reduced credit card approvals from five minutes to fifty-six seconds then, by the 1990s, down to seven seconds.

This directly affected the music industry because people increasingly used their credit cards to purchase music; overall, about 30 percent of music sales comes from credit card purchases.

Several other important factors also helped make country music big business during the 1985–1995 period. First, the introduction of the compact disc in 1983 helped create a boom in sales of recorded product because consumers no longer just purchased a current album but also purchased their favorite catalog items. Labels also aggressively marketed catalog items, repackaging them into boxed sets or compilation albums.

Next, there was a change in image for the term *country*. In 1940, when Eddy Arnold joined the Golden West Cowboys, approximately 23 percent of the population lived on farms but by 1950 only 15 percent lived on farms; by 1960 that figure had dropped to eight percent (in 1995 it was around two percent). During the first twenty years after World War II the image of the rural person was that of a country bumpkin, a hayseed, hick, or rube, as shown by the national media's stereotype of country music and country fans. The image of the city dweller was that of someone cultured and sophisticated, or at least streetwise. So the term *country* had negative connotations for people who were or wanted to be "citified," and these connotations likewise applied to country music.

The 1990 census showed the United States to be an urban nation, although more people actually live in the suburbs that surround a city than anywhere else. Nevertheless, about 80 percent of the U.S. population is now to be found in metropolitan areas. By 1990, however, the cities had acquired a negative image and were viewed as areas of widespread violence, rampant crime, crowded living conditions, and—for many inner-city dwellers—hopelessness. Country living, on the other hand, had gained a lot of appeal. To live in the "country" meant having fresh air and freedom from inner-city conditions. A home in the country became a status symbol, and country clothing, furniture, and music became increasingly popular.

Helping establish this change of image has largely been the work of the media, especially television. The Nashville Network (TNN) and Country Music Television (CMT) both went on the air in 1983. This brought country music into homes on a regular basis and destroyed the old image of country bumpkins in country music. The change also came within the industry as country music executives increasingly looked for good-looking young men and women ("hunks and babes") to sign.

Eddy Arnold had to obtain a spot on network television, competing against every major musical act in all genres, and then travel to New York, Chicago, or Los Angeles in order to appear on television in his heyday. By 1985, a country artist in Nashville only had to make the short drive to The Nashville Network offices at Opryland, where country music shows were broadcast seven days a week. Or, an artist might spend two days shooting a video that would be played over and over for a national audience. That was an opportunity artists like Eddy Arnold never enjoyed.

In addition to the increase in regular television exposure, there was a huge growth in radio exposure for country music. In 1961, the first year for which the Country Music Association compiled data on radio stations, and the year that probably marked the low point for country music programming (numerous stations had switched from country to rock 'n' roll between 1956 and 1961), there were only 81 stations playing country music full-time. By 1969, however, there were 606, and during the 1970s that figure grew to 1,434. In 1980 there were 1,534 country stations, but by the end of that decade there were 2,108. By 1994 that figure had risen to 2,427 radio stations programming country music full time. In order for Eddy Arnold to be a successful artist on the radio he had to obtain exposure on the networks in the 1940s and early 1950s. During the 1960s he had to be a "crossover" act, or get played on pop and rock music stations to achieve mass appeal. By the 1990s, a country artist only needed exposure on country radio in order to achieve a large national audience.

The dominant area for country music radio stations and sales of country records is the South, and during the 1980s and early 1990s there was a huge influx of people moving into the South. In fact, in 1995 the population of Nashville showed that a fourth of the people had not lived there a decade earlier. This was indicative over the whole region as people moved from the Northern rust belt into the South in a population shift that was comparable to the Great Migration during and immediately after World War II.

The shift to the South was helped by several factors. First, in 1980, 80 percent of the homes in the South had air conditioning; without air conditioning so widely available, people would not have moved. The hot muggy South of Eddy Arnold's youth was still there, but people didn't really notice it as they drove their air-conditioned cars to air-conditioned offices and then went home to air-conditioned houses. Computers have transformed businesses, making it possible to do business anywhere so companies could conduct business for less money in the South but with the same efficiency, thus precipitating a number of moves.

The growth of long-distance phone service also increased since World War II. In 1945 only 46 percent of the population had a phone but direct-dialing for long-distance calls did not begin until 1951. When Chicago publisher Fred Forster called Frank Walker at Victor in New York to obtain a recording contract for Eddy Arnold in 1944, or when Steve Sholes in New York called Eddy Arnold in Nashville in 1945 to discuss his recording career, an operator had to place the call. It was not until 1965 that most long-distance calls were dialed directly; by the mid-1990s over 150 million calls were dialed directly, a result of technology which made it possible and the breakup of AT&T in 1984 which caused other phone companies to come into the market and drive down prices. In 1995 Eddy Arnold only needed to punch eleven digits to talk to his manager in New York, and a FAX machine kept Arnold informed of his upcoming concert dates and television appearances.

The growth of interstate highways, which account for 20 percent of traffic in the United States although they are only one percent of the roads, made it easier to be mobile—and that made it easier for country artists to travel throughout the country on large custom buses. Jet travel also played a role in increased country exposure because it allowed a number of country artists to travel by jet. In 1940 United States airlines transported 3.5 million passengers; by the mid-1990s that figure had increased to over 400 million.

In terms of the country music audience, there were, essentially, two different audiences. First are the record buyers, who are essentially younger (18 to 45) and these buyers have been getting younger because of country music videos and the change in image of country music. The audience for live shows is often older (25 to 65), and the demand for older country artists—even those who haven't had a hit in years— remains strong, giving rise to places like Branson, Missouri, who cater to an older audience. The prime reason for this is Social Security. In 1948 about half the men over 65 worked; by the mid-1990s most of those over 65 were retired on Social Security and private pensions—a number that exceeded 26 million. The very idea of a person retiring while in their 60s, still active and potentially productive, is essentially a new idea which came into being in the late 1960s. This audience has the time and money to travel to country music shows, and they do so.

To some, it might appear that Nashville is no longer the center for country music, but in reality, Nashville has grown stronger as the corporate center for country music while it has declined as a tourist attraction. Country music was never really centralized; prior to World War II, Chicago, Los Angeles, Atlanta, Dallas, and other cities all had a strong country music industry, generally based on a radio show. But during the 1945–75 period country music's center became Nashville. However, with the mobile middle class, country music performances can be found in a number of towns, such as Branson, Missouri, and Myrtle Beach, South Carolina.

During the 1980s there were a number of corporate mergers: RCA, Eddy Arnold's long-time label, was purchased by the German-based Bertlesman Group (BMG); CBS Records was purchased by the Japanese company, Sony; the Japanese firm Matsushita purchased MCA; Time, Inc. and Warner Brothers merged. The increase in size of these multinational firms meant that Nashville offices had more autonomy and thus they had marketing departments. In the past, Nashville was a corporate outpost where country music acts were signed and recorded but the marketing decisions came from New York and Los Angeles; by 1995 each Nashville office had its own marketing division.

> *Officially, Eddy Arnold has only a few Gold albums, yet he has sold 85 million recordings.*

The growth of country music can perhaps best be demonstrated in the number of "gold" and "platinum" albums awarded for country sales. Since the Recording Industry Association of America (RIAA) instituted the "gold" record in 1958 to represent a half million albums sold or one million singles sold, there has generally been a steady increase in the number of gold and platinum awards each year. Before 1968 only a few country albums or singles went "gold," but in 1968 and 1969 ten albums went "gold" each of those years. It dropped to less than ten until 1973, when ten country albums again achieved "gold" status before dropping below ten again. Then, in 1976 a breakthrough occurred when country music received a platinum album (selling a million copies) for "The Outlaws," a compilation featuring Waylon Jennings, Willie Nelson, Tompall Glaser, and Jessi Colter, who headed the "outlaw" movement.

The following year, 1977, there were 14 albums certified gold and two platinum. From this point on, the number of country albums certified gold has always been in double digits with the high watermarks being 1978 (22 gold, 6 platinum), 1980 (22 gold, 8 platinum), 1981 (30 gold, 6 platinum) 1983 (21 gold, 5 platinum) and 1987 (20 gold, 9 platinum and 1 multi-platinum). Then, in 1991 when SoundScan was introduced to the industry's trade charts, there were 28 gold albums, 22 platinum albums and 11 multi-platinum albums. In 1992, the first full year for SoundScan, Country music had 40 gold albums, 24 platinum, and 20 multi-platinum albums. That number has continued to increase since that time.

Officially, Eddy Arnold has only a few gold albums, yet he has sold 85 million recordings. But his success came at a time when it was a lot harder to sell country music. If Eddy Arnold had his big-selling years from 1985–95 instead of 1945–55, he would probably not have room enough on his walls to hold all his gold and platinum albums.

32

The Show Goes On

The last song by Eddy Arnold that charted in *Billboard* was "The Blues Don't Care Who's Got 'Em" in 1983. Arnold had 145 of his single records chart during his career. That same year he was given the Pioneer Award by the Academy of Country Music. There were still fans who bought his albums; in 1985, *Reader's Digest* gave him a Gold album for selling almost a million copies of an album marketed through their magazine. And awards continued to come in; in 1987, the Songwriters Guild gave him their President's Award.

In 1987, Arnold purchased a getaway place in south Florida, where he would go in the winter. And two days before his seventieth birthday, he and his close friend Bobby Campbell went back to Henderson, Tennessee, where they visited the farm where Arnold grew up and Pinson Elementary School where Arnold had gone to school.

Although he was still active in his businesses and still performed occasional concerts, his health caused some concerns. On March 28, 1990, he underwent double-bypass heart surgery at St. Thomas Hospital in Nashville; he was released on April 6 and began a regimen of walking and exercise. The following year he became a spokesman for the American Heart Association.

In 1983, the compact disc was introduced in the music industry, putting music on digital recordings. Arnold recorded some for the new configuration and some of his older recordings were repackaged, although his earliest material—from 1945 to 1955—remained mostly unavailable. Part of that was Arnold's choice; he much preferred the recordings from the 1960s era when he hit his stride as an artist in both country and pop, singing smooth love

Eddy Arnold with Garth Brooks.

songs in a lower register than his earlier work of more traditional country songs as a tenor.

In 1995, the United States celebrated the fiftieth anniversary of the end of World War II. It was also the fiftieth anniversary of the first record released by Eddy Arnold, "Mommy Please Stay Home with Me," that began his remarkable career. Also in 1995, a press announcement proclaimed that Garth Brooks had just become the biggest selling country artist of all time. The man he replaced was Eddy Arnold.

At the time of the Garth Brooks announcement, Eddy Arnold was seventy-six years old, living a busy, active life, still going to his office every day. On May 15, he celebrated his seventy-seventh birthday by working in his office and attending a small birthday party at lunchtime at Campbell's Glass Company, owned and run by his best friend, Bobby Campbell. There he ate some barbecue and birthday cake, then went back to his office.

In Eddy Arnold's office is a sheet tacked up that says "The Customer." Under this heading are statements such as, "Remember that you are nothing without your customer" and "You must always take care of your customers or they will find someone else who will." This paper on the wall shows that Eddy Arnold is a salesman—and he's proud of it. His ambition was to sell recordings—and indeed he did sell them.

> *"I like the love songs. That's what people relate to."*

During the summer months, Arnold usually leaves his office early on Friday afternoons and heads out to the lake where he keeps his boat. The *Sally K.* is a fifty-three-foot yacht where Eddy likes to spend summer weekends cruising around Nashville area lakes.

In October 1995, he performed at the Alabama Theater in Myrtle Beach, South Carolina. At 11:00 A.M. on the day of the concert, Eddy Arnold and the group of musicians who would perform with him arrived and began rehearsals. Since Arnold doesn't do many concerts, he doesn't have a band, although he keeps guitarist Jim Lance on retainer. Instead, he hires his group of musicians whenever he has a concert booked. The band consists of an arranger, who plays a baby grand piano, two female background singers, two guitar players, a bass player, a drummer, and two electronic keyboard players who play the synthesized sound of an orchestra.

Eddy Arnold loves a great song—and he demands it be performed right. During the rehearsal he practiced the songs and made sure the tempo was right. He got excited when the band got in a groove, and he even did a shuffle dance step when rehearsing "Mountain Dew." He let the sound man know when he wanted to hear more guitar or vocals. And he asked the musicians to play a song over if it didn't feel quite right. He wanted the fans to get full value for their money; they paid to hear him sing, and he was determined to give them a top-notch show.

There is a real sense of excitement and energy when a song moves him. He was especially excited about "You Again," a song by the Forester Sisters that he performed that evening. "I like the love songs," he admits. "That's what people relate to." At the concert he gave them a whole range of love songs. "I'm a sentimentalist," he says. "I believe in holding hands."

He remembers the old days with fondness. "I wanted to sell *records*," he says—and he did! He learned early that you had to look

Eddy Arnold relaxing on his boat.

for the best songs. "I never played politics with songs," he says. "I always picked the best I could find and I didn't care who wrote 'em or who published 'em." And he still does that.

The highlight of the concert came when he sat alone with his guitar in front of the curtain and sang some of his old hits: "Lovebug Itch," "I Really Don't Want to Know," "I'll Hold You in My Heart," "Turn the World Around," "What's He Doing in My World," "Bouquet of Roses," and "Make the World Go Away."

He sang "Cattle Call," and there was a collective gasp from the audience—that has always been his trademark song. He paused. "You didn't think I could still do it, did you?" he said after that patented yodel. They laughed.

In truth, Eddy Arnold's voice isn't as strong as it used to be. "I've lost some of my high notes," he confesses. But that's not why people go to see Eddy Arnold. They go to see him because he is a legend and, somewhere along the line, he has touched their lives. It is an audience that is very comfortable with him because his performances exude comfort and geniality.

Eddy Arnold's boat.

The other reason people still come to Eddy Arnold concerts is that he is one of those rare, remarkable performers who bonds with his audience. The large theater could be a living room, and Eddy Arnold an old friend. He sings songs for them, tells stories and jokes, and makes them feel comfortable. He has a sense of style that comes across as elegant and down home at the same time—the country boy who made it big but never forgot his roots.

He finished the concert with two songs that were autobiographical: "If I Had My Life to Live Over (I'd Still Fall in Love with You)" and "I've So Much to Be Thankful For."

Backstage afterward he said, "I don't mind telling you I'm tired." Still, he met with some fans and old friends. He gave hugs, signed autographs, and talked with some of his fans who had driven for miles just to see him. During the concert one woman wept, and backstage after the show there were men and women of all ages clearly flabbergasted to be in the same room with Eddy Arnold.

During the latter half of 1995, he went into a studio as a favor to his longtime friend Mike Curb and recorded a duet of "Cattle Call" with a thirteen-year-old singer. When the album was released in 1996, LeAnn Rimes became the hottest new story in country music, and Eddy Arnold was becoming a "star" all over again. Suddenly, a whole new group of people became acquainted with Eddy Arnold, and young fans found out who he was. Producer Chuck Howard's young sons pronounced him "cool," and that delighted Arnold, who sent each an auto-graphed picture.

> ➤ *On his seventh-eighth birthday he spent the afternoon at his office rehearsing songs with Lance that they would record.*

In February 1995, Arnold performed in Laughlin, Nevada, for a week to packed houses. *Reader's Digest* released a three-CD set, and Arnold went back into the studio with guitarist Jim Lance and recorded a number of his old songs acoustically, which would become an album of duets. On his seventy-eighth birthday he spent the afternoon at his office rehearsing songs with Lance that they would record. He also picked three Christmas songs to record for a Christmas release.

In May 1996, Eddy Arnold boarded a plane in Nashville headed for Pittsburgh. He had collected the plane ticket in his office from his secretary, Roberta Edging, who has been with him since 1967. At the Pittsburgh airport he met his manager of thirty-two years, Jerry Purcell, and musicians who would perform with him. They all drove to Wheeling, West Virginia, about an hour and a half away, where he would appear at the Capitol Theater, home of the *Wheeling Jamboree.*

Like the *Opry*, the *Wheeling Jamboree* is a live radio program of country music. It is younger than the *Opry*, having first broadcast on January 7, 1933. But unlike the *Opry*, the *Wheeling Jamboree* has not remained at the forefront of country music. A band performed cover songs for about an hour and sang commercials for sponsors, then the thick red velvet curtain was closed and the stage prepared for Eddy Arnold.

Earlier in the day, at 11:00, the band had come to the theater to rehearse; Arnold joined them at noon and did a run-through of his show. Around 2:30 everyone took a break, and Arnold joined a small group for lunch where he had a steak salad and talked about the National Basketball Association play-offs between the Chicago Bulls and Orlando Magic. Arnold had been watching the games. He was a fan of the Atlanta Braves as well, and he watched their games on tele-vision. He talked of Greg Maddux's pitching, "a real artist." Around 3:30 he went back to his room to rest before the concert.

Eddy Arnold and the author.

The *Jamboree* began at 7:00 P.M. and the first portion ended just before 8:00. Around 8:15 the curtain opened to an overture of Eddy Arnold's past hits, and Arnold walked on stage in a tuxedo with a powder blue jacket. The two thousand people in the audience stood and applauded while Arnold took a bow and began his show. A little over an hour later, he finished his show.

The next morning, Sunday, Eddy Arnold, his manager, and the group of musicians got in a van and headed back to the Pittsburgh airport where Arnold bought a Pittsburgh newspaper and turned to the sports page to read about the Bulls-Magic game the day before. He had managed to catch a little bit of the action the day before in his hotel room and wanted to read about the game. Back in Nashville, his wife of fifty four years, Sally, picked him up at the airport, and they headed home. A few weeks earlier their son, Dick, had gotten married.

Eddy Arnold was busy and active, in his office every day overseeing his real estate business, recording in the studio, and meeting with a number of people. He had talked with his old steel guitar player, Roy Wiggins, at the funeral of Wiggins's father in May, and he had talked with Tom Parker by phone. He still kept in touch with old friends and associates.

In August he spent several days with a television crew taping "The Life and Times of Eddy Arnold," a summary of his career that would be broadcast over The Nashville Network.

He had read a biography of Dizzy Dean that spring and then purchased a copy of David Brinkley's *Memoir* for his nighttime reading. Each morning he woke early and walked about two miles at a nearby shopping mall before he started his day by going to the post

Eddy and Sally Arnold.

office, then into his office. And he had several concerts scheduled for the fall.

In many ways Eddy Arnold is the Cal Ripken of his field, the Iron Man of Country Music. No other country music artist has been so popular for so long and remained so active. He has a new perspective on his recordings and concert appearances. "I used to be so keyed up about recordings," says Arnold. "I was so concerned that if I didn't have a record on the charts, playing on the radio, people would forget me." That, obviously, is not true; whenever he gives a concert, a whole concert venue is certain to fill up.

The fact that audiences remember and love him was obvious on Monday, October 14, 1996, when he appeared on TNN's *Prime Time Country* and received two standing ovations. It had been almost fifty years to the day since his first big hit, "That's How Much I Love You," had entered the charts, and that evening he would perform "Cattle Call"—a song he first recorded in 1944—with fourteen-year-old LeAnn Rimes, the hottest star in country music at the time.

Sitting in a dressing room backstage before the show, Arnold chatted with Mike Curb, his close friend who had moved to Nashville and established the headquarters for his label, Curb Records. Curb had first thought about LeAnn doing "Cattle Call" in a dream—he had heard her do "Cowboy's Sweetheart" and been searching for a song where she could do a voice "break." Then Curb had played a tape of LeAnn singing some songs for Eddy Arnold in a car tape player after Curb and Arnold had finished lunch at the Green Hills Grille in Nashville. Arnold was impressed and agreed to sing "Cattle Call" with LeAnn when she recorded it. Later, in the Green Room at TNN, LeAnn told of how Mike Curb had sent her the tape of "Cattle Call," then, before the session, Curb, LeAnn, and Arnold had all gone out to dinner where they got to meet each other and talk a bit before recording the duet.

The performance came off well, and after the show, Arnold gathered his belongings to head home and watch the play-off game between the Atlanta Braves and the St. Louis Cardinals. He needed to record some more songs for his Christmas album and was concerned that time was slipping away. The evening was another highlight in the remarkable career of Eddy Arnold mixed with plans for future projects and activities.

It has been a good, full life for Eddy Arnold. It is tempting to say he was the Garth Brooks of country music in his time, but that statement holds only a grain of truth. The fact of the matter is that there

Eddy Arnold and his manager, Jerry Purcell.

has never really been anyone in country music quite like Eddy Arnold, and perhaps there never will be. Perhaps those thousands of young hopefuls who stream into Nashville each year, attracted to the city because it is the magnet for country music hopefuls, may not know all he's done. But if it weren't for Eddy Arnold, there is a good chance that Nashville wouldn't be the center for country music. Or that country music might not be quite the same as it is today—the music of the American middle class.

Bibliography

BOOKS

Ambrose, Stephen E. *Eisenhower: Soldier and President.* New York: Touchstone, 1990.

Arnold, Eddy. *It's a Long Way from Chester County.* Tappan, N.J.: Hewitt House, 1969.

Carr, Patrick, ed. *The Illustrated History of Country Music.* New York: Dolphin, 1980.

Crumbaker, Marge, and Gabe Tucker. *Up and Down with Elvis Presley.* New York: G. P. Putnam's Sons, 1981.

Davis, Louise Littleton. *Nashville Tales.* Gretna, La.: Pelican, 1982.

Doyle, Don H. *Nashville Since the 1920s.* Knoxville: University of Tennessee Press, 1985.

—————. *New Men, New Cities, New South: Atlanta, Nashville, Charleston, Mobile, 1860–1910.* Chapel Hill: University of North Carolina Press, 1990.

Editors of Country Music Magazine. *The Comprehensive Country Music Encyclopedia.* New York: Times, 1994.

Escott, Colin, with George Merritt and William MacEwen. *Hank Williams: The Biography.* Boston: Little, Brown, 1994.

Gentry, Linnell. *A History and Encyclopedia of Country, Western and Gospel Music.* Nashville: Clairmont, 1969.

Goodwin, Doris Kearns. *No Ordinary Time: Franklin and Eleanor Roosevelt: The Home Front in World War II.* New York: Touchstone, 1994.

Graebner, William S. *The Age of Doubt: American Thought and Culture in the 1940s.* Boston: Twyane, 1991.

Green, Douglas B. *Country Roots: The Origin of Country Music.* New York: Hawthorn, 1976.

Guralnick, Peter. *Last Train to Memphis: The Rise of Elvis Presley.* Boston: Little, Brown, 1994.

Hagen, Chet. *Grand Ole Opry: The Complete Story of a Great American Institution and Its Stars.* New York: Owl, 1989.

Hall, Wade. *Hell Bent for Music: Pee Wee King.* Lexington: University of Kentucky Press, 1996.

Hemphill, Paul. *The Nashville Sound: Bright Lights and Country Music.* New York: Simon and Schuster, 1970.

Horstman, Dorothy. *Sing Your Heart Out, Country Boy: Classic Country Songs and Their Inside Stories by the People Who Wrote Them.* New York: Dutton, 1975.

Ivey, Bill. "The Bottom Line: Business Practices That Shaped Country Music." In *Country: The Music and the Musicians.* New York: Abbeville Press, 1988.

Jackson, Kenneth T. *Crabgrass Frontier: The Suburbanization of the United States.* New York: Oxford University Press, 1985.

Kingsbury, Paul. *The Grand Ole Opry History of Country Music: 70 Years of the Songs, the Stars, and the Stories.* New York: Villard Books, 1995.

————, ed. *The Country Music Reader.* Nashville: Vanderbilt University Press, 1996.
———— and Alan Axelrod, eds. *Country: The Music and the Musicians.* New York: Abbeville Press, 1988.
Langdon, Philip. *A Better Place to Live: Reshaping the American Suburb.* Amherst: University of Massachusetts Press, 1994.
Malone, Bill C. *Country Music U.S.A.* Austin: University of Texas Press, 1968.
———— and Judith McCulloh, eds. *The Stars of Country Music.* Urbana: University of Illinois Press, 1975.
————. *Singing Cowboys and Musical Mountaineers: Southern Culture and the Roots of Country Music.* Athens, Ga.: University of Georgia Press, 1993.
McCloud, Barry. *Definitive Country: The Ultimate Encyclopedia of Country Music and Its Performers.* New York: Perigre, 1995.
McElvaine, Robert S. *The Great Depression: America 1929–1941.* New York: Times, 1984.
Morris, Edward. "New, Improved, Homogenized: Country Radio Since 1950." In *Country: The Music and the Musicians.* New York: Abbeville Press, 1988.
Nash, Alanna. *Behind Closed Doors: Talking with the Legends of Country Music.* New York: Knopf, 1983.
Nocera, Joseph. *A Piece of the Action: How the Middle Class Joined the Money Class.* New York: Simon and Schuster, 1994.
Oermann, Robert. *America's Music: The Roots of Country.* Atlanta: Turner Pub., 1996.
Porterfield, Nolan. *Jimmie Rodgers: The Life and Times of America's Blue Yodeler.* Urbana: University of Illinois Press, 1979.
Pugh, Ronnie. *Ernest Tubb: Texas Troubadour.* Durham, N.C.: Duke University Press, 1996.
Reynolds, David. *Rich Relations: The American Occupation of Britain, 1942–1945.* New York: Random House, 1995.
Rose, Frank. *The Agency: William Morris and the Hidden History of Show Business.* New York: HarperBusiness, 1995.
Rosenberg, Neil V. *Bluegrass: A History.* Urbana: University of Illinois Press, 1985.
Rumble, John Woodruff. "Fred Rose and the Development of the Nashville Music Industry, 1942–1954." Ph.D. diss. Vanderbilt University, 1980.
Sanjek, Russell. *American Popular Music and Its Business: The First Four Hundred Years.* Vol. 3. New York: Oxford University Press, 1988.
Schlappi, Elizabeth. *Roy Acuff: The Smoky Mountain Boy.* Gretna, La.: Pelican, 1978, 1993.
Sears, Richard S. *V-Discs: A History and Discography.* Westport, Conn.: Greenwood Press, 1980.
Tichi, Cecelia. *High Lonesome: The American Culture of Country Music.* Chapel Hill: University of North Carolina Press, 1994.
Tilley, Nannie M. *The R. J. Reynolds Tobacco Company.* Chapel Hill: University of North Carolina Press, 1985.
Tosches, Nick. *Country: The Biggest Music in America.* New York: Delta, 1977.
Westbrooks, Bill, with Barbara M. McLean and Sandra S. Grafton. *Everybody's Cousin: Cousin Wilbur.* New York: Manor Books, 1979.
Whitburn, Joel. *Top Country Singles 1944–1988.* Menomonee Falls, Wis.: Record Research, Inc., 1989.
————. *Top Pop Singles 1955–1990.* Menomonee Falls, Wis.: Record Research, Inc., 1991.
Williams, Roger. *Sing a Sad Song: The Life of Hank Williams.* New York: Ballantine, 1973.

Wolfe, Charles K. *Tennessee Springs: The Story of Country Music in Tennessee.* Knoxville: University of Tennessee Press, 1977.

————. "The Triumph of the Hills: Country Radio, 1920–1950." In *Country: The Music and the Musicians.* New York: Abbeville Press, 1988.

ARTICLES

"American Folk Tunes." *Cowboy and Hillbilly Tunes and Tunesters,* April 5, 1947.

Antrim, Doran K. "Whoop-and-Holler Opera." *Collier's,* January 26, 1946.

"Arnold Denies He's a Western Singer." *Albuquerque, New Mexico Journal,* September 17, 1968.

Arnold, Eddy. "My True Romance." *True Romance,* 1949.

Barron, Mark. "Eddie Arnold Homesick During New York Visit." *Rapid City (S.D.) Journal,* April 22, 1945.

Barthelme, Don. "Disc Sounds Familiar," *Houston Post,* May 14, 1949.

Betz, Betty. "Arnold Gets Marriage Bids in Mail." *Houston Post,* 1949.

Blachar, Ted. *Ottawa Journal,* August 30, 1968.

"Bull Market in Corn." *Time,* October 4, 1943.

Bumpass, Gina. "Eddy Arnold." *Fort Worth Star-Telegram,* March 16, 1948.

Churchill, Allen. "Tin Pan Alley's Git-Tar Blues." *New York Times Magazine,* July 15, 1951.

Clovis, Kathryn Kirkham. "Radio's Famous 'Wranglers' Spread Good Will of Sooner State" Clovis (New Mexico) *News-Journal,* 1948.

Concert Review from Panama City, Fla., January 20, 1968.

Concert Review from Monroe, La., January 21, 1968.

Coon, Dick. *Great Falls Tribune,* July 27, 1968.

"Corn of Plenty." *Newsweek,* June 13, 1949.

"Country Disc Craze Grows; Arnold Nabs Another Hit!" *Record Bulletin* C. M. McClung & Co., Knoxville, Tennessee, May 2, 1949.

"Country Music Goes to Town." *Mademoiselle,* April 1948.

"Country Music Is Big Business, and Nashville Is Its Detroit." *Newsweek,* August 11, 1952.

"Country Music Snaps Its Regional Bounds." *Business Week,* March 19, 1966, 96–103.

"Country Music: The Nashville Sound." *Business Week,* March 19, 1956.

"Country Musicians Fiddle Up Roaring Business." *Life,* November 19, 1956.

Duff, Morris. "Make Way for the Country Sound." *Toronto Daily Star,* March 21, 1964.

"Eddy Arnold Halts Traffic in Bradenton." *Bradenton, Fla.,* August 15, 1948.

"Eddy Arnold Opened Record Shop in Murfreesboro, Tenn." *Variety,* May 17, 1948.

Eddy Arnold's Radio Favorites Song Book No. 1, Adams, Vee & Abbott (1946) song folio.

Eddy, Don. "Hillbilly Heaven." *American Magazine,* March 1952.

"Fort Knox No Longer Has Exclusive on Pot of Gold; WSM, Nashville, Talent Corners a Good Chunk of It." *Variety,* October 26, 1949.

Gleason, Ralph J. "Eddy's the Man Who Helped Bring the Country Song to the Big Town." *San Francisco Chronicle,* July 15, 1951.

"Gold Guitars, The." *Newsweek,* April 4, 1966.

Gordon, Jack. "Eddy Arnold, Former Plow Boy, Is Visitor." *Fort Worth Press,* March 16, 1948.

Gray, Dick. Column in *Atlanta Journal,* February 9, 1968.

Hanna, Charlie. Concert review of Portland show. *Oregonian,* June 6, 1968.

Harris, Roy. "Folk Songs." *House and Garden,* December 1954.

Hefferman, Harold. "Studio Nips Flight of Lonely Balladeer." *Detroit News,* 1949.

Hicks, Ida Belle. "Eddie's Country Boy, Not Singing Cowboy." *Fort Worth Star-Telegram,* March 16, 1948.

Hilburn, Robert. *Long Island Press,* October 6, 1968.

"Hillbilly Fans, Including Tuck, Acclaim Eddy Arnold's Show." *Richmond Times-Dispatch,* March 31, 1948.

"Hoedown on a Harpsichord." *Time,* November 14, 1960.

Humphrey, Hal. "Cowpokes Shout 'Boycott.'" *Oakland Tribune,* August 10, 1953.

Jarman, Rufus. "Country Music Goes to Town." *Nation's Business,* February 1953.

Jones, Paul. "Hillbilly Sound Attaining Dignity." October 30, 1968.

Kaliff, Joe. *Brooklyn Daily,* May 29, 1968.

King, Larry L. "Inside Grand Ole Opry." *Reader's Digest,* July 1968.

King, Nelson. "Hillbilly Music Leaves the Hills." *Good Housekeeping,* June 1954.

Kittsinger, Otto. Liner notes for *Pee Wee King* (Bear Family Records).

Langley, Frank. *Boston Herald,* June 30, 1968.

Lieberson, Goddard. "Country Sweeps the Country." *New York Times Magazine,* July 28, 1957.

MacKenzie, Bob. "On Television." Oakland newspaper, April 25, 1968.

Marek, Richard. "Country Music, Nashville Style." *McCall's,* April 1961.

Marvin, Wanda. "Hillbillies Win in New York: Much Mazuma Found in Mountain Music-Making." July 22, 1944.

Montana, Kay. "About Eddie Arnold." *Silver Star Song Club Bulletin,* fall and winter 1948.

"Pistol Packin' Mama." *Life,* October 11, 1943.

Portis, Charles. "That New Sound from Nashville." *Saturday Evening Post,* February 12, 1966, 30–38.

"RCA in Promotion Tie on Arnold Disk for Divorce Squelching." *Variety,* December 28, 1949.

"Record Date with Eddy Arnold, A." *Country Song Round Up,* 1949.

Scherman, Robert. "Hillbilly Phenomenon." *Christian Science Monitor,* March 13, 1948.

Singer, Samuel. Concert review of Philadelphia show, April 20, 1968.

"Songs from Texas." *Time,* March 24, 1941.

Stone, Jack. "Millions in Music—Hillbillies in Clover." *American Weekly,* February 6, 1945.

"Strictly by Ear." *Time,* February 11, 1946.

Teeter, H. B. "Nashville, Broadway of Country Music." *Coronet,* August 1952.

Terry, Bea. "Folk Music and Its Folks," 1949.

Waldron, Eli. "Country Music: The Squaya Dansu from Nashville." *The Reporter,* June 2, 1955.

Wilson, Eleanor. "Tennessee Plowboy Plows Right to Top of Billboard's Popularity Chart." February 25, 1949.

Zepela, Monte. "I'm Really a Pop Music Artist." *Charlotte Observer,* December 8, 1968.

Zolotow, Maurice. "Hayride." *Theater Arts,* November 1954.

———. "Hillbilly Boom." *Saturday Evening Post,* February 12, 1944.

Billboard Chart Singles from Eddy Arnold

(YEAR AND HIGHEST POSITION)

1945: Each Minute Seems a Million Years (#5)
1946: All Alone in This World without You (#7)
1946: That's How Much I Love You (A Side) (#2)
1946: Chained to a Memory (B Side) (#3)
1947: What Is Life without Love? (#1)
1947: It's a Sin (A Side) (#1)
1947: I Couldn't Believe It Was True (B Side) (#4)
1947: I'll Hold You in My Heart (Till I Can Hold You in My Arms) (#1)
1947: To My Sorrow (#2)
1948: Molly Darling (#10)
1948: Anytime (A Side) (#1)
1948: What a Fool I Was (B Side) (#2)
1948: Bouquet of Roses (A Side) (#1)
1948: Texarkana Baby (B Side) (#1)
1948: Just a Little Lovin' (Will Go a Long, Long Way) (A Side) (#1)
1948: My Daddy Is Only a Picture (B Side) (#5)
1948: A Heart Full of Love (for a Handful of Kisses) (A Side) (#1)
1948: Then I Turned and Slowly Walked Away (B Side) (#2)
1949: Many Tears Ago (#10)
1949: Don't Rob Another Man's Castle (A Side) (#1)
1949: There's Not a Thing (I Wouldn't Do for You) (B Side) (#3)
1949: One Kiss Too Many (#1)
1949: The Echo of Your Footsteps (#2)
1949: I'm Throwing Rice (at the Girl I Love) (A Side) (#2)
1949: Show Me the Way Back to Your Heart (B Side) (#7)
1949: C-H-R-I-S-T-M-A-S (A Side) (#7)
1949: Will Santa Come to Shanty Town? (B Side) (#5)
1950: There's No Wings on My Angel (#6)
1950: Take Me in Your Arms and Hold Me (A Side) (#1)
1950: Mama and Daddy Broke My Heart (B Side) (#6)
1950: Little Angel with the Dirty Face (A Side) (#3)
1950: Why Should I Cry? (B Side) (#3)
1950: Cuddle Buggin' Baby (A Side) (#2)
1950: Enclosed, One Broken Heart (B Side) (#6)
1950: Lovebug Itch (A Side) (#2)
1950: Prison without Walls (B Side) (#10)
1951: There's Been a Change in Me (#1)
1951: May the Good Lord Bless and Keep You (#8)
1951: Kentucky Waltz (#1)
1951: I Wanna Play House with You (A Side) (#1)

1951: Something Old, Something New (B Side) (#4)
1951: Somebody's Been Beating My Time (A Side) (#2)
1951: Heart Strings (B Side) (#5)
1952: Bundle of Southern Sunshine (A Side) (#4)
1952: Call Her Your Sweetheart (B Side) (#9)
1952: Easy on the Eyes (#1)
1952: A Full Time Job (#1)
1952: Older and Bolder (A Side) (#3)
1952: I'd Trade All of My Tomorrows (for Just One Yesterday) (B Side) (#9)
1953: Eddy's Song (#1)
1953: Free Home Demonstration (A Side) (#4)
1953: How's the World Treating You? (B Side) (#4)
1953: Mama, Come Get Your Baby Boy (#4)
1954: I Really Don't Want to Know (#1)
1954: My Everything (#7)
1954: This Is the Thanks I Get (for Loving You) (A Side) (#3)
1954: Hep Cat Baby (B Side) (#7)
1954: Christmas Can't Be Far Away (#12)
1955: I've Been Thinking (A Side) (#2)
1955: Don't Forget (B Side) (#12)
1955: In Time (A Side) (#6)
1955: Two Kinds of Love (B Side) (#9)
1955: Cattle Call (A Side) (#1)
1955: The Kentuckian Song (B Side) (#8)
1955: That Do Make It Nice (A Side) (#1)
1955: Just Call Me Lonesome (B Side) (#2)
1955: The Richest Man (in the World) (A Side) (#10)
1955: I Walked Alone Last Night (B Side) (#6)
1956: Trouble in Mind (#7)
1956: Casey Jones (The Brave Engineer) (#15)
1956: You Don't Know Me (#10)
1957: Gonna Find Me a Bluebird (#13)
1959: Chip Off the Old Block (#12)
1959: Tennessee Stud (#5)
1961: Before This Day Ends (#23)
1961: (Jim) I Wore a Tie Today (#27)
1961: One Grain of Sand (#17)
1962: Tears Broke Out on Me (#7)
1962: A Little Heartache (A Side) (#3)
1962: After Loving You (B Side) (#7)
1963: Does He Mean That Much to You? (#5)
1963: Yesterday's Memories (#11)
1963: A Million Years or So (#13)
1963: Jealous Hearted Me (#13)
1964: Molly (#5)
1964: Sweet Adorable You (#26)
1964: I Thank My Lucky Stars (#8)
1965: What's He Doing in My World (#1)
1965: I'm Letting You Go (#15)
1965: Make the World Go Away (#1)
1966: I Want to Go with You (#1)
1966: The Last Word in Lonesome Is Me (#2)
1966: The Tip of My Fingers (#3)

1966: Somebody Like Me (#1)
1967: The First Word (#51)
1967: Lonely Again (#1)
1967: Misty Blue (#3)
1967: Turn the World Around (#1)
1968: Here Comes Heaven (#2)
1968: Here Comes the Rain, Baby (#4)
1968: It's Over (#4)
1968: Then You Can Tell Me Goodbye (#1)
1968: They Don't Make Love Like They Used To (#10)
1969: Please Don't Go (#10)
1969: But for Love (#19)
1969: You Fool (#69)
1970: Since December (#73)
1970: Soul Deep (#22)
1970: A Man's Kind of Woman (A Side) (#28)
1970: Living Under Pressure (B Side) (#28)
1970: From Heaven to Heartache (#22)
1971: Portrait of My Woman (#26)
1971: A Part of America Died (#49)
1971: Welcome to My World (#34)
1971: I Love You Dear (#55)
1972: Lonely People (#38)
1972: Lucy (#62)
1973: So Many Ways (#28)
1973: If the Whole World Stopped Lovin' (#56)
1973: Oh, Oh, I'm Falling in Love Again (#29)
1974: She's Got Everything I Need (#24)
1974: Just for Old Times Sake (#56)
1974: I Wish That I Had Loved You Better (#19)
1975: Butterfly (#47)
1975: Red Roses for a Blue Lady (#60)
1975: Middle of a Memory (#86)
1976: Cowboy (#13)
1976: Put Me Back into Your World (#43)
1977: (I Need You) All the Time (#22)
1977: Freedom Ain't the Same as Being Free (#53)
1977: Where Lonely People Go (#83)
1978: Country Lovin' (#23)
1978: I'm the South (#91)
1979: If Everyone Had Someone Like You (#13)
1979: What in Her World Did I Do (#21)
1979: Goodbye (#22)
1979: If I Ever Had to Say Goodbye to You (#28)
1980: Let's Get It While the Gettin's Good (#6)
1980: That's What I Get for Loving You (#10)
1980: Don't Look Now (But We Just Fell in Love) (#11)
1981: Bally-Hoo Days (A Side) (#32)
1981: Two Hearts Beat Better Than One (B Side) (#32)
1982: All I'm Missing Is You (#30)
1982: Don't Give Up on Me (#73)
1983: The Blues Don't Care Who's Got 'Em (#76)

Index